NTRY LINKS
R 1942 – JULY 1944

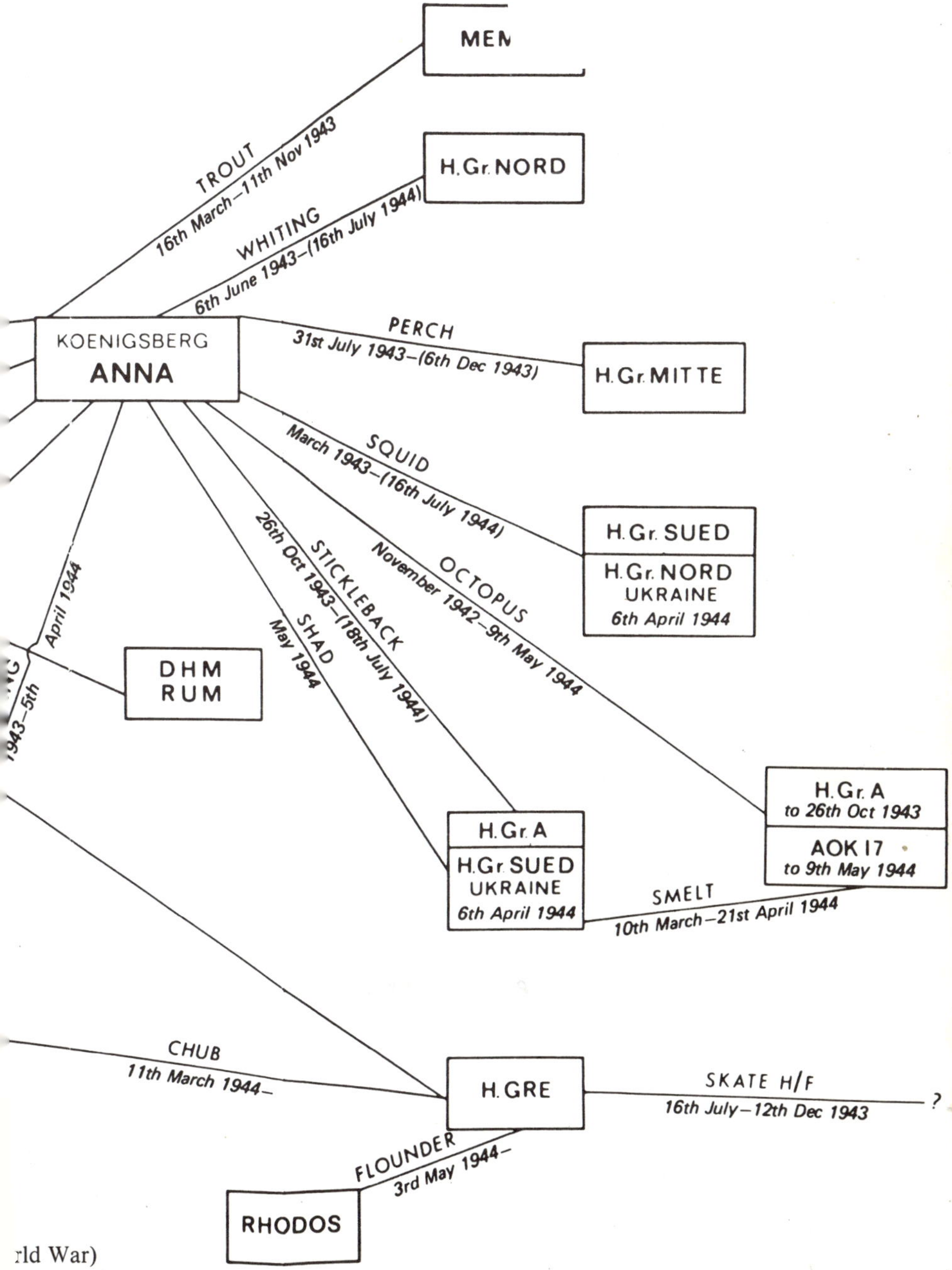

```
                              ┌─────────┐
                    TROUT     │  MEN    │
              16th March–11th Nov 1943
                              └─────────┘
                              ┌──────────┐
                    WHITING   │ H.Gr.NORD│
              6th June 1943–(16th July 1944)
                              └──────────┘
┌──────────────┐      PERCH
│ KOENIGSBERG  │──31st July 1943–(6th Dec 1943)──┐
│    ANNA      │                                 │ H.Gr.MITTE
└──────────────┘      SQUID
              March 1943–(16th July 1944)
                                                   H.Gr. SUED
                    OCTOPUS                        H.Gr. NORD
              November 1942–9th May 1944           UKRAINE
                                                   6th April 1944
```

- TROUT 16th March – 11th Nov 1943 → MEN
- WHITING 6th June 1943 – (16th July 1944) → H.Gr. NORD
- PERCH 31st July 1943 – (6th Dec 1943) → H.Gr. MITTE
- SQUID March 1943 – (16th July 1944) → H.Gr. SUED
- OCTOPUS November 1942 – 9th May 1944 → H.Gr. NORD UKRAINE 6th April 1944
- STICKLEBACK 26th Oct 1943 – (18th July 1944)
- SHAD May 1944
- ...G ...1943 – 5th April 1944

DHM RUM

H.Gr. A / H.Gr. SUED UKRAINE 6th April 1944

H.Gr. A to 26th Oct 1943
AOK 17 to 9th May 1944

SMELT 10th March – 21st April 1944

CHUB 11th March 1944 –

H.GRE

SKATE H/F 16th July – 12th Dec 1943 ?

FLOUNDER 3rd May 1944 –

RHODOS

(rld War)

£15.95 (less⅛)

Library Service

RIDGE AVENUE
LIBRARY
RIDGE AVENUE
LONDON N21 2RH
081-360 9662

	14. SEP 99
	22. JUN 00
	11. DEC 00
23. NOV 95	13. DEC 01
11. JAN 97	12. JUN
	05. AUG 97
	05. MAR 98
04. FEB 98	02. OCT 98
30. 28	05. JUN 99
FEB 91	30. SEP 99
03. JAN 98	

ease remember that this item will attract overdue charges if not
rned by the latest date stamped above. You may renew it by
nal call, telephone or by post quoting the bar code number and
ersonal number. I hope you enjoy all of your library services.

Peter Herring, Head of Arts and Libraries

30126 00968983 4

ENIGMA
and its
ACHILLES HEEL

HUGH SKILLEN

First published in Great Britain 1992
By Hugh Skillen, 56 St Thomas Drive
Pinner, Middlesex HA5 4SS
to whom all enquiries should be addressed.

By the same author:
    Spies of the Airwaves (1989) ISBN 0 9515190 X
    The Y Compendium (1990)
    Knowledge Strengthens the Arm (1991) ISBN 0 95150190 1 8

All rights reserved. No part of this publication may be reproduced, stored in a retrieval system, or transmitted, in any form or by any means, electronic, mechanical, photocopying, recording or otherwise, without prior permission of the author/publisher. Such permission, if granted, is subject to a fee depending on the nature of the use.

Typeset and printed by Hobbs the Printers of Southampton

© Copyright by Hugh Skillen
   ISBN 0 9515190 2 6

British Library Cataloguing-in-Publications Data.

A catalogue record for this book is available from the British Library.

Contents

Chapter		Page
	Foreword	vii
	Acknowledgements	ix
1	The Enigma Video by Gilbert Bloch	1
2	A Short History of the ENIGMA Machine	22
	The Audio Tape-Recorder	29
3	A Modern Odyssey. Bertrand's search for Allies 1931–1939	35
4	Lieut-Colonel Langer's Report on the French campaign	48
5	The Battle of Britain	62
6	Bletchley Park	72
7	The Ordeal. Bertrand in the Hands of the Abwehr 1944 as D-Day approached. His interrogation, and terms for surrender of his Y sections and links with London	108
8	Straight from the Horse's Mouth by a German ENIGMA/Geheimschreiber Operator	145
9	The Impact of Ultra on the Conduct of the Second World War	162
App. 1	The Enigma Video by Gilbert Bloch (in French)	
App. 2	User Instructions for the Cipher Machine ENIGMA (German) (The first documents supplied by Hans-Thilo Schmidt). Illustrations of operating systems of 'Rudolf' and 'Michael'.	
	Index	

'The game,' said he 'is never lost till won'.

This book is dedicated to all those who took part in the Great Game, to the men and women of the three services and the civilians who laboured at Bletchley Park and in its satellites across the seas, members of the Army, Navy and Air Force Y Sections, who served at home and overseas, and our comrades in the American, Australian, Canadian, French and Polish intercept services.

My special thanks are accorded to Lucienne Hermelin (now Edmondston-Low) of the Hut 6 Registration Room at Bletchley Park for her editing advice and careful proofreading.

Foreword

It was clear to the organisers of an Enigma Reunion fifty years on that there would be many and probably a great majority of those present who had worked in various aspects of the Y Service at Bletchley Park, Chicksands Priory, Beaumanor and Harrogate and so on, and in the field in Special Wireless Sections and SCUs who did not have any clear idea of the Enigma machine itself, its history and the problems involved in solving clues every day of the war in order to arrive at decryptions.

When it was mooted that there should be several short talks on various aspects of the work, by an operator, by a member of the Wireless Intelligence Section, by slip-readers, (and what was a slip reader?) a translator, I proposed that a demonstration of the Enigma machine itself would be a boon and a blessing. Major R.W.M. Shaw, curator of the Intelligence Corps Museum was very quick to offer to lend their Enigma for this purpose and Bill Edwards offered to bring along his own machine and give a 'hands-on' demonstration. To my mind, having studied books by Gordon Welchman and others, the presentation of the excellent Video by Gilbert Bloch, made for the Memorial Museum in Caen, and subsequently presented by him to the Imperial War Museum, would tell the complete story very simply in forty minutes if we had an English translation of the Video. This was not simple and took a long time but it has been done.

What about the many who would have given so much to be there but lived across the oceans or were not fit enough to undertake the journey to Bedford or who had unfortunately other commitments already made for these dates? I came to the conclusion that a book based on the video text with good photographs of the machine and its essential parts, plus some vital information by Gordon Welchman and others, including a German operator of the Enigma and the Geheimschreiber at Hitler's HQ and at Stalingrad, would provide a permanent record for those able to attend the reunion and especially for those unable to do so. The series of Geheimschreibers is described with photos and the invention of the Colossus to decrypt them.

For those who have read *Spies of the Airwaves* and *Knowledge Strengthens the Arm* and have been fascinated by the trials and tribulations of Gen. Bertrand in his years-long attempts to interest the British and French governments in the steps necessary for their own survival, there is the final chapter in the story of his arrest and imprisonment in Paris by the Abwehr, his interrogation under threat of death and the offers made to him to betray his comrades and act as a double agent with Germany against Bletchley Park by keeping open his radio link with London and Algiers—all this before D-day with London and BP at panic stations.

The decisive role of Ultra and the Y services in the Battle of Britain is examined and in conclusion Sir Harry Hinsley's Liddel-Hart Lecture of February 1992 on the 'Impact of Ultra on the Conduct of the Second World War' asks the question 'What would we have done without Ultra?'

Acknowledgements

Bertrand G. Enigma ou la plus grande Enigme de la Guerre 1939–1945 (1973)

Bloch G. The Enigma Video made for the Peace Memorial Museum, Caen.
La Contribution Française à la Reconstitution et au Décryptement de l'Enigma Militaire Allemand en 1931–1932 (Revue historique des Armées No. 4—1985).
Rapport sur le Travail de l'Equipe du Lieut-Colonel Langer pendant la Campagne de France du 1.10.39 au 24.06.40

Hinsley H. The History of British Intelligence in the Second World War.

Lewin R. Ultra Goes to War.

Paillole P. Notre Espion chez Hitler.

Rohwer und Jaeckel Die Funkaufklaerung und ihre Rolle im Zweiten Weltkrieg

Trenkle F. Die Deutschen Funknachrichtenanlagen bis 1945

Trenkle F. Vol. 1. Die ersten 40 Jahre.

Trenkle F. Vol. 2. Der Zweite Weltkrieg.

Ellissen H. Vol. 3. Funk- und Bordsprechanlagen in Panzer-Zeugen.

Rusbridger Betrayal at Pearl Harbor.

Welchman G. The Hut Six Story.
From Polish Bomba to British Bombe. The Birth of Ultra. (Intelligence and National Security Journal (Jan 1986 No. 1 Vol. 1)

West N. GCHQ.

CHAPTER 1

THE ENIGMA VIDEO

Made for the Peace Memorial Museum, Caen, by Gilbert Bloch

(Translation from the French by Hugh Skillen and Jean Scoffoni)

You have before you a model of the Enigma machine in use by the German Armed Forces from 1 June, 1930, well before the coming to power of Hitler, until the end of the war in May, 1945 (Page 1).

I am going to explain to you the nature of the machine, how it was born and developed and how it functions.

The ENIGMA is a machine for *en*-ciphering and *de*-ciphering messages practically which means, that is, if you put into the machine the CLEAR TEXT of a message by typing it in on the key-board, that you see before you—Page 2—the clear text goes in here as you type—and the enciphered text of the message is going to appear letter by letter on the lamps which are here and that I shall demonstrate to you. (Pause)

You see that the lamps have exactly the same pattern as the keys on the keyboard—and each lamp represents one letter—but the letters light up on a little lamp. Each lamp represents a letter and can be lit up by a small bulb below—you will see it presently. The clear text is entered here—the enciphered text appears letter by letter on these lights. But inversely, as the machine is one for enciphering and deciphering, with the same arrangement, you will see later what this means—if the operator taps out the enciphered text on the keyboard he will see on the lamps, letter by letter, the clear text will appear. The machine can encipher and decipher and you can see that the use of the machine from now on is plain. The sender of the message enciphers his message on his Enigma and the recipient or addressee reads the

Wehrmacht ENIGMA (Courtesy of Pierre Lorain)

Wehrmacht ENIGMA E (Courtesy of Pierre Lorain)

enciphered text: he has his own machine and knows what configuration he must select. He deciphers the message by entering the enciphered text and recovering the clear text on the lamps. (Pause) You have just made acquaintance with the essential characteristic of the Enigma which is its great reversibility, that is to say the capacity of the machine for enciphering and deciphering. Notice that the machine plays no part in transmitting the message. It enciphers and deciphers but the enciphered text must be passed to a radio operator who will then transmit it by wireless normally in Morse code, while at the other end the radio operator who receives the enciphered text in Morse will write it down and pass it to the Enigma operator who deciphers it. This machine has not only good points. First, it is labour-intensive—it demands two persons at least at either end: one to type the letters while the other reads off the enciphered text on the lamps letter by letter—I repeat it is typing letter by letter—and transcribes what he reads on the lamps on to a special message form. It is NOT rapid. This means that for each letter to appear in cipher you need to wait two seconds.

A message, therefore, of 250 letters takes about 10 minutes to encipher or decipher (pause) for as you see the Enigma is slow and this slowness is accentuated still more by another factor because you see that the keyboard has only letters. If I have numbers to transmit—and God knows if there are numbers to transmit in military messages—I shall have to spell out the figures—I shall not transcribe 7 but S-E-V-E-N.

This lengthens the message—and will lengthen the encipherment and decipherment. It is a serious disadvantage in the machine. A last disadvantage is a further inconvenience—besides being slow and labour-intensive, failing to transmit figures, the machine leaves no tangible record of the message it takes in. All modern machines put out a paper strip on which the message is printed. Here there is not a thing—only what the second operator takes down by hand.

The Germans were well aware of the shortcomings, and set to work to create an improved machine. This is a Military Enigma Machine Type 1. The Germans worked to perfect a Type 2 which would be the same machine coupled with a printer. With the later improved type you could get a much faster strike with only one operator and with a print-out. Apart from the lack of figures on the keyboard all the other disadvantages would disappear. Hum! This Type 2 was finalised in

1932 and tested in a campaign. It was a complete failure. The machine would break down most of the time. Well, things being as they were the Germans decided to stick with Type 1. And 100,000 were to be manufactured between 1930 and 1945. (Pause)

Of course the machines designed and used afterwards by the foreign forces—the British Typex which came into commission in 1935 and the US Sigmaba which would be finalised in 1940—did not possess the disadvantages of the Enigma. But this was nevertheless a remarkable machine for its time and the Germans would start the war with a marked superiority over their adversaries in that domain for not only did they have a machine but they had really thought out their system of transmission.

They had set up a whole set of regulations, a whole network—they did not wait for General Guderian to say that modern warfare would demand far-flung inroads by armoured divisions which means rapid continuous secret informative communications. They had really perfected their system so that they would begin with, in that war, a marked superiority. (Page 5)

Meanwhile what about France? Well, France limited herself to ordering about a thousand copies of cipher machine C36, from the Swedish manufacturer Edward Adler. These machines were badly and little used in the course of the 1939–40 campaign.

How is the enciphering done inside the machine? The CLEAR TEXT of the message is transformed by alphabetic substitution method, which means simply that each letter of the clear text is replaced by another letter.

There exist a lot of alphabetic substitution methods—the simplest method you certainly know consists in writing down the alphabet A B C D E F in the normal order and writing below it in random order a substitution alphabet for example K below A, Z below B etc and replacing in the enciphered text each letter of the clear text by its substitute which means that A will always be enciphered by K, B by Z etc.

It is obvious that such a mono-alphabetic substitution system offers no guarantee of security: with a fairly long message, say a hundred letters or so, it will take under ten minutes to trace back to the substitution alphabet and read the message, inasmuch as you can find out in which language it was written, but nothing prevents you from having a go. Therefore if a substitution alphabet is to present much

Colonel-General Guderian in his command car with the ENIGMA machine in the foreground. Behind the two ENIGMA operators, one manipulating the machine and the other writing the deciphered text, is the radio operator at the controls of his set (Collection for the Archives of the Bibliothek fuer Zeitgeschichte, Stuttgart).

chance of giving you security you must use several substitution alphabets.

From the 16th to the 18th century it was thought that the most elegant and safest method to construct a polyalphabetic substitution system was to use what is called the Vigenère Square, which supplies you with 26 substitution alphabets. You can understand why it is termed 'square': 26 alphabets each of which fills up a 26 compartment column will result in 26 lines (as there are 26 letters)

```
A B C D E F G H I J K L M N O P Q R S T U V W X Y Z
B C D E F G H I J K L M N O P Q R S T U V W X Y Z A
C D E F G H I J K L M N O P Q R S T U V W X Y Z A B
D E F G H ............................................................ C
E F G .................................................................. D
F G H ................................................................. E
..............................................................................
..............................................................................
Z A B C D ............................................................ Y
```

With 26 alphabets at his disposition the user selects the alphabets to be used and the random order in which they are to be used by means of a keyword and the keyword determines the alphabets to use and their order. All this seemed faultless until 1863 when a German mathematician demonstrated by a very simple reasoning and some calculations that were not very complicated that these periodic polyalphabetic substitutions, inasmuch as the period was not too long, were perfectly decipherable, and then the polyalphabetic substitutions method was given up. Then came the war of '14–'18 during which a good many novelties appeared including the use of radio.

Everybody, friend or foe, can intercept radio messages—so keeping messages secret became a particularly acute problem, a problem of unmatched importance and each of the belligerents strove to work it out by using various systems for enciphering—manual enciphering—but it was soon found that they presented serious inconveniences among which, in many cases, security was shown to be illusory, so in different countries it occurred to some people that a machine would do the work better, and that it would be possible to make a machine do the enciphering . . . Hum . . . to begin with, some plans were made, then the armistice came in 1918 and none of these plans had been carried out in practice. But on the European side in engineer named Hugo Koch took out a patent—actually he took out a patent for a design of a machine. He did not make it, but a German engineer named Arthur Scherbius made that machine. He really constructed it in 1923 and called it 'ENIGMA'.

And he began its manufacture with a view to having it used for the secret communications of commercial firms and private people—in fact it seems he was a bit naive—anyway he never claimed that his machine could be used for military purposes. As a matter of fact the machine was a total fiasco on the commercial plane, and Dr Scherbius died in 1926 at the precise period that the military authorities were taking an interest in his invention. How did that commercial Enigma work? Well, that is what I am going to show you with the help of this Military Enigma machine although the military machine differs in some respects from the commercial model.

Well, the commercial Enigma has an entry keyboard of 26 letters in the normal typewriter order. Here is the entry mechanism, and it has a lamp-board (26 lamps) in the same order as the keys on the keyboard. (Pause).

Wehrmacht ENIGMA showing lampboard
(Courtesy of Pierre Lorain)

This is the exit mechanism. What happens between the entry and the exit mechanism? That's what I am going to show you. These 26 keys on the keyboard—you can see better like that. You can see the rows of lamps lighting up . . . If I press a key I close an electrical circuit . . . which links the key to the entry disc, which is here. This entry disc has on either side 26 electrical contacts corresponding to the 26 keys of the entry keyboard, the contacts being activated in the order of the keyboard, that is to say Q W E R T Z etc. Then there are 3 mobile rotors chocked on the same axis. (Bloch lifts them out) There! Here they are! These 3 rotors are numbered *I, II* and *III* in Roman numerals. (Page 8). Here is one! It presents 26 electrical contacts that are springy studs on the right side, and on the left 26 electrical contacts which are small pads. These rotors are hollow and inside each rotor the contacts on either side are linked together by internal cables. Each rotor has a unique cabling system. No. *II* is different from No. *I* and No. *III* has internal cabling different from Nos. *I* and *II*. But in all the Enigmas all rotors *I* have the same cabling system, all rotors *II* have the *same* cabling system, all rotors *III* have the same cabling system. You can see that the way these rotors are assembled ensures the electrical continuity with the entry disc.

On the left of the machine is a fixed drum . . . here it is! which is marked B called the Return Drum (Umkehrwalze). This drum presents on its left side—and only on the left—26 electrical contacts (spring studs) and these are linked two by two inside the drum by

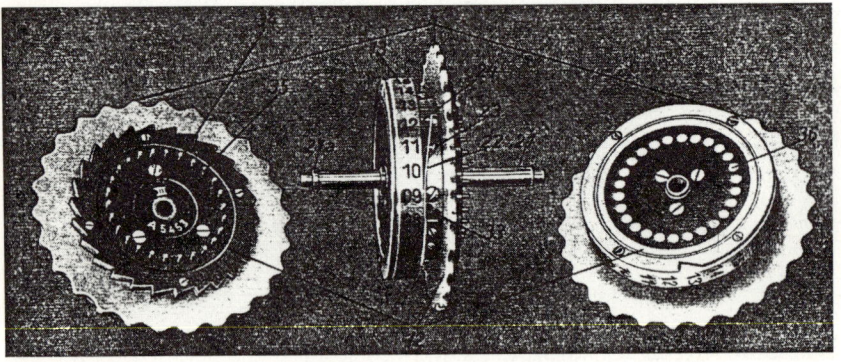

The three rotors

internal cables. Therefore you have got 13 connections—26 divided by 2. What is the role of this Return Drum? Let us put the rotors back in place!

I depress a key . . . Then the current will pass through the Entry Disc, through the 3 rotors from right to left, it will pass through the return drum which will reflect it back from left to right through the 3 rotors following quite a different pattern from the entry pattern. It will finish up at the entry disc which becomes the exit disc (it is an entry/exit disc); from there it will be sent back from the exit disc to the lamp-board where the depressed key will light up one lamp. The circuit followed by the current is therefore quite clear. Now what happens if I depress key A? A lamp on the lampboard will glow. What will happen then if I depress key A again?

The pressing of the key determines the rotation of the right-hand rotor . . . by one position. The electrical circuit will be completely different from the one which took place on the first typing, and though I depress the same key A it will not be lamp C that will glow, it will perhaps be . . . K. The only thing that cannot happen if you press key A is the lighting up of A on the board. The way the machine is constructed the enciphering of a letter by itself is utterly impossible. If I continue to type on the keyboard, still letter by letter, on the entry-keyboard, the right-hand drum will continue to move around. When it reaches a certain position a pawl will operate and make the central rotor move round by one position. And then so will the central rotor which after some typing will make the left hand rotor move round by one position. It is exactly like the counter on a water, gas, or electricity meter. It is not any more complicated.

Now let us consider things carefully: I continue to type or more exactly I have started typing when the rotors were in a certain position: if I type every day on the keyboard there will come a moment when the drums return to the initial position. When will this happen? Each rotor has 26 possible positions; then it will happen after 26 strikes to the power of 3, that's to say 17,576 strikes. And these 17,576 strikes correspond to 17,576 different positions of the rotor. Now at each of these different positions of the rotor a different substitution alphabet comes into use. So with 17,576 substitution alphabets you realise we are very far from the 26 alphabets of the Vigenère square.

But that is not all. The rotors are interchangeable. I can change their order. With 3 rotors I have 6 possible orders then I can use 17,576 × 6 substitution alphabets—i.e. over 105,000. And when on December 15, 1936, the Germans have added to the three mobile drums numbered *I, II* and *III*, two more drums numbered *IV* and *V* the possible arrangements of three mobile drums out of a series of 5 will come to 60. Then I shall have at my disposition more than one million alphabets—enough to discourage the most courageous cryptanalyst. And besides, each message, (but prior to that there is something else) (he closes down the machine). The machine is not powered by any motor at all: it is only by depressing the keys that you switch off the electric circuit and stop the rotating rotors—the electric current is supplied by a 4.5 volt battery—you can see it here, but there is no motor. Each message will have its own key. Which key shall it be? It shall be at the position where the rotors start moving around. Indeed, (let us close down the machine!) the rotors can be moved round their axes and present on their right sides a little cogged part which enables me to move them round by hand. (He turns the rotor) Therefore I can move them round until one of the 26 figures on each rotor appears in the tiny windows which are here. In fact each of these figures corresponds to a letter. The corresponding system is quite simple $1 = A$, $2 = B$, $3 = C$, etc. I am going to choose a starting position, for example, H S B this corresponds to (H = 08, S = 19, B = 02). It is the key that has appeared. I can now start typing my message. Yet there is some slight difficulty. If I want all that to work it is absolutely necessary that the addressee at the other end should know that I have started with H S B as the key to the message. Therefore I will notify in the directions of the day that today the keys of the message will be typed on the machine with another starting position which will be the same for all messages today. (p. 19).

I will choose for example Z A H: then I will set the machine to Z A H which comes to $Z = 26$ $A = 1$ $H = 08$. I will type H S B on the keyboard then I will make the corresponding figures for H S B appear on the tiny windows, and I will start typing the message. Then I have 26 to the power of $3 = 17,576$ possible starting positions. But there again, there is a clever dodge, you can see here the crown which is on the rotor—the crown with the 26 figures—well there is a small clip— by means of which I can free the crown and cause it to be mobile— which is very difficult to do the other way round—and I can block it at 26 different positions. This does not alter the number of starting

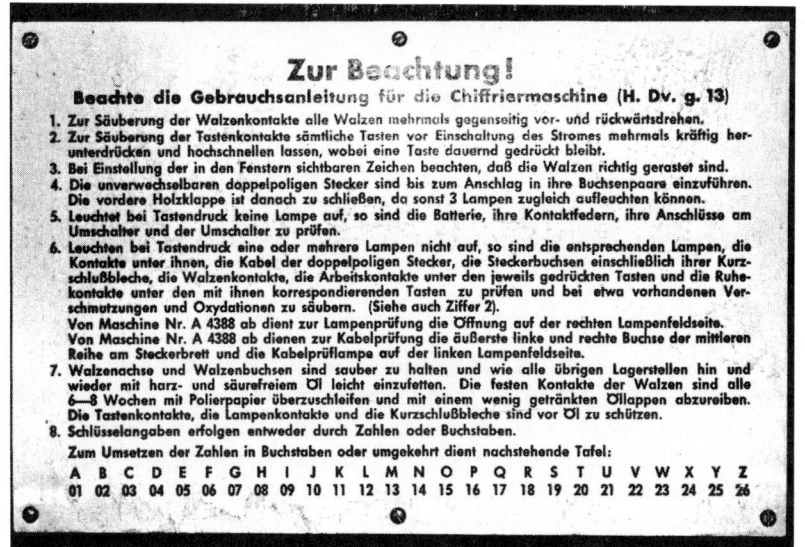

Maintenance instructions for Wehrmacht ENIGMA inside the lid showing numbers corresponding to letters of the alphabet (Courtesy of Pierre Lorain)

positions, 17,576, but it means that I have another 17,576 ways of making completely different substitution alphabets correspond to my starting position. Therefore the number of possibilities of setting the machine is multiplied by an incredible number. In short, with that commercial Enigma I have on one hand the configuration for the day, the order of the rotors and the setting of the crowns, and on the other hand for each message the specific key of the message . . . I am going—to put it together . . . like that . . .

You can understand that with such provisions the machine aroused a keen interest with military authorities who sought a means of transmitting secret messages, especially the German military authorities. On 9 February 1926 the German Navy adopted a derivative of the commercial Enigma—there was no question of adopting the commercial Enigma directly—this was Model C while the Army followed suit on July 15, 1929, and adopted Model G. But still, Colonel Erich Fellgiebel, responsible for German Signals for the Wehrmacht, did not feel comfortable about the security offered by the machine. He decided to 'open the umbrella' (which meant that he would transfer the responsibility to others in case the machine failed to ensure secrecy). In every country in the world as in any administration to 'open the umbrella' consists in appointing a committee of experts to check whether the machine can be trusted as to secrecy. The Colonel did that in 1928 and then one day in 1929 the experts called on the Colonel with a surprising verdict: they said 'This machine is not to be trusted. First of all your period of 17,576 is not as big as all that' and above all the experts found out a mathematical method, a rather complicated one indeed, which enabled them, with the help of the enciphered text of the message—a great deal of enciphered text—to reconstitute the configuration. Mathematical experts were asked to decrypt the messages and reconstitute the setting of the keyword? Their verdict: 'This machine is not fool-proof'. Consternation? No! To make it absolutely safe there is a simple method: we must add a table of connections (26 plugs) Here it is! (p. 13) This panel has 26 plugs—double ones—corresponding to 26 letters—and these plugs can be connected two by two to mobile plugs called 'Steckers'. Here are some! you can see two more mobile plugs. By linking them two by two you can obtain a double superencipherment, as you send the electric current through these plugs—the current then passes twice; it passes from the entry and it passes from the exit discs so you have a double superencipherment which not only frustrates the mathematical method the German experts had found out (and they called it the 'stick' method) but in addition multiplies the possible combinations by an enormous factor. Indeed suppose we consider only 11 connections, not 13, we can have a maximum of 13 connections (26 divided by 2 is 13)—if I consider 11 plugs and I count the different possible ways of linking 11 connections—eugh—linking 26 letters by 11 connections which comes to exactly 2—well, I find that the number of possibilities amounts to 2 followed by 14 noughts—(200,000,000,000,000). Therefore, according to the experts, the adoption of this table of connections or Steckers made it utterly reliable as to security. Let us see now how we can assess the secrecy capability of this machine. This is ensured at several levels. The first level is the machine itself—even if you can read a description of the machine you can by no means reconstitute it. For a very simple reason: as you know the machine presents 5 mechanisations with two internal cabling systems, the three rotors, the Return Drums and the cabling

View of the Stecker-Board (Courtesy of Pierre Lorain)

system linking the keys of the keyboard to the entry/exit disc, well the different possibilities of arranging the cabling system amounts to 10 (hum—sorry)—to 5 followed by 92 noughts: 500,000,000,000,000, 000,000,000,000,000,000,000,000,000,000,000,000,000,000,000,000, 000,000,000,000,000,000,000,000,000,000. Therefore even if you know, if you can study at leisure a general description of the machine, it is out of the question to reconstitute it. The Germans are aware that this success will not last forever. One day in peace or war a machine will fall into the hands of the enemy, or worse a traitor will smuggle abroad the designs of the cabling system. Meanwhile they take extra security measures for the machine and these measures will be efficacious. Never will the designs of the cabling system leave the secret safes of the Reichswehr or the Wehrmacht and we have to wait until the Norwegian campaign to learn that 3 Enigmas were captured by the British forces. So the secret about the existence of the machine was well kept.

But even if you have the machine, if you know it, if you have got its cabling systems, you still have to work out a problem concerning its configurations or settings (indicators). Now the possible configurations of the machine—and remember they have added the Steckers—amount to a number of possibilities expressed by 27 followed by 22 noughts, 270,000,000,000,000,000,000,000 only for one day (because the mechanisms are set differently every day) so again it is impossible to get into these combinations to try to find out which one has been used for messages you have intercepted: the machine cannot be reconstituted, nor can its messages be deciphered. And yet the machine will soon be reconstituted and its messages deciphered! When the German experts parted company they were quite certain that the Military Enigma machine could guarantee the absolute secrecy of their transmissions. Mind you, considering the level that technique had reached at that time they were perfectly right—I am not speaking ironically—and yet the machine was to be reconstituted and its messages deciphered owing to four reasons—a combination of four causes—

1. An error in the setting up of the encipherment procedure
2. Treachery—an act of treachery
3. The intervention of a mathematical genius
4. Errors of German operators

First cause An error in the setting up of the encipherment procedure. The Germans had not gone into enough detail in prescribing how to proceed with the machine. This was done by other experts, the specialists. These new experts, these specialists had quite different purposes from the former ones: they had been told that the machine was perfectly secure as to secrecy so they took it for granted. What **they** were interested in was how to proceed for transmitting: and one fear kept obsessing them, namely the errors that were bound to occur some time or other—in the encipherment procedure. They knew the errors would occur; they were reconciled to the idea—anyway, how could they help it? But these errors, at least the serious ones—they wanted to be able to detect them very quickly.

Well, one of the serious errors is the one which may occur when you encipher the specific key of the message: Suppose I have chosen the key HSB and it is necessary that the addressee at the other end recuperates clearly H S B. To be certain, what do the specialists do?

They say: 'we shall not transmit it once, we shall transmit it twice': HSB HSB—this will be enciphered by six letters, (hum) say . . . for example XKY WAC.

So the message will begin with a group of six letters in which, if I am acquainted with the procedure I am sure the first letter and the 4th letter the 2nd and the 5th, the 3rd and the 6th all result from the encipherment of the same letter of the clear text. It is a redundancy, it looks perfectly innocent but it will wreck the security of the whole system.

Second cause An act of treachery. In October 1931 a civil servant in the German Defence Ministry Cipher Office offers the French Intelligence Service delivery of some documents, and so on 8th November 1931 at Verviers in Belgium an Intelligence Service officer, Captain Bertrand, meets a traitor codenamed Asche (his real name being Hans-Thilo Schmidt) and Asche delivers two documents to Captain Bertrand. These two documents—Here they are! (See Appendix)

There is the Instruction Manual for Enigma Operators, and there is the description of the Operations Enciphering Procedures used at that time. Of course the latter is a general description of the machine, complete with photographs if you please, but obviously contains no clue as to the internal cabling.

Gebrauschsanweisung fuer die Chiffriermaschine ENIGMA. Instruction Manual for Operators: It describes the machine but not the internal cabling, and there are several pages of photographs of the machine.

Schluesselanleitung fuer die Chiffriermaschine ENIGMA. Instruction Manual for Operators: this one gives the operational procedures.

Bertrand travels back to France carrying the documents, shows them to the French Cipher Service which, after examining them, comes to the same conclusions as the German experts: 'The machine', they say 'cannot be reconstituted nor its messages deciphered, so the documents are useless'. Of course Bertrand is very disappointed but he gets permission from his superiors to communicate the documents to the Allied Services in order to find out whether they could unite their efforts and exploit the documents jointly. He first gets in touch with the British late in November 1931: the British are not interested;

the Germany of 1931 does not look dangerous and as ASCHE costs a lot of money they are not keen to pay their share of the expenses. Then from 7 to 11 December 1931 Bertrand goes to Poland where he meets the representatives of the Polish Cipher Service—Major Langer and Captain Cieski who is in charge of the Cipher Bureau and deals especially with Germany. Bertrand gets an enthusiastic welcome: the Poles have been floundering on the matter since 1923 and have made practically no headway: the documents will enable them to go on researching with a better chance. They come to some kind of agreement: Bertrand shall continue to supply the Colonel with documents, Asche shall deliver, and the Poles—'Cross your heart and hope to die'—shall keep Bertrand up to date as to progress in the work.

Then the Polish officers set out to solve the problem of Enigma. They knew—we were in 1931—they knew the Germans had been using a machine; they were certain the machine was a commercial Enigma which had been modified but they did not know at all which modifications had been made: moreover they also noticed that the first six letters of each message had some elements in common, and that it must be the keyword.

Third cause The intervention of a mathematical genius. Then, armed with Bertrand's documents, the Polish officers launched into the attack. To no avail—another complete failure—it was impossible to reconstitute the machine. Then in desperation they came to a heroic decision: since the military people have failed, let us try civilian mathematicians! The Cipher Bureau have been employing 3 civilian mathematicians who came from Poznan University in 1929. They were named Marian Rejewski, Jerzy Rozycki and Henryk Zygalski and in September 1932 these three mathematicians who had been working in German for the Cipher Service are posted to the Cipher Bureau in Warsaw. They are tested and then, early in October the Bureau picks the brightest of them, Rejewski (p. 17) who is given the ultra secret task of reconstructing, and if possible, deciphering the Enigma machine. He has at his disposition a commercial Enigma and the two documents bought from Asche and a continuous supply of messages intercepted daily by the Polish intercept unit. Rejewski ponders the matter for a time; he strives to get acquainted with the

The Polish mathematician Marian Rejewski who was first to reconstitute the ENIGMA machine and decrypt its messages.

machine and concentrates his effort on the first six letters of the messages.

I shall not take you into the arcane mathematical reasoning of Rejewski but I can reconstitute for you the steps of his intellectual approach to the problem and you'll see that actually it is simple. These first six letters of each message which correspond to the double encipherment of the specific key of the message—Rejewski reflects that . . . that they set in motion the right-hand rotor by six positions. We know that only one move of the right hand rotor can set in motion the middle rotor therefore in 20 cases out of 26 these six letters will be enciphered with the movement of the right hand rotor alone. And in these 20 cases you can consider the rest of the machine as a fixed ensemble. As you know this concerns the duplication of the key which has the same letters twice, you can express the encipherment of these six letters by six successive equations of permutation of which certain properties are known, if you take into account the duplication, and in that case this 6 equation system can be 'determined' (in the mathematical sense of the word) i.e. it can be solved.

Theoretically—YES because in practice, owing to the means of calculation at one's disposition at that time, early in the Thirties one could by no means come to a practical solution. But Rejewski sticks to his idea. If he could solve these equations then he could reconstitute the cabling of the right-hand disc. As the three discs are at different periods placed on the right he could reconstitute the internal cabling of the three rotors. Once he has got the cabling system of the three rotors he could then reconstitute the cabling system of the Return Drum and therefore he could reconstitute the whole of the machine. I insist, this is sheer theory. But Rejewski goes and imparts his findings to his fellow mathematicians who are dazzled by the ability of the young mathematician—he is then 27—and Cieski tells him 'Well, if it is so, we can give you something more' and they give him other documents that they had received from Bertrand. They are monthly sheets of the discriminants.

Rejewski has the message enciphered for the corresponding days. He knows, thanks to the monthly sheets passed by Bertrand, the order of the rotors, the setting of the crowns and of the Steckers. (p. 19) Now he can simplify his equations and having simplified them he can work them out and come to the practical solution. By the end of 1932 Rejewski has reconstructed the entire internal linkage system—it was not so easy because the early calculations of Rejewski had been a failure and Rejewski wondered why they had although his reasoning had been sound. And he thought that—concerning the scheme of linking between the keys and the entry/exit disc—he had adopted the same pattern as the one in the commercial Enigma, that is the usual order of the keys Q W E R T. Well, he reflected, suppose the Germans have altered that order? As the Germans are logical people with logical minds it is a dead cert they have not done the linking in random pattern. If they have altered the order why wouldn't they have done the linking in alphabetical fashion A B C D E etc. Rejewski had a try and in fact it was exactly the way the Germans had altered the pattern.

VIII. Beispiel.

17. Gültiger Tagesschlüssel:
(Ausschnitt aus der für die Verschlüsselung des Klartextes
in Betracht kommenden Schlüsseltafel, z. B. ....
Maschinenschlüssel für Monat Mai.)

Datum	Walzenlage	Ringstellung	~~Grundstellung~~
4.	I III II	16 11 13	~~01 12 22~~

Steckerverbindung	Kenngruppen-Einsatzstelle .... (Gruppe)	Kenngruppen
CO DI FR HU JW LS TX	2	ndq nuz opw vxz

Nach diesem Tagesschlüssel ist die Chiffriermaschine einzustellen (vgl. Ziff. 4 und 5).

Der im nachfolgenden Beispiel eingesetzte Schlüsseltext ist aus Geheimhaltungsgründen nicht mit der Chiffriermaschine getastet, sondern willkürlich gewählt worden.

A. Verschlüsseln.

18. Zu verschlüsselnder Spruch:

Tag 4. 5.,
Abgangszeit 17,55 Uhr
Korpskommando VI
angreift 5. Mai 0445 Uhr mit 3. und 10. Div. Feind bei Maisach.
Gef. Stand: Milbertshofen Nordausgang

19. Für die Verschlüsselung ist der Klartext des Spruches gem. H.Dv.g. 7, Ziff. 40 wie folgt niederzuschreiben:

Korpskommando roem x s e q s angreift fuenften mai null drei
vier fuenf uhr mit dritter und zehnter div x feind bei maisach x
gef stand x milbertshofen nordausgang

20. Auf dem Spruchformular bezeichnet der Schlüßler die im Tagesschlüssel vorgeschriebene Einsatzstelle (im Beispiel 2. Gruppe) für die Kenngruppe und spart diese Gruppe beim Eintragen des Spruchschlüssels bzw. des Schlüsseltextes aus.

Der Schlüßler wählt für jeden Spruch bzw. bei mehreren Teilen eines Spruches für jeden Teil eine besondere Grundstellung, z.B. wie (23 05 16) und stellt diese

21. Der Schlüßler wählt den Spruchschlüssel, z. B. XFR (24 06 18), und tastet diese 3 Buchstaben zweimal nacheinander, wobei sich die Buchstaben hfikl klli ergeben, die unter Berücksichtigung der nachträglich einzusetzenden Kenngruppe (vgl. Ziff. 20) als erste Buchstaben des zu befördernden Spruches niederzuschreiben sind.

22. Nunmehr stellt der Schlüßler bei sonst gleichbleibender Einstellung der Chiffriermaschine in den Fenstern die als Spruchschlüssel gewählten Buchstaben XFR (24 06 18) ein und tastet den Klartext. Die sich ergebenden Buchstaben werden im Anschluß an die 6 Buchstaben, die beim Tasten des Spruchschlüssels entstanden sind, niedergeschrieben. Dabei werden gleichzeitig Gruppen zu je 5 Buchstaben gebildet.

Es ergibt sich folgender Schlüsseltext:

hfikl	.....	bsgex	nnfop	(hfikl ..... b
rsalm	cydrj	qqarz	ubhfe	verschlüsselter
mooxz	lgred	lfijy	acivd	Spruchschlüssel)
gnhye	xmjyr	aqztl	ssiwf	
uwfhe	lnarz	qeduw	jvsfa	
bskqu	dihsg	nejpf	afohw	
egaim	fojrl	ekhbd	lpbme	
binge				

23. Zur Bezeichnung der für die Schlüsselung des Spruches verwendeten Schlüsseltafel ist aus dem Tagesschlüssel eine der 4 Kenngruppen, z. B. snuze, zu entnehmen, die z. B. in znu umgestellt wird und unter Voranstellen zweier Füllbuchstaben, z. B. eul-, als Kenngruppe an der ausgesparten Stelle einzusetzen.

Unter gleichzeitiger Voransetzung des Spruchkopfes (vgl. Ziff. 12) lautet der zur Übermittlung fertige Spruch:

0405 – 1755 – 145 – oep wep –

hfikl	ulznu	bsgex	nnfop
rsalm	cydrj	qqarz	ubhfe
mooxz	lgred	lfijy	acivd
gnhye	xmjyr	aqztl	ssiwf
uwfhe	lnarz	qeduw	jvsfa
bskqu	dihsg	nejpf	afohw
egaim	fojrl	ekhbd	lpbme
binge			

Early in 1933 the machine was entirely reconstituted and the Poles could start the industrial production of the military Enigma machine in Warsaw.

Fourth cause Some errors made by the German operators.

In the course of the year 1932 the German operators were so careless in selecting specific keys for the messages that they would choose . . . hum . . . keys in the order of the keyboard, they would choose some letters ABC SSS . . . or things like that—they were so careless that Rejewski and his colleagues were able to elaborate some generic systems which allowed them (still starting from the mistake that was the duplication of the specific key of the message) . . . generic systems which allowed them to reconstitute both the configuration of the machine and the specific key of the message. Early in 1933 not only had the Poles reconstructed the machine, but also they could decipher its messages currently.

CHAPTER 2

A Short History of the Enigma Machine

Although Dr Arthur Scherbius pioneered the first commercial Enigma machine and gave it its name when he was on the board of directors of the Chiffriermaschinenaktiengesellschaft established at 2, Steglitzerstrasse, Berlin, in July 1923, it was an American Edward H. Hebern in California who first advertised a glow-lamp machine operated by revolving wheels or rotors for encipherment in 1921. The enciphered letters were illuminated on an alphabetical panel and he claimed that without changing code wheels the machine could devise '40,303,146,321,064,147,046,400,000 entirely different codes'. The US Navy purchased some models from time to time and some were actually in use until after Pearl Harbor, when two were captured by the Japanese. The British examined one and the Italians purchased an early version, but the Enigma machine as used by the German Armed Forces derived from the Scherbius model.

The Germans, the Poles, the Americans and the Japanese purchased some models and adopted them in their own way. A Captain Koot, a Dutch Army staff officer, tested one for two months in 1926–27 and declared 'even possession of an equal machine with the same electrical connections both in the ciphering cylinders and in other parts of the machine will not enable an unauthorised person, although he may be an expert in deciphering, to decipher a certain document or find out its solution by scientific methods, unless he knows the whole key.'

The US military attaché in Berlin, Colonel Conger, forwarded this report to Washington on 17 October, 1927, together with copies of

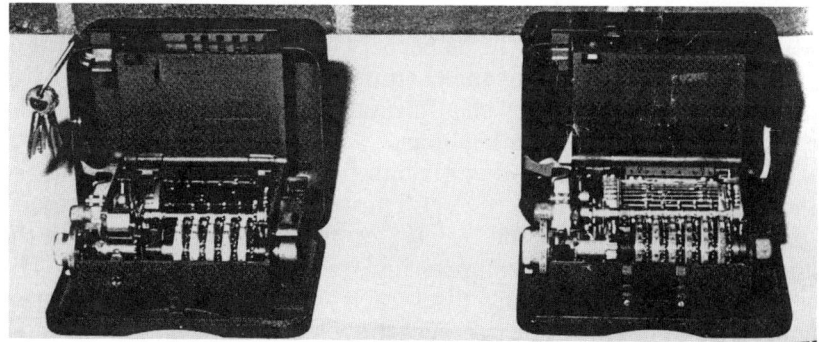

On the left, the Hagelin Cipher Machine C.36 used by the French Army, and the machine on the right, one of the 14,000 models further developed in the USA of the M209

the glow-lamp pamphlet as a result of which the chief signal officer purchased for 144 dollars a Scherbius machine to be shipped from Bremen to New York on the SS President Harding. Japan purchased a Scherbius in 1931 and after modifications it was used by the Japanese Navy in 1937 as the Model 97-skiki-o-bun in-ji-ki (Alphabetical Typewriter 97) which became known as the Purple Machine which the Americans broke and read during the war.

The assistant military attaché of the United States in Berlin, Major P.W. Evans, sent a report to Washington on 4 October 1930 on the signals communications on recent German Army manoeuvres and stated that they were 'using a typewriter type of enciphering device in the field'. Having been invited to view their latest devices by the overtly confident German Staff he sent a report on 2 July 1931 headed *'German (military) Subject: Ciphers used in Army signal communications'*. He described the machine as similar to the commercial Enigma machine and made by the same company. 'It has three enciphering wheels each of 25 numbered points on its periphery and the keyboard and lampboard are the same. The only difference in the military machine lies in the fact that at the front of the machine, just beneath the keyboard, there is a series of jacks with double contact plugs with cord connections which can make variable electric circuits in the machine.' He then went on to describe the Geheimschreibers in use: 'At the German War Department in the principal station of the German Army radio net there is another 'Enigma' machine of more elaborate design. This larger machine weighs approximately 200 lb and has ten enciphering wheels each of 25 points. This machine is built to give a typed copy of the enciphered message in groups of five characters or to give a typed clear message when the operator puts the enciphered message on the keyboard.'

He further describes another machine which may have been the one which the Allies never broke: 'A still more elaborate machine is in use in the message center of the Naval Communications which is in the same building (Reichswehrministerium) as the War Department. The machine has 20 enciphering discs each with 50 numbered contact points. The whole machine occupies the top of a table and must weigh 400 to 500 lb. Its operation is apparently similar to that of the War Department radio station.' While the British were not treating the German threat as serious, the Poles had been intercepting German Army signals at Poznan, Starograd and Krzlawice quite happily until they noticed in 1926 that the Germans on manoeuvres were employing a mechanical cipher which defeated their best cipher experts. According to Col Lisicki they were able to study that year a German military Enigma for a weekend by abstracting one from a box addressed to the German Embassy in Warsaw from the Railway Parcels Custom Office on a Friday afternoon and returning it before the following Monday morning. They also acquired a Scherbius machine and their subsequent complete success has already been related.

If the British had sent someone round to the Patent Office in 1927 they could have learned all about the Scherbius machine, with a technical description in English because the Chiffriermaschine Aktiengesellschaft of 2 Steglizerstrasse, Berlin W 35 applied on 17 January for a patent to cover British rights in the German invention which was accepted and registered on 11 August 1927. The most minute technical details were revealed as they had to be. The importance of being able to change round the three rotors was stressed. 'It is also possible to replace one or all of the ciphering drums 1, 2 and 3 by other ciphering drums which are differently interconnected. In case of war there is the further advantage that, for instance, when surprised by the enemy it is only necessary rapidly to remove the set of drums or even only one drum, thus rendering the ciphering machine useless for deciphering purposes.'

A further patent: 'Improvements in Coding Machines' (registered in Germany in 1928) was accepted by the British Patent Office on

16 February 1931, a bare nine months before Hans-Thilo Schmidt handed over the Enigma manuals to Bertrand.

The Italians also used a variant of the commercial Enigma machine, whose ciphers the British read in the Spanish Civil War and until the battle of Matapan. Then the Italians settled for the Hagelin. Its inventor had escaped from Sweden to New York with the blueprints and two machines in 1940 after a journey through Germany and the last peace-time crossing of the Atlantic on an Italian liner. It was adopted by the Americans who began its mass-production in 1942 and put 140,000 into service. The Converter M-209 was called C.36 in its European form.

In Sweden during the second half of the Second World War a six-rotor enciphering machine was built, which in spite of very slight adjustments printed the cipher- and clear-text on paper strips. This Hagelin-Cipher Machine BC-543 was subsequently built in the latter part of the war by Wanderer-Weke in Chemnitz, Germany, under the designation SG-41 (and also C-41). Unfortunately it was produced only in small quantities.

It is evident that the Americans could have made a serious impact on the reconstitution of the German military Enigma if they had not been distracted by the danger of the Rising Sun in the Pacific. They concentrated their interest and their cryptanalytical energies on breaking the Purple Machine, and lost their initial advantage over the British in their knowledge of the German progress in enciphering machines. In the upshot it was to the advantage of both countries that they each concentrated on one main adversary.

Having made the first replica of the German Military Enigma machine the Poles launched the industrial manufacture of the machine which was entrusted to A. Palluth, one of the directors of the AVA factory for radiophonic equipment in Warsaw. He had been closely linked with the work of the 'Biuro Szyfropw' or cipher bureau and it was he who translated the ideas of Rejewski into parts of equipment. The first industrial replicas came out of the factory in 1934 and by 1939 the Poles had 17 complete machines two of which were handed over to the French and British in August 1939. Considering the number of rotors incorporated in the cyclometres and bombas invented by the Poles it is calculated that the number of machines or essential parts which came out between 1934 and 1939 was four or five times that quantity.

After the fall of France in June 1940 Bertrand made some hazardous trips into occupied France to collect parts of the Enigma machine which he was having constructed in various suburbs of Paris, and before his capture by the Abwehr he had sufficient parts to build four Enigma replicas to use at his new HQ at PC Cadix near Uzès in the unoccupied zone. One of these machines survived the war and is now in the Sikorski Museum in London. The latest estimate of Gilbert Bloch (*Enigma Avant Ultra 1930-1940*) in September 1988 is that the Germans did not build 100,000 Enigma machines between 1930 and 1945, when the distribution was thought to be 60,000 simultaneously in service, with 30,000 for the Army, 20,000 for the Luftwaffe, 6,000 for the Navy and 4,000 for other services, Gestapo, SS and civil administration. A reasonable estimate for the number in operational use at the beginning of the war in 1939 was 40,000. Now his latest research puts the number manufactured between 1930 and 1945 at 50,000.

The complexities of the naval Enigma machine are highlighted by Gilbert Bloch. When the Army and the Luftwaffe had five rotors at their disposition at the end of 1938, the Navy had two extra, making seven, and an eighth was introduced shortly before the war began. In addition these extra rotors had two pawls instead of one, one being fixed, and their movement was therefore different. They did not duplicate the discriminant of the key as did the others and so the measures which were effective against the Army and Luftwaffe machines before 1 May 1940 did not pertain to the naval version.

The Royal Navy made great efforts to capture naval versions of the Enigma and also charts, special codes and a dictionary of abbreviations. They made a raid on the Lofoten Islands for this purpose on 23 February, 1941, and captured two meteorological trawlers, the Muenchen on 7 May 1941 and the Lauenberg on 25 June, as well as submarines with the naval Enigmas.

It has often been stated, erroneously, that the naval Enigma M4 incorporated four rotors. As Gilbert Bloch points out, this would have been impossible as it would have entailed increasing the width of the Enigma machine rendering it incompatible with the other versions. The modification was ingenious. The M3 had a relatively thick Umkehrwalze about 4 cm, against 2.5 for the rotors. They gave the M4 a thinner Umkehrwalze 2.5 cm and baptised it Umkehrwalze B. They added to the right of this thin fixed drum a new very slim

Left: Marine M-4 Enigma
Right: The Five additional rotors in carrying case.

additional drum, a Zusatzwalze, only 1.2 cm, called a Greek drum as it was designated by a letter of the Greek alphabet—Beta. This Greek drum did not revolve during encipherment or decipherment of a message and therefore needed no mechanism but could be turned manually to 26 different positions. Thanks to the combination of the Umkehrwalze b and the Greek drum the original single return drum was replaced by a modifiable return drum offering 26 possibilities. Moreover, in a certain position of the Beta drum, the conjunction of this drum and the Umkehrwalze b had the same characteristics as the former B drum thus assuring compatibility of M4 with the previous types of machine used by all arms of the German forces. Only in appearance did M4 seem to have four rotors.

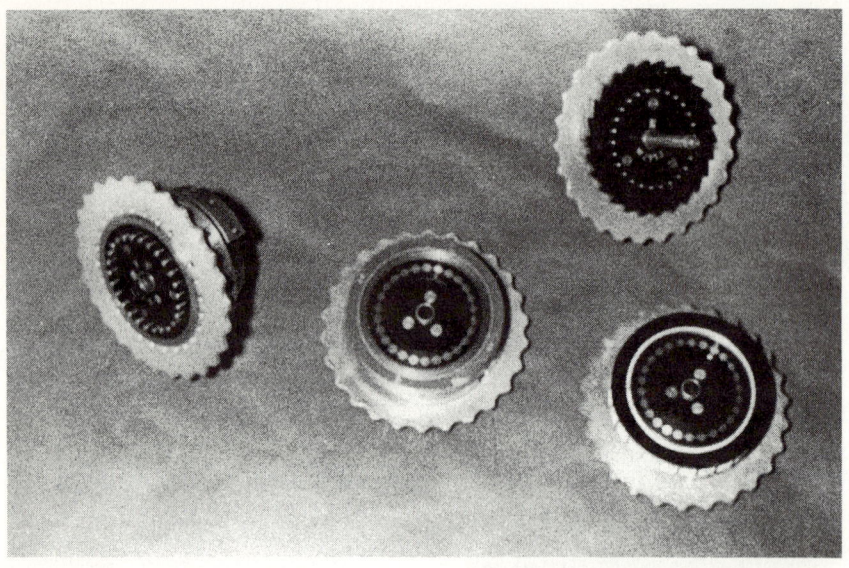

The Marine M-4 Enigma introduced 1.2.1942 for the Atlantic U-Boats caused the 'black-out' at Bletchley Park until December 1942 because of the fourth Greek rotor on the left.
(Courtesy BIBLIOTHEK fuer Zeitgeschichte Stuttgart)

From 1 February to December 1942 it was the great black-out for the Admiralty. But with tremendous cryptological efforts, the introduction of high-speed bombes, and the recovery of equipment and documents from damaged submarines, especially the U.559 on 30 October 1942, Bletchley Park was able to resume decryption in December 1942 and apart from rare temporary interruptions was not to lose mastery of it again.

The German Navy continued to make modifications. After the Beta drum came the Gamma drum to alternate with the Beta drum. An alternative to the thin return drum B was created with the bringing into service of a similar drum called C. A third Greek drum Delta should have been brought into operation in 1945 but did not materialise.

The Tape Recorder—Magnetophone

It had been thought until recently that the ubiquitous tape-recorder, first encountered by the Allies at Radio Luxembourg by Capt Henry of the Army Y service in 1944, had come into use late in the war. In the second volume of his history of German radio apparatus up till 1945 entitled 'Der Zweite Weltkrieg' Fritz Trenkle reveals details of the development of the machine for commercial and military purposes from 1935 till 1945. It is now clear that this was another of the successful German secret weapons.

'From 1935 the Magnetofon developed by AEG along with IG-Farben was taking its place in sports commentaries along with the wire sound recorder of Lorenz. From the portable version for broadcasting corporations AEG developed for military purposes the "Tonschreiber a". This was for predominantly stationary use within the intercept service for the recording of transmissions of all kinds (e.g. High speed Morse) but also for surveillance of long-distance calls.

Tonschreiber b was for field use in a Tornister case with a playing time of at first 30, later 60 minutes. With a frequency range of 50–10,000 Hz it served for recording foreign languages, fast telegraph and impulse transmissions After the fixed Intercept Service from 1939 the field intercept companies were also equipped with it. Its rotating sound-knob facilitated the slow playback of fast telegraphy in the original modulation (pitch).

Tonschreiber c had been developed as an especially light version with clockwork drive for the war correspondents who jumped with the Paras in Crete and for close reconnaissance units. From mid-1942 Y-platoons were equipped with it and the recording unit operated with a spring drive and DC current magnetisation while the playback had a 12-volt electric motor, three RV 12 P 200 valves and editing facility.

Tonschreiber d was developed from c especially for use in Propaganda Companies, for microphone interviews, recording of enemy propaganda, diffusion of counter-propaganda and for recordings for radio broadcasts of front-line reports.

Tonschreiber e was ordered by the Luftwaffe as the precursor of the flight recorder, with a long play-time for the recording of data and the clarification of aircraft crashes. The Luftwaffe gave up its development at the end of 1944.

Tonschreiber f was equipped with remote control for the surveillance of partisans and resistance groups in the west which started automatically with the dialling of certain telephone numbers and switched off at the end of the conversation. Up till the end of 1944 twenty production models had been delivered over and above eighty for Hans-Thilo Schmidt's "Forschungsamt".

Tonschreiber g was ordered for the recording of data on several sound-tracks but the development was soon halted.

Tonschreiber h was ordered by several departments and especially for the German Navy, to record higher frequencies in the 30 or 100 kHz band, but could not be developed because of shortage of personnel'.

Tonschreiber(=Magnetofon) Ton.S.a

Tonschreiber b mit Laufwerkteil (oben) und Verstärkerteil (unten)

Tonschreiber c (A) Aufnahmetell (links) und Wiedergabetell Ton.S.c. (W) (rechts)

Tonschreiber C(A) Recording section on the left and Replay Ton S.C.(W) on the right.

Photos: Courtesy Fritz Trenkle

Photos: Courtesy
Fritz Trenkle

Sound Tape Recorders.

Top Tonschreiber d on the left with microphone amplifier in the middle and receiver on the right.
Middle Tonschreiber d
Bottom Commercial GRUNDIG TK 8 Tape Recorder c.1960.

FORSCHUNGSAMT[1]
(Organisation générale en 1940)

SERVICE CENTRAL – BERLIN. 116 À 126 Schillerstrasse

1er Bureau
- 1re Section – Organisation, Sécurité.
- 2e Section – Administration.

2e Bureau
- 3e Section – Personnel.

3e Bureau
- 4e Section – Centralisation et Répartition des recherches.
- 5e Section – Centralisation et Répartition des rapports.

4e Bureau – Cryptographie
- 6e Section – Question scientifique – Codes.
- 7e Section – Affaires anglo-saxonnes, espagnoles, portugaises, Asie.
- 8e Section – Affaires francophones, Italie, Pays-Bas, Belgique, Suisse.
- 9e Section – Affaires slaves, nordiques et autres.

5e Bureau – Exploitation
- 10e Section – Synthèses, Rapports.
- 11e Section – Politique extérieure.
- 12e Section – Politique économique.
- 13e Section – Politique intérieure.

6e Bureau : 14e Section – Recherches techniques. – 15e Section – Réalisations techniques.

SERVICES EXTÉRIEURS

Sept Forschungsleitstellen (F.L.S.)
(même organisation interne que le Service Central)

Centralisation régionale (fichiers-archives).
Direction du travail des postes spécialisés (F.S.).
Exploitation locale :
Berlin   München
Hamburg   Breslau
Köln   Wien
Stuttgart

Forschungsstellen (F.S.)
Postes spécialisés dans les écoutes et contrôles

F.S. A – Écoutes et contrôles téléphoniques (A_1 et A_2 langues étrangères, A_3 allemand). Berlin, Königsberg, Dantzig, Litzmannstadt, Kattowitz, Stuttgart, Breslau, Stettin, Dresden, Wien, Köln, Nürnberg, Nordhausen, München, Frankfurt, Hamburg. (A partir de 1941 toutes les grandes villes occupées).

F.S. B – Écoutes et contrôles radios intérieurs.
   C – Écoutes et contrôles radios extérieurs.
Templin, Glienicke, Lübben, Leha, Lissa, Eutin, Köln, Deutz, Konstanz. (A partir de 1941 : Sofia, Amsterdam, Plodiv, Reval.)

F.S. D – Contrôle télégraphique et télex } Bureaux de postes du Reich et aux
F.S. F – Contrôle postal   armées (y compris pays occupés).

Nota. En 1941 des postes d'écoutes téléphoniques ont été installés à Paris, Bordeaux, Bayonne, Dijon, Lille. En 1943 à Lyon et Marseille.

---

1. Tableau réalisé en partant des informations et documents fournis par H. E. et par les services historiques allemands.

Notre espion chez Hitler (Courtesy of Col. Paillole)

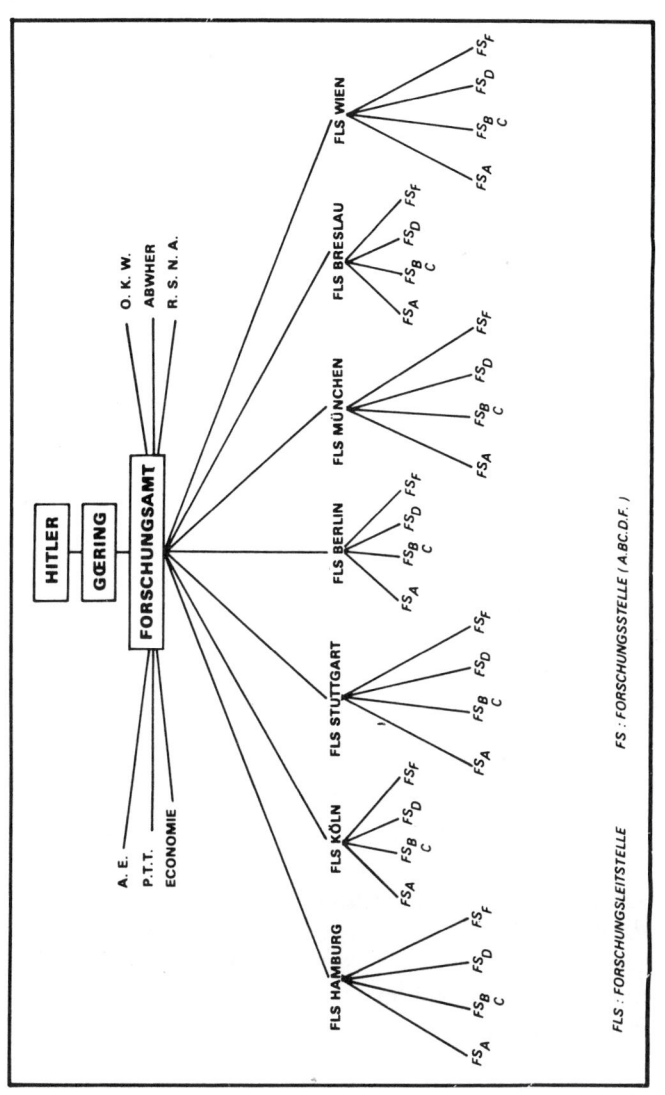

ARTICULATIONS ET LIAISONS
DU FORSCHUNGSAMT (1940)

Notre espion chez Hitler (Courtesy of Col. Paillole)

The Germans gained a great advantage by the invention and development of the magnetofon. The BBC had improved on the recording of sound on wax discs with the Blattnerphone but the wire made editing impossible or very laborious. It is now evident that with the Magnetofon the Germans were able to tape countless private conversations and filled up the concentration camps, with a great economy in man-power, and to tape diplomatic ciphers.

In *Spies of the Airwaves* the organisation of the Forschungsamt under Goering is described with the locations of the various intercept sections or Forschungsstellen:

Forschungsstellen A —intercept of telephone messages
Forschungsstellen B —radio intercept (internal)
Forschungsstellen C —radio intercept (external)
Forschungsstellen D1—intercept of teleprinters
Forschungsstellen D2—intercept of telegrams
Forschungsstellen F —intercept of letters.

There were six divisions of the FA—administration, personnel, research, cryptography, exploitation and technical research. The most important was IV—cryptography with two friends of Hans-Thilo Schmidt in charge of 240 technicians and cipher specialists.

Goering appointed Prince Christopher von Hesse, uncle of Prince Philip, in April 1935, as head of the FA and in December 1935 they decrypted often in less than 24 hours 2,200 messages mainly of French, British and Italian origin. In 1935 they intercepted 34,000 internal and 8,400 external communications (radio, telephone and others), to be exploited by the Abwehr, Foreign Affairs Ministry, Gestapo, High Command, Finance Dept, etc. It was calculated they must have made more then 30 million intercepts of all kinds. The table of organisation compiled by Col Paillole in his book *Notre Espion Chez Hitler* shows to what an extent the FA had grown by 1941. With many millions of messages being registered, many at very high speeds, one wondered how this was achieved. No longer. It was the Magnetofon which made it possible.

CHAPTER 3

A Modern Odyssey

Between 1931 and 1939 Gustave Bertrand made 19 trips abroad to meet the traitor Hans-Thilo Schmidt (Asche) to purchase documents mainly about the Enigma machine and its monthly issues of daily keys:

Belgium	4
Denmark	1
Switzerland	12
Czechoslovakia	1
France	1

He also made 13 visits to Poland to carry this indispensable material to the Polish cryptographers. Having failed to interest the British allies in this intelligence coup he also visited other Allies in Czechoslovakia and the Baltic States as he was not receiving any direct confirmation from Warsaw that they were breaking Enigma. His colleague Colonel Langer (Luc) had not been able to reveal this to Bertrand because Poland had signed non-aggression pacts with Russia in 1932 and the Third Reich on 26 January 1934, and Marshal Pilsudski and Colonel Beck, the head of the Polish Intelligence Services, had ordered complete secrecy in their success with the Enigma machine.

According to Bertrand (*Enigma—1973*)(p. 36):

> 'So, I am alone facing this situation, and my cryptographic knowledge will never be sufficient, especially as there is nothing to be expected from the French side, where all documents received are being submitted to the Head of Cipher section and carefully filed by him.

I must therefore seek elsewhere among friendly intelligence services; and as relations between these are never disinterested whatever the degree of confidence and friendship presiding there, one must present oneself "with hands full" in order to dominate the situation; this is so.

But who are the others? Some discreet soundings of the Polish Intelligence Service shows a study of the question with a certain desire to succeed but there is no possibility of espionage in this matter. The Czech service is also seeking, but without much hope. As for the British, which it is said possesses a technical team, important in quality as well as in numbers, it appears to be disinterested, (which does not mean that it is not working at it!) the threat from Germany being neither certain nor immediate, therefore requires evidence before believing. St Thomas would have been worthy of such a match!'

At the first meeting with Hans-Thilo Schmidt he established his credentials and said he could produce documents on the Enigma machine and military information emanating from his brother General Rudolf Schmidt. At the next meeting a week later on 8 November 1931 in the same Grand Hotel at Verviers on the actual frontier of Holland and Germany he produced for Major Bertrand a hundred documents from a concertina portfolio which included:

— a diagram and plan of the organisation of the Berlin Cipher Office;
— a radio code as all messages enciphered by Enigma are transmitted by W/T;
— a book of manual ciphers with keys used by the Wehrmacht HQs;
— a War Office study on toxic gases, use and protection, from his brother;
— a short technical note about the Enigma Type 1 in service, with variable connections;
— a numbered copy of the User Manual for Enigma 1, Gebrauchsanweisung H. Dv.g.13 und L.Dv. g.13 (See 1937 issue of the same in Appendix);
— a numbered copy of the Enciphering Procedure for Enigma 1.Schluessel—Anleitung H.Dv.G 14.L.Dv.G.14 und M.Dv.G.168 (1937 issue in Appendix).

The last two documents were indispensable for the reconstitution of the service Enigma machine, complete as they were with plans and photos. Bertrand took this treasure trove to the Cipher Office of the Army Command and their verdict was that it was unbreakable. Bertrand insisted they should acquire a commercial Enigma, try to reconstitute the military version and decrypt intercepted Enigma messages. The Head of the Cipher Office took away the documents and gave his verdict on 20 November. They had not the means to attempt such a monumental labour. It was a day of mourning for Bertrand, and his chiefs in the Intelligence Service were equally glum.

'With their agreement I decided to consult our English friends. In Paris I entrusted the photographs of the two manuals for the "Use of and for the Encipherment of the Enigma Machine" to Cdr Wilfred Dunderdale, the SIS representative. I requested him to inform his chiefs of the possibilities being offered to us. I proposed to go to London to examine with the British specialists the common approach to our research work. If my venture succeeded I had the secret hope it would stimulate the interest of the French decryption services. Dunderdale, a natural enthusiast convinced of the importance of my supplies, left at once for London on 23 November. He was back on the 26 November and from the consternation of his face I realised he had obtained no more success than I had in France. On the advice of my "Patron" who was as determined as I to exploit Asche's resources to the full, I sought an interview through the Polish Embassy with Lt Col G. Langer, head of the Cipher Office in Warsaw. I sent the documents by diplomatic bag and recovered them on 7 December 1931 at the French Embassy in Warsaw'.

The Poles succeeded in less than a year in reconstituting the military Enigma and decrypting it.

'There is nothing more for it but to have a go, with all due desirable diplomacy in these different directions although it is in fog that I have to go to Warsaw, Prague and London, with the approval of my superiors—my own superior and his "Patron" the head of Army GHQ—to whom I have to expose my plans and the results I hope to achieve. I have complete liberty of action, and the assurance that all my initiatives in this undertaking will be appropriate "under my own responsibility".

Warsaw. It would be as well to remember that there existed at that time no technical liaison with the Polish HQ: sure, results of interception on the two networks was exchanged but on the French side, at least, little came out, at most some texts enciphered manually, i.e. double transposition when optimum conditions were present, i.e. three texts of the same length enciphered with the key for the same day. The remainder was enciphered by mechanical process whether it was German army or navy traffic.

The first liaison took place in Warsaw from 7–11 December 1931. On my arrival at the Central Station Gopwna I find a representative of the "House" in Warsaw who takes me immediately to the hotel designated by the Polish service then to their Deuxième Bureau (EMG) on which the service depends and with which I have to deal and whose chief is Luc (Lt Col Langer). Very well received in all respects, à la Polonaise. I at last make the acquaintance of Luc: a historic moment as will be seen in due course: first impression is excellent. Asche's documents are welcomed like manna in the desert and all doors are immediately opened. A new era opens for Luc in the study of the Enigma enciphering machine—his supreme aim as well—and he promises to keep me constantly au courant with results obtained, which were going to increase ipso facto because, for the moment, these were shown to be rather weak. In fact Luc's service is admirably set up and equipped with mathematicians who have been studying the question since 1928 solely through intercepted messages without any other documentation.

A collaboration sure and durable (the interest of each was at stake) to become friendship and to enter history unknowingly. Thus there will be thirteen liaison visits of mine to Warsaw and as many by Luc to Paris before arriving at the final result. Henceforward, Study—work on cipher—texts for Luc and for me Research.

In addition, from the intercept point of view we divide up German territory so as to obtain the maximum enciphered messages each day which will be communicated in each diplomatic bag—same procedure for direction-finding plots to locate the army network transmitters whose call-signs vary every day. It is full steam ahead at Warsaw.

London. Same kind of contact but London maintains no liaison with Luc and, moreover, is on bad terms with the Polish IS. Confidence does not reign there. Even so the day will come when the IS will wake up and will want to have double rations then—almost on the eve of war.

Prague. In agreement with Luc we must find out where Prague stands in his domain: but Poles and Czechs are not on good intelligence terms, firstly naturally, and secondly because of Teshen. They rely on me to try to find out what is going on in Prague and also to try to patch it up between the two Services: I shall on the whole succeed.

The same procedure as in Warsaw: the Chief is Raoul, basically Austrian like Luc, which eases matters. There the Establishment is weak. But it is rather an information exercise without Asche's documents—with promises, however, so as to have a clear picture. Raoul is very interested in this collaboration and attracted by the promises. Suddenly he puts his cards on the table: he has not much to offer but one quickly has the feeling that he wants to succeed and had been working on the question for a fairly long time already. His ideas are not negligible, nor are his deductions. As for the intercepts they are different from ours and it seems desirable to obtain them, which is immediately accepted. It is agreed that Raoul will come to Paris, which delights him, and we will walk hand in hand for the future, even with Luc in a common aim.

Nevertheless, this collaboration was being established with the greatest circumspection for the Prague EMG (like the French IS) was very exposed to German "penetration"—in agreement with Luc besides—to such good effect that technical notices will be entrusted to Raoul. And so I retain the "key" to the problem and we must endeavour to arrive at the solution as soon as possible for events are moving quickly. With time confidence increased. At a reunion in Paris, with Luc and Raoul I launched the idea of technical information only—one with Prague and the other with Warsaw to be used in emergency—the code being composed and supplied by myself. This was the BLR link (using the initials of the three nicknames, Bolek being mine in Poland), which was ready to function from 1 January 1938.

The Baltic States. To complete our interception of German radio traffic I had to go to Lithuania, to Riga, where there was a Radio Intercept Network mounted by the "House"—with the agreement of the Latvian EMG—which had a good reception of German transmissions: but it was necessary to steer it because it made chance interceptions being unaware of the question. I set off one day from Paris for Riga, with the Nord-Express to Berlin, from where the Wagon-Lit in which I was alone, with two Russian diplomatic couriers as neighbours, was attached to the Moscow train at the Schlesischer Bahnhof. Then it was Kustrin, Schneidemuhl, Fuerschau, the Polish Corridor . . . and then East Prussia . . . Lithuania with . . . Virbalis . . . and finally Latvia with . . . Riga. The Baltic States are situated on the East coast of the Baltic Sea. Latvia occupies a central position among them at the cross-roads linking Western and Eastern Europe: it is the "Baltic Riviera" while in the interior is the "Latvian Switzerland". The Letts are not Slavs but represent with the Lithuanians a separate branch of the Indo-European family: their language is near to Sanskrit.

Attended at Riga station by the "House" representative of the Baltic intercept service, I am taken to a hotel room reserved for me. Then come the Protocol visits to the French as well as to the Latvians: Then to work—because tomorrow is the national holiday which I shall have to attend and above all the review of the Riga Division.

Then a tour of Estonia, where they know nothing at all about interception. Riga, Valka, Tallinn (the former Russian Reval) 430 km, one night. A day in Tallinn, just time to see the Estonian Military Authorities with which there is nothing to do from the intercept point of view, and visit the city. It is the month of May, it is no longer freezing or one could cross the ice to go to Finland on the other side of the Gulf of Finland.

At last, return via Lithuania, to complete the prospecting trip. Same mission with the Lithuanian intercept service and same result: no organisation of this kind and then . . . it is still a delicate matter

But I have to return via Warsaw and the railway line between the Lithuanian frontier and Wido has been cut since the affair with Poland: then I have to return to Koenigsberg, and hence via Prostken, Grajewo and Bialystok one can reach Warsaw. . . A detente is necessary away from work for one cannot allow oneself to become besotted, ceaselessly, with the Enigma machine. On my tenth liaison with Warsaw—the preceding one having left a bad impression of Berlin—I judged it preferable not to take the Nord-Express and to go round via Vienna and Prague. I was accompanied this time by Arnaud, the chief of Transmissions of the "House" invited by Luc to finalise the BLR link.

On arriving in Vienna 11 March 1938 in the evening, intending to go to Warsaw, while crossing the city by taxi from one station to the other, great commotion at the Estbahnhof and armed troops awaiting—surely a VIP, not us, naturally. Already since Linz the train had been invaded by an excited crowd going to Vienna talking of events to come and suggesting something was going to happen. Crossing

Vienna the taxi-driver said: "Hitler ist da!" (Hitler is here!) And from all sides the SA were occupying the city, in threes on one motorcycle. At the Ostbahnhof, at the Warsaw train, great surprise, Luc was waiting to escort us to the Polish frontier for "the march of events was unforeseen". But there was also the French Military Attaché who had just received telegraphic orders to turn us back at once to return to the "House". However we obtained after a long discussion (how can one discuss the order of a military attaché especially in a foreign country) about being able to pass the night and next morning to see what was going to happen, on condition of telephoning the "Patron" at once to ask for his instructions. And so, before going to look for a lodging—which did not look good, as almost all the hotels having been requisitioned for Hitler's arrival, we had to go to the Embassy to telephone. We succeeded in these terms:

— "Hello, Colonel, would you be good enough to authorise us to stay a little in Vienna instead of returning immediately?"
— "in Vienna, what Vienna? " (either he had got out of bed on the wrong side or he had forgotten we were passing through Vienna to go to Poland!)
— "In Austria, of course! And we would like to be present when Hitler will arrive tomorrow morning".
— "Return at once by the first train!"
— "All right!"

As the first train was leaving the next day after lunch the match was won but it was the last train, as will be seen. After visiting a certain number of hotels, by taxi, we managed to obtain lodging until next morning "Before 8 a.m.!"—all Vienna's hotels being booked from that time onwards for Hitler's entourage. All night an orgy of singing and shouting and laughter: Twenty-four hours sufficed to win over those who were hesitating to welcome National-Socialism! Next morning, up early and down to the street, very quickly so as to miss nothing. The streets are littered with the tracts of the Patriotic Front dropped by Austrian aircraft in view of the plebiscite foreseen by Chancellor Schussnig for 13 March, but who, faced with the threat of German invasion, had to give in and yield his position to a minister Seyss-Inquart.

About 10 a.m. a large group of three-engined Heinkel aircraft flies over Vienna on its way to the Aspern Airport to disembark their cargo of German troops; on the way they sprinkle the city with tracts and a rain of little multi-coloured paper swastikas. Immediately there are processions and the Hitler flag is hoisted above the Chancellery. Moreover Swastika tie-pins are sold everywhere and it is good if not prudent to buy one and to stick on your jacket lapel. In front of the Opera an immense crowd processes in front of a life-size effigy of Hitler, not without kneeling in front of it and making the sign of the cross: He's the new God.

But the news spreads during the morning that Hitler will make his entry in Vienna the day after tomorrow (14th), and all rail traffic will be suspended for 48 hours—while the Gestapo is going to "clean up" the city.

Nevertheless on leaving the Left Luggage where we had just deposited our bags as we left the hotel I heard someone behind me say "Es sind zwei Juden!" (These are two Jews). It is true that Arnaud has a nose a teeny-bit·sheeny but it seems desirable not to hang about all the more because having checked it out, it is indeed

Top left Feb 1967 at the Invalides, General de Gaulle decorates General G. Bertrand DSO as Grand Officer of the Legion of Honour.
Top Right Commander Wilfred Dunderdale known as "Bill".
Bottom April 1940 at P.C. Bruno Left to Right: Lt-Col Langer Head of the Polish Cipher Bureau, Major Bertrand, Captain MacFarlane of the Intelligence Service.

the last train! And we take it: on the way control after control by the Hitler Youth, by police in mufti recognisable by their mien in all countries of the world and we did not feel safe until we crossed the Swiss frontier at Buchs. Our arrival in Paris dissipated all worries they had about our safety. Our families were there to welcome us for they were all already wondering what our fate had been in Vienna, in Austria.

Back in Warsaw Luc will send me this missive:

"Warsaw
11 April, 1938

Dear Captain,

Infinite thanks for your last letter and also all that you sent me (understood: monthly keys for Enigma). I much regret you were not able to continue your journey because I would have been very happy to see you among us. Now we do not know when we shall see each other again next time. It is written—but nevertheless at the Gare du Nord it was for us a historic moment. Now we are going through a very rough time. After the Saar and after Austria—who? The colonies, Czechoslovakia or us?

We can only see that a lot of explosive has been collected together in Europe. And after it explodes? An alteration of frontiers, perhaps a change of ideas, heavy losses and again divergences of opinion and new perils. It is History, it is true, but this is not the aim of Humanity.

After this digression I must thank you for your great work. Your last piece is so well done that I must congratulate you on it (understood: the BLR link). As I am on the subject of this piece, I would like to ask you if it is possible for you to fix MEZ (Middle European Time) for the surveillance exercise, as at present we have an immense load of traffic. For the other exercise—no change. The Station in the Wood is functioning already. Before closing I should like to say a word to you. You are a great worker and for men like you life is not very easy,—one eats one's bread by the sweat of one's brow—very often there are disappointments but the end crowns the work".

In the course of a liaison visit to Prague I had expressed the wish to see this Sudeten region of which so much was spoken as it was one of the principal objectives of Hitler. Indeed encouraged by the admirable success of his methods of demoralisation and internal intimidation, Hitler, after swallowing up Austria, attacked Czechoslovakia, the forward bastion of France. Three and a half million Germans in the Sudetenland are for him an admirable instrument to blow up the framework of this country which projects like a wedge into his new Empire. The scenario is always the same: Hitler uneconomical with German blood pushes his partisans to the most extreme acts of violence to cast the responsibility back upon the government of Prague. He summons to Berchtesgaden Henlein, chief of the Sudetens, and gives him instructions to undermine Czech unity while he affirms he will not interfere in the conflict which opposes the Bohemian Germans to the Government of Prague.

The "minorities" in Czechoslovakia consist of:
Hungarians – 1 million
Ruthenians – ½ million
Germans – 3½ millions

These people cast nostalgic glances at their respective "mother country", Hungary, Russia and Germany, although the Ruthenians had never belonged to the German Reich (except when it was part of the Germanic Holy Roman Empire the composition of which was moreover rather vague), but only to Austria. These minorities desired at least a greater autonomy than that which they enjoyed. But in 1933 when Hitler became Chancellor the virus of National Socialism seeped into the Germans of the Sudetenland. We saw the German Sudeten Party (SDP) created at the instigation of a mild-mannered gymnastic teacher named Konrad Henlein. In 1935 he had enrolled the majority of the Sudetens except the Social-Democrats and the Communists. At the Anschluss this party which had been receiving directives for three years from Berlin was ready to carry out Hitler's orders. Henlein himself summed up the ideas of the Fuehrer: "We must always formulate demands so exorbitant that they can never be satisfied." The situation of the German minority in Czechoslovakia was therefore for Hitler only a pretext to prepare a coup in a country he coveted, to ruin the land, bring trouble and confusion into the minds of the nations friendly to this country and to mask the true aims he was pursuing.

Last souvenir of Poland, on 27 May, 1938, Luc invites us to visit the "Station in the Wood" at Mokotov, baptised in the conventional language as Wycher, which means the "Wind".

There everything is under a concrete shelter from the radio station to the cryptologues' offices: it is the brain of the organisation where they work night and day in silence. Woods there are and one is forced to conserve them to camouflage the concrete works which disappear totally from the sight of aircraft: one has to think of everything.

This mission will be my last but one in Poland, a souvenir which will never desert me! for it seems clear that "Enigma" has had it! so high is morale . . . but still no avowal!'

The indefatigable Bertrand travelled far and worked hard to find allies for his research into the conquest of the Enigma after his rebuttal by the British in 1931. In all, his journeys totalled 63,100 km or 38,125 miles, one and a half times round the world, almost entirely by rail and the people with whom he discussed the problems of interception were in countries subsequently overrun by the Germans or the Russians or both. There were risks of leakage. In addition he made thirteen fruitless journeys to Holland to confer with a self-styled member of the Russian Intelligence Service, nicknamed Walter Scott who was in the market for purchasing foreign codes and ciphers. Taking Rex (Lemoine), France's expert in buying ciphers, with him to the Hasenkamp in Rotterdam for their usual meetings

The literary trio: William Shakespeare (Lemoine), Walter Scott ('W. Scott'), Victor Hugo (Bertrand)

with Walter Scott, Bertrand could not establish whether W.S. was real or a fake and as he skilfully avoided offering anything worthwhile that corresponded with what Bertrand had to offer, Bertrand considered W.S. only wanted to know what they had in their possession. He had sniffed him out. The trio adopted literary names for their cover and so Rex became W. Shakespeare and Bertrand Victor Hugo. They were snapped by a street photographer in the Hague all three in step.

According to Bertrand the British woke up after the Anschluss and he was able at last to propose a meeting with the Poles under the aegis of the French in Paris.

'With this aim in mind I go to London and the enthusiasm I raise with the British cryptologists (these sphinxes that nobody has the right to see) is delirious. The documents from Asche are all the rage, even doled out in driblets and they want still more! Besides Luc asks no more questions: is it because Asche can no longer answer them following his change of job, or is it rather that he needs nothing more having in hand all he needs? As for me I wait patiently for Luc to open up, for I have learned from contacts with them that a maximum of diplomacy is always necessary with the Poles.'

By December 1938, after Munich, there was a danger they would be overtaken by events and Bertrand decided that it was time for the British technicians, always omniscient, to be convinced that they must meet their Polish counterparts. Relations between the British and Polish Intelligence Services had been rather cold—this was before the Anglo-Polish pact of May 1939 which re-established friendly relations—and so Bertrand went to London to pave the way.

The first meeting took place on 9 and 10 January 1939 in the offices of the Service de Renseignement in Paris and included Polish experts, of which Luc was the leader, British experts with Denniston, and a French 'expert' who attended only the first meeting and decided it was not even worthwhile attending another. Bertrand summarises the results of these meetings:

> 'Each representative explained his methods and researches and his results obtained up to 15 September 1938 when the system was modified by the Germans probably by the introduction of mobile cylinders in the machine. Although the methods used were a little different from each other and the ideas exchanged had proved useful to everyone, the work undertaken seemed to have reached an impasse in which only information from agents will enable a solution to be found: for this purpose a technical questionnaire had been established as simple as possible to be handed to such an agent suitable to accomplish such a mission. Moreover the research work had been split up the best possible way and these missions will be pursued thoroughly.
>
> In conclusion, the opinion of the best technicians in this question who moreover find themselves united in a sincere desire to succeed is that this question is not insoluble if certain external elements can be obtained while the reconstruction of the machine solely through the study of texts appears practically impossible: that was, moreover, the opinion of the German technicians who set themselves the same task before putting their machine in service.'

Hope was born, and the satisfaction of the British team was expressed in a stirring letter from Cdr Denniston Head of the Decryption Service amplified naturally by the Head of the IS. 'M' himself, Colonel Stuart Menzies.

They parted having fixed the next meeting for Warsaw and the one after in London but only if something new came up.

By May, London with nothing on the horizon was becoming impatient. Bertrand calmed them down for Luc was not yet ready for the meeting.

The French High Command thought everything was going well and now pinned its hopes on the efforts of the 'technicians' and Asche having founded their greatest hopes on him following the special missions and technical liaison visits of which it had been kept informed.

'Then came the great moment in July 1939—Luc's invitation by telegraph—there was "something new" relating to the conclusions of the last meeting.

Nevertheless Denniston in London is taking a lot of coaxing: perhaps he wants to arrive at the tape alone, with the halo of glory, taking his time of course. But faced with my insistence and the orders of his chief he weakens and yields.

On 24 July 1939 everyone arrives in Warsaw, Braquenie and I by the Nord-Express and those from London by air—all anxious for the morrow. The same evening without waiting for the meeting on the morrow Luc revealed to me that his efforts had not been in vain and that not only had the secret of the Machine been pierced (thanks to Asche's documentation) but that some copies of the Machine had been reconstituted, of which he had two for my disposal, one for me and one for the British, which I should take myself to London—the surprise being kept for the morrow.

Next morning everyone was led to the "Station in the Woods" where the real interviews took place, following which Luc presented the reconstituted Machine. It was a moment of stupefaction for Denniston and Knox and it was then for the first time perhaps that the pride of the British technicians succumbed to the results obtained by the Polish technicians. They had to recognise nevertheless that in six months Great Britain was profiting gratuitously from eight years of Franco-Polish friendship, forged at the price of a dozen liaisons maintained in mutual confidence. But Denniston and Knox wanted to draw up plans of the instrument and immediately summon from London specialist mechanics and electricians: they could not believe their ears that two models were destined for us, one for Paris and one for London which would be handed to me before my departure: up to me to make arrangements with London!

Unfortunately the Germans had just modified their system by bringing into service already on 1 July 1939 the mobile rotors (Walzer) and more research was needed, but this time on solid foundations for the machine was there.'

Bertrand and Braquenie returned to Paris by air but with a stopover in Berlin. They made a cultural tour of the sights and joined the hysterical crowd in front of the Chancellery waiting to greet Hitler. The Germans stood with photos of their leader and a pen for his autograph. They mingled with the crowd for half-an-hour but he was late and they did not wish to miss their plane. They changed planes again at Cologne, to a Dewoitine 338, and dined in the air before reaching le Bourget.

'The machines arrived in the first Diplomatic bag and on 16 August 1939 I was on my way to London accompanied by Uncle Tom—the diplomatic courier of the British Embassy in Paris—who was carrying a diplomatic bag with the Enigma Machine. At Victoria Station Colonel Menzies, Head of the IS wearing the rosette of the Legion of Honour in the buttonhole of his dinner-jacket (he was going to a soirée) was waiting for us: triumphal welcome! Which occasioned him to say one day to a "Patron" of the "House" that the SR had done him a *"considerable service on the eve of war"*.

'As for the Polish Cryptologists, to them and them alone all the merit and all the glory of having taken to a successful conclusion, technically, this incredible adventure, thanks to their knowledge and tenacity unequalled in any country in the world!'

CHAPTER 4

Report on the work of Colonel Langer's team during the campaign in France

On 27 Sept 1939 I arrived at Calimanesti where, at about 11 a.m., Capt de Winter of the French Army came to me to warn me that the French Mission had received a telegram from Paris announcing that 'Bruno' (Capt Bertrand of the Ve French Section) was inviting me and my comrades with our families, in the name of his Chief, to Paris. I informed Lt Col Mayer who gave his agreement for our departure taking into account the possibilities of the continuation of our work.

On 1 October 1939 I arrived in Paris and announced my arrival next day to our Embassy, obtaining the agreement of the Polish military authorities, to continue our work at the French Headquarters. In January our attachment appeared in the Journal Per. Nr 1—(Placed at the disposal of the Bureau Personnel Militaire—without pay).

For the first weeks we remained in Paris because at that moment PC Bruno was being organised in the Chateau de Vignolles near Gretz (35 km SE of Paris). On 20 Jan 1940 we arrived at our new workplace. Our principal task was to pursue studies to determine the eventual changes in the use of the Enigma machine. (Note of the translator from the Polish—Gilbert Bloch—On 15 Dec 1938 the Germans had added rotors *IV* and *V* to the series of three rotors formerly used (*I*, *II* and *III*). On 1 Jan 1939 they had increased the number of mobile plugs—Steckers—to be engaged daily. The Poles thought, wrongly as it turned out, that other modifications could have been brought in on the same date for the German procedures in the use of Enigma).

To explain the problem I would like to sum up the situation in a few words. After several years of labour we had managed to reconstitute the German methods of encipherment. For quite a long time we were able almost daily to decrypt German telegrams coming from different networks. In January 1938 for two weeks exercises took place in near-war conditions to judge the possibilities of decryption and of reading messages intercepted by permanent listening stations. The result was that we were capable of deciphering 75% of the communications of the various networks. Towards the end of 1938 the French took the initiative in organising in Paris, with the participation of the representatives of the HQs of the countries interested (France, Poland and Great Britain), to discuss problems involved in decryption. This conference took place and I went on this occasion to Paris accompanied by Major Ciezki. My superiors had forbidden me to reveal the results that we had obtained.

As the political situation did not cease getting worse the Commandant of the Second Section obtained the agreement of our HQ to reveal our secrets to our future Allies, which was done in the second part of the month of July, 1939, in Warsaw. So as to accelerate research I gave, with the agreement of my Chief, to the British as well as to the French, one Enigma machine.

On my visit of August 1939 to Paris I confirmed that matters stood like this: no study had been engaged by the French, while the British, as I had learned during my stay in England (December 1939), had begun studies at once and also allotted the sum of £12,000 for the construction of machines and auxiliary equipment. We had been able to save from Poland two machines which we arranged to be brought to France and we had therefore begun work with three machines. Research proved to be long and we had lived through difficult moments. When all seemed lost on 17 January 1940 (during the stay of one of the British in our workplace) our team succeeded in determining the setting of 28 October 1939. And so we knew henceforth that no change had taken place (in the German procedures) until that date.

The question of an eventual change after 1 Jan 1940 continued to be faced but it was resolved in the negative at the end of the month of January. This was all the more important because the British had meanwhile found in a German submarine rotors VI and VII used by the Navy.

(Translator's note: Lt Col Langer is certainly referring to the capture on 12 Feb 1940 of the three rotors (effectively the rotors *VI* and *VII*) when the U-Boat U.33 was destroyed) by HMS Bulldog.) The German Air Force was using the series of 5 rotors as during the period which had preceded the war. (Previously all arms of the service used 3 rotors. It was only a year before the war in Warsaw that Colonel Zychon had warned us of the use of 5 and thanks to that we had undertaken studies which permitted us to reconstitute the internal cabling of the 2 new rotors).

Results obtained

During our stay in France were decrypted:
- Norwegian Campaign : 1,151 messages
- French Campaign : 5,064 messages
- clandestine (working for the Germans) : 287 messages
- others : 1,918 messages

Langer displays a table of dates of transmission of messages and the corresponding date of establishing the setting for the day, either at PC Bruno or received from England.

These begin on 6 July 1939 when it took 50 days, gradually speeding up until 9 March 1940 when it took 2 days, then it became one day until the procedures were changed on 15 May and resuming on 20 May it took only one day on most days until operations ceased on 16 June.

Summary

—number of days for which settings were determined   110
—number of settings determined   126
—percentage of settings determined by the British   83%

The difficulties

(1) 'When I went to England in December 1939 we brought up the possibility of collaborating. The British demanded specialists. Personally I thought that we at that time should stay where our army was being formed. The proposal of the British to create a common cell as at PC Bruno was rejected by the French. We finally decided we ourselves were going to conduct our researches and that the British were going to busy themselves with technical work and exploitation. As I mentioned at the beginning we had three machines at our disposal to start with. One of these three machines was taken to pieces in January 1940 to facilitate plans

for reconstruction of new machines. On the second a team of three persons was conducting researches. There remained therefore only one machine for decryption. That may explain the high percentage of settings determined by the British. When the Battle of France really began, we were busy 24 hours out of 24 hours decrypting telegrams based on the settings sent by the British.

(2) The lack of machines derived from the fact that their production had not been envisaged from the beginning on the French side. I do not know if that was due to difficulties met with in finding an appropriate factory or if they were waiting to see the results of the work. But, even when we had obtained conclusive results the beginning of production was slow although the main plans for construction had been ready since 12 February 1940 (they had been drawn up by 2/Lieut Palluth assisted by his pupil Fokczynski).

I must point out that none of the materials in the course of manufacture fell into the hands of the Germans because we were dealing with a conscientious factory with which Bolek liaised. Now only at the end of July they delivered three machines to us.

(3) The delay in delivery of the listening material and the irregularity in the reception of settings had also a negative influence on the output. It often happened that we had not yet received the intercepts when already the news of the decryption of a new message by the British came in. Sometimes the date was not yet decrypted when the following setting would arrive. In that case when we were in possession of the intercepts we decoded first of all the telegrams emanating from stations considered to be very talkative, based on signatures like: Cartes, Hess, Neuber, Paschka as well as on messages indicating situation reports and which were transmitted either before or after midnight'.

Welchman refers to Colonel Langer's List of 126 Broken Enigma Keys in the report he wrote probably in Algeria in the autumn of 1940.

Date of Daily Key (Date sent)		Date of Break (at PC Bruno or of reception from UK)	
1939	06.07	26.08	**1939**
	02.08	?.01	**1940**
	10.09	17.03	
	13.09	17.03	
	19.09	28.02	
	29.09	23.02	
	30.09	13.02	
	25.10	17.01	
	28.10	17.01	

It starts with the daily key broken in Poland before the war—a key for 6 July 1939, broken on 26 August, 1939. The other entries are daily keys of 1939 broken at Bruno or at Bletchley in 1940. Polish breaks would have been recorded at once but Bletchley breaks could not be entered until they had been communicated to Bruno, which evidently took many days in the early months of collaboration.

'Unfortunately Langer's list does not indicate which of the German crypto nets (Red, Green or Blue) was involved in each break. Nor does it say which of the breaks were achieved at Bruno. But we have clues, and it is intriguing to speculate on what may have happened.'

In his rebuttal of much of the content of Hinsley's Appendix 1 to Volume 1. 'Rejewski agrees that 83 per cent of the keys in Langer's list were broken at Bletchley. This means a score of 105 for Bletchley and 21 for Bruno. He also points out that at Bruno everything had to be done by Zygalski, Rozycki and himself, whereas Bletchley already had far more people at work. Indeed the Polish achievement of 21 breaks is quite remarkable, remembering that this same team of three would be deciphering messages on daily keys broken at Bletchley.

It seems clear that the first break at Bruno was the daily key for 28 Oct 1939, broken on 17 Jan 1940 immediately after the arrival of perforated sheets from Bletchley. This was the Green key used by the administrative centres of the German army. It also seems clear though surprising to me, that the Green key for 25 October 1939 was broken at Bletchley at about the same time. Apart from this one key I suggest that the remaining nine daily keys of Table 1 were Polish breaks.

In the period covered by Table 2 there are 16 cases in which two different daily keys for the same day were broken. I suggest that the Poles broke the first of the keys shown on the table for the following seven days: 6, 16, 18, 26 January, 24, 27 February and 20 March; also that they broke the second keys on five days: 18 January, 21 February and 2, 21, 27 March. This accounts for the Bruno score of 21 breaks. Much of this is pure conjecture but it may well be pretty accurate.

It appears that after the sheets were received on 17 January 1940 the Polish three-man team worked backwards, leaving work on current keys to BP. I suspect that they concentrated on Green traffic while we concentrated on Red. As I discovered in my studies of September and October 1939, the French intercept stations were better placed for the interception of Green traffic than was our station at Chatham under Commander Ellingworth. Furthermore I found that the call-signs

DELAYS IN DAYS BETWEEN THE DATE OF A DAILY KEY OF 1940 AND ITS ENTRY ON LANGER'S LIST OF BROKEN KEYS

Date of Daily Key	Delays Jan	Delays Feb	Delays March	Delays April	Delays May	Delays June
1			14		1	0
2			6(24)		0	
3				1	1	
4			7(14)		2	0
5					7	0
6	19		5		1	0
7			4		2	0
8		15	4	1	1	0
9			2	3(6)	1	
10				4(4)	1	
11				1	1	0
12		15	4(5)	4	1	0
13		14	4(8)		1	0
14		9		2	1	1
15				1		6
16	43	10	2	1		5
17	11			1		
18	34(41)			2		
19				1(5)		
20		6	17	1	1	
21		7(23)	2(19)	1(1)	0	
22	12	4	8(11)	1(1)	1	
23		8	3	1(2)	1	
24	15	23		1(2)	1	
25			8	1()	0	
26	28			1	1	
27		31	2(15)	0	0	
28				2	1	
29	10	4		1	0	
30	14	X	9	1	1	
31	5	X		X	0	

The figure in ( ) allows for cases in which two different keys for the same day were broken.

were repeated monthly, so the French traffic analysis, as a result of observation over a long period would have been able to provide a complete forecast of call-signs for each day. This would have been a great help to intercept operators because, as Ellingworth explained to me, the German radio net carrying Green traffic used an unusual method of operation which made it difficult to intercept. Anyway, using available Green intercepts the Poles attacked the Green key for 6 January 1940 which they broke on 19 January, only two days after the arrival of the perforated sheets. Next, on 28 January, having no doubt spent a lot of time decoding messages on the two broken keys, they broke the Green key for 3 September 1939. In February and March of 1940 they went back to Green traffic of 30, 29, 19, 13 and 10 September 1939. They also managed to attack current traffic of several days in January, February and March of 1940 as shown in Table 2, a truly remarkable achievement by Rejewski, Zygalski and Rozycki.'

The Polish Contribution to the Defeat of Enigma

The individual contributions of the three Polish mathematicians Rejewski, Rozycki and Zygalski have already been mentioned in the chapter on the Enigma video and in *Spies Of The Airwaves*. Lt Col G. Langer also gave, in his report on the work of his team in the campaign in France from 1 October 1939 to 24 June 1940, the breakdown of the staff, mainly Polish at PC Bruno, and the dates of their arrival there after escaping from Poland.

	Date of Arrival		Date of Arrival
Lt Col Langer	01.10.39	Civilian Palluth	06.05.40
Major Ciezki	08.10.39	Civilian Gaca	06.05.40
Major Michalowski	18.03.40	Civilian Krajewski	10.05.40
2 Lt Pashowski	10.10.39	Civilian Fokczynski	08.10.39
2 Lt Palluth	08.10.39	Captain Gralinski	12.02.40
Civilian Rejewski	27.09.39	2 Lt Szachno	12.02.40
Civilian Rozycki	27.09.39	Civilian Smolenski	08.03.40
Civilian Zygalski	27.09.39		

Langer also gives the staff position on 12.05.40:

PC Bruno

Director — Major Bertrand
Polish Army Representative — Lt Col Langer
British Army Representative — Captain MacFarlan

German Section
Head: Major Renard
Deputy: Major Ciezki
Intercept: Lieut Annequin
Chief: M. des I. Siedenmeyer
Intercept: M. des L.
Classification Fokczynski

Russian Section
Head: Capt Couey
Deputy: Capt Chasles
Decryption: Capt Gralinski
2 Lt Szachno
Civ. Smolenski

Clandestine Section
Head: Capt Marlière
Deputy: Capt Chadapaux
Sorting: Sgt Eclancher
Decryption: 2 Lt Palluth

Decryption

Manual Procedure
Capt Larcher
Major Michalowski
2 Lt Palluth

Mechanical Procedure
Capt Braquenie
M. Zygalski
M. Rejewski
M. Gaca
M.S. Palluth
M. Paszkowski
M. Krajewski

When Germany launched its blitzkrieg on Poland on 1 Sep 1939 Bertrand's first concern was for Langer's Polish team of cryptographers. The emergency link BLR which had been functioning normally ceased on 10 September. It was essential to save them before they could be taken prisoner. The British were also anxious to get them out, he knew. The search began on 18 Sep and ended on 1 Oct when Luc and his team arrived in Paris, some by the Orient-Express and some by air. They had been traced to the Kalimanesti Camp in Rumania and their escape organised. They brought with them two Enigma machines after destroying the others before their escape.

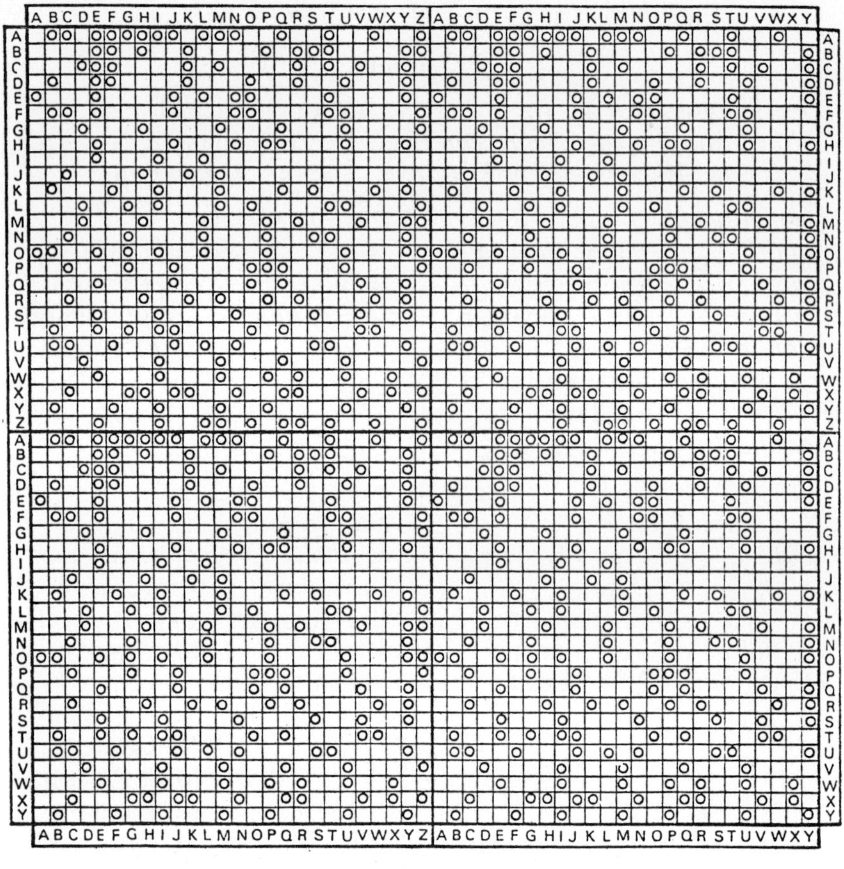

Bild 8: Lochkarte

The perforated sheet invented by ZYGALSKI. For each position of the rotor N a card with 26 × 26 squares representing all possible positions of rotors L and M were prepared for each rotor situation. 26 cards were needed.

Bertrand was delighted to augment his team at Gretz by fifteen Polish experts, a potential of inestimable value. The Polish team became Equipe Z led by Langer (Luc). He already had a foreign team Equipe D which was the Spanish team of five officers and two political commissars specialising in cryptography recruited by him in

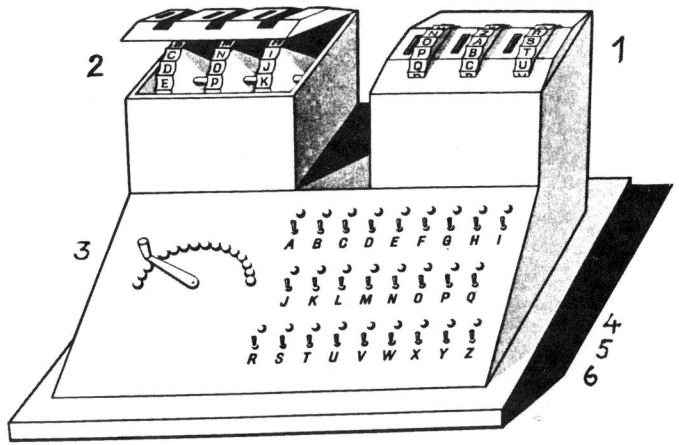

Bild 6: Polnischer Zyklometer: 1 „Enigma"-Walzen mit geschlossenem Deckel, 2 „Enigma"-Walzen mit geöffnetem Deckel, 3 Rheostat, 4 Lampen, 5 Schalthebel, 6 Alphabet
(Rekonstruktion: T. Lisicki)

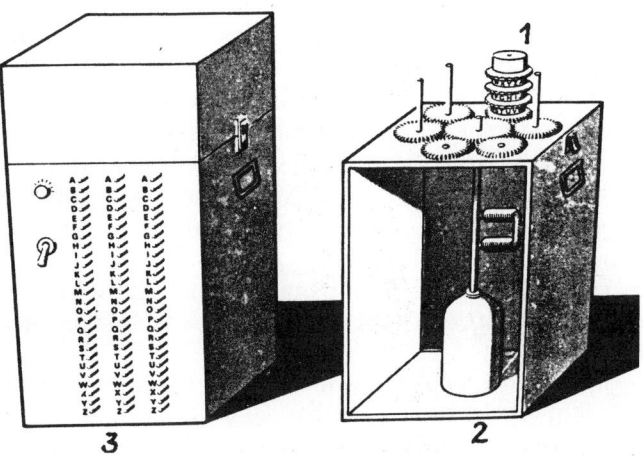

Bild 7: Polnische Bomba: 1 „Enigma"-Walzenlage mit drei Schlüsselwalzen, auf den restlichen fünf äußeren Zahnrädern sind die anderen bei drei verwendeten Walzen möglichen Walzenlagen angeordnet; 2 Elektromotor; 3 geschlossener Kasten mit drei Reihen Schalthebeln.
(Rekonstruktion: T. Lisicki)

January 1939 when the Republican Army was defeated by Gen. Franco. With his indigenous French experts he now had 70 'technicians' and could set to work, supplying intelligence to French GHQ through the Command Post of the 5e Bureau set up also near Gretz at Château Pereire, called PC Victor.

In this heterogeneous think-tank were a dozen officers plus Luc (Polish Colonel) and 'Pinky' MacFarlan (British Major as liaison with London and the British GHQ at Arras) aged 35 to 50 and not all with the same ideas or tastes, especially culinary ones.

To regularise the situation Bertrand had the Equipe D enrolled in the Foreign Legion and Equipe Z in the Polish Army in France but paid by France.

At PC Bruno the Intercept Control consisted of the **Network for Listening and Direction-finding of Foreign Radio-Electric transmission** and the **Control Network of Radio-Electric Transmissions of the Interior and Search for Clandestine Stations created at Mobilisation**.

The intercept stations were linked to PC Bruno by teleprinters for the rapid transmission of the most important intercepts and a fleet of liaison cars went to GHQ and PC Victor and Paris when required.

Bertrand paid a visit to London in December 1939 to organise the pooling of intercept information and the transmission of Enigma keys by teleprinter and radio. He also ordered 40 models of the Enigma machine, in parts of course, to be assembled by the specialists in Equipe Z and soon the Poles were able to assemble the 'bomba' a combination of six Enigma machines owing primarily to Rejewski and the 'Cyclometre' which consisted of two interconnected Enigmas, which they had used in the 'Station in the Woods' in Poland. The invention of Henryk Zygalski, who was the last of the Polish trio to die in 1978, after retiring from the Mathematics Dept of the University of Surrey, was the system of 'feuilles perforées', perforated sheets.

The Cyclometer (p.57) shown in Colonel Lisicki's reconstruction consisted of two linked Enigma machines without the keyboard using only the interior wire links and the lamps. The procedure to reconstruct the Key for the Day lasted only a few minutes with this method. When the Germans introduced a new key system on 15 September 1938, and on 15 December a fourth and fifth rotor, the Poles countered quickly by building the purely mechanical Bomba in

November 1938. The encoder, instead of using a ring setting for the whole day, chose arbitrarily a key of three letters for each message, which he sent in clear for the recipient to use and then sent the same letters enciphered.

Knowing that the fourth letter was the enciphered first letter, and the fifth the second, and the sixth the third, a machine could work through the 26 different combinations for each pair, the Poles built six bombas one for each rotor-position. It took only 110 minutes to find the setting for all three rotors. One Bomba is shown on p.57.

Henryk Zygalski's system of perforated sheets was re-invented at BP in the autumn and winter of 1939. Re-invented because Gordon Welchman did not know that Dillyn Knox had seen these in use in Warsaw and was using them without Welchman knowing. These were stacks of 26 sheets with up to 51 holes designed to detect any cipher pattern that could enable an Enigma key to be identified, whatever the plugboard connections. A light from below shone through the perforations to enable the viewer to see the pattern. This worked with three rotors but the introduction of two more meant using at least 50 stacks to break one key.

During the 'phoney war' most of the Enigma messages were GAF (German Air Force) as the Army were using teletype machines connected to landline. The GAF traffic which was considerably heavy offered more possibilities in reconstituting the keys and in addition when the shooting war started they supplied a deal of information on military formations through air liaison officers.

The main Army intercept station at Chatham was too far to take German Army Enigma but Bertrand at Gretz and the British No.1 Special Wireless Group with its three sections with the BEF were sending back Enigma to BP—in quantity. Bertrand was to make contact with the British Field Y Sections when he was summoned to Lille on hearing that a German agent had been caught with a transmitter. His sets as well as those of the Y Sections were on the lookout for clandestine radios as part of their normal duties. It was Whit Sunday and traffic was low. He had just come back from a religious service in a village 2 km away when he had a phone call from his 'Patron' in Paris.

'Your colleagues are already on the spot—there are "boites de sardines" and some "recettes pour s'en servir". Report back to me on your return!'

As the civil lines could be tapped and as especially in the rear areas the SR used this jargon, where 'boites de sardines' meant illegal transmitters and 'recette pour s'en servir' meant all indispensable ciphers and radio procedures in use, he drove the 250 km to Lille and there was an air-raid alarm in progress. This was the period of scares of enemy parachutists and rumours of spies. A certain Otto had given up one of his agents in Belgium, whom he had provided with a suitcase radio. This agent, a 70-year-old man with his wife, a pretty Javanese lady of about 40, were in a train evacuating German diplomatic personnel from Brussels to Germany whose transit through France was authorised under diplomatic immunity but passport control was carried out in Lille. The train was found not to contain real diplomats so who were they? Surely personnel of the German espionage fraternity in Belgium.

Otto was one of those on the fringe of the diplomatic service who seemed to have good relations with the French Counter-Espionage personnel and after the agent had been arrested denying he was a spy but only a radio amateur carrying some toys for his amusement. Otto supplied Bertrand with all the information he required on the set. He said it was the standard model issued by the Abwehr to anyone who wished to work with them. The documents, especially, interested Bertrand very much as they were still usable as others were in possession of them as well. When he thanked Otto the latter shook his hand effusively and added: 'Perhaps we shall meet again one day!' 'What a prophet!' says Bertrand for the next time they were to meet it was the gallows or the firing squad that awaited Bertrand. The next day he was back at Gretz and heard that the spy had made a full confession during the night.

When Bertrand went to Paris during the Occupation in January 1944 to pick up a radio which had been parachuted from London and stocked ready for his collection by an agent in Paris, it was his 101st mission and things went wrong. When he followed instructions to meet Paul between 9 and 9.30 a.m. on 3 Jan 1944 in the Sacré-Coeur he was given another rendez-vous for 5 January and he met his wife Mary and his brother who had come from Algiers by submarine on a special mission along with some friends he had invited to dinner at the Hotel du Printemps. On the 5th he was arrested and it transpired that Paul had been arrested on 2 January and had probably betrayed him. It had been his wont to remove incriminating documents from his pockets and wallet before going on these missions but on this occasion there was in his greatcoat pocket a list of Gestapo call-signs which an agent had passed to him the previous day. This was pushed under his nose as a secret document, proof of espionage and a Frenchman also took the 20,000 francs he had with him. Handcuffed, he was taken to the hotel Continental for interrogation. The Chief, who was Masuy, told him he was lucky to have been arrested by the Abwehr, the German Counter-espionage and not by the Gestapo.

CHAPTER 5

The Battle of Britain

An international conference on *Wireless Reconnaissance and its Role in the Second World War* was held in Bonn—Bad Godesberg 15 and 16 November and in Stuttgart University on 17 and 18 November 1978. Under the chairmanship of Professor Juergen Rohwer there were many American, Canadian and German historians, cryptographers and even inventors such as Boris Hagelin from Orsa in Sweden, Russian-born, whose M209 was sold in 140,000 machines to the US Army for the use of the Allies. Also Erkki Pale from Helsinki who had great success with Finnish cryptography against Russia.

Among the British representatives who addressed the conference were:

    Patrick Beesly RNVR Submarine Tracking Room, Admiralty
    Peter Calvocoressi RAF Member of Hut 3 Bletchley Park
    Sir Norman Denning Operational Intelligence Centre
    Ronald Lewin, author of *Ultra Goes to War*
    Sir Herbert Marchant Leader of Hut 3 Bletchley Park
    Mrs Mary Pain Intelligence Evaluation, Bletchley Park
    Vice-Admiral Schofield RN Dir. Trade Division, Admiralty.

Among the wide-ranging revelations were several mentions of the value of Ultra in the Battle of Britain.

The first speaker, David Kahn author of *The Codebreakers*, said: 'The deciphered Bletchley messages known under the general heading of Ultra played a significant role for the first time in the Battle of Britain. This is not surprising for Britain stood with her back to the wall and had to rely for her defence mainly on reconnaissance (including Radar systems). To sum up the role of Ultra briefly one can say that it put Britain in the situation to use her meagre forces with optimum effect which is nothing more than the task which reconnaissance in war has really to fulfil. The best examples are the events of the so-called Eagle Day, the dramatic 15 August 1940 when Goering concentrated his whole strength on destroying the Royal Air Force. His plan was to attack in waves in the hope that the RAF would mobilise all its planes to strike down the first wave of the attack and then be helplessly delivered up to the following attacks. But Ultra uncovered these tactical plans and enabled the Commander of Fighter Command to operate his few aircraft in such a way that they were armed for all the attack waves. And so Ultra played a decisive role in one of the most decisive battles of the war'.

Dr Harold Deutsch, historian at the US Army War College, Carlisle, Pennsylvania: 'Other aspects of Ultra's role in the Battle of Britain deserve our attention. First the example of Eagle-Day (15 August) the day of the first conflicts of the opponents, in which Air Marshall Dowding was able to spread out his aircraft as far as the then possibilities permitted, to defend the seven airfields indicated by Ultra as threatened. Ultra's support was far above the normal because the messages of the Luftwaffe, child's play for the British Cipher service, came as a gift from Heaven when the air battle was in full progress.

Much fuss was made about the fact that highly placed witnesses like Air Chief Marshall Sir John Slessor and Vice-Admiral Sir Norman Denning did not answer the direct question about the Battle of Britain being lost but for Ultra. Those whom one cannot designate as Ultra-partisans have deduced the opposite from it, namely that the Battle could have been won without Ultra—which Slessor and Denning had not meant. Churchill learned through Ultra at what moment Hitler called off Sealion and was therefore in the position to throw into the scales the weight of Britain's then scarce Fighting forces into North Africa. So the transition from one war phase to another was facilitated by Ultra, quite apart from the fact that only a victory on the home front put Britain in a position to influence the events of the war.' Another pointed out that victory in the Battle allowed the many British warships, locked up in southern harbours to repel Sealion, to be liberated for convoys and especially for the protection of the armada sailing to N. Africa.

Dr F. Pogue of the Eisenhower Institute, Washington, spoke of the importance of building up an enemy Order of Battle. It was essential to keep a record of messages which at the time were not of tactical importance to accumulate later to build up the picture of 200, 250 or even 350 divisions. To this Dr Rohwer replied that the Germans had not sufficiently appreciated this or they would have forbidden publication by wireless of the daily communiqué of the Luftwaffe.

Dr Rohwer went on to point out that the Allies could not be omniscient through Ultra even if they deciphered everything. It was an axiomatic principle that information of the top grade should be communicated by the most secure system: this meant landlines for teleprinters and telephone. He recalled that Fellgiebel General of the Intelligence at the outbreak of war had told his colleagues: 'Gentlemen, using radio is high treason!' Dr Rohwer said they had once calculated statistics of marine radio, and the percentage of the total intelligence communications network sank from 20% before the war to 12% in 1940 and 15% in 1941. With the increased power base and shortage of telephones this rose from 25% in 1942 to 29% in 1943. The share of teleprinters on the other hand lay between 32 and 43%, telephone between 41 and 50%. The British cryptography was admissible to only the 15 to maximum 29% of the long distance traffic enciphered in Enigma. He pointed out that the network of OKW and supreme Command of the Army, Navy and Luftwaffe used radio teleprinters and telephones for essential high-ranking intelligence traffic; and only tactical traffic between Army and divisions and below, especially in a war of movement, and between ground stations, and flying formations or ships and their landbased controls went by radio.

Dr Hubatsch of Bonn University reminded hearers that a considerable proportion of intelligence traffic was sent by post. No one from the Hut 3 delegation mentioned that most of the Fish traffic (radio teleprinters) was read by the British and that the French intercepted telephone calls.

In his postscript Dr Rohwer answers the question 'was Ultra decisive for the war?' with a clear 'No'. The inequality of the Coalition and Germany was too great in respect of human and industrial capacity, raw materials, etc. The picture is built up through Intelligence, by reconnaissance, beginning with agents' observations or diplomatic reports on optical observation, by one's own efforts or aerial reconnaissance, and other means down to Wireless Reconnaissance with its three branches: Traffic Analysis, D/F and Deciphering. Important as these are with their innumerable little pieces of mosaic it depends on the decisions of a political or military leader. The behaviour of Roosevelt and his military leaders in the last days before Pearl Harbor serves as an example. On the other hand a single little suitable 'stone' in an open situation which offers several options, can give the push in this or that direction, as the example of the intuitive Churchill on 17 September 1940. . . . The closest bond of confidence between Commander and Intelligence Officer and the most precise Intelligence can not make good insufficient suitable forces at the place of action . . . It (intelligence) can only be used when it is available at the right time. Thus General Freyberg failed in Crete in spite of exact knowledge of the German plans, while Admiral Nimitz was able to concentrate his vastly inferior forces at Midway in the right place at the right time.

Thus seen, Intelligence, and in its framework especially wireless reconnaissance, strongly influenced the strategy of the Western Allies in the Second World War. Ultra had the effect of not alone deciding the issue but at least of shortening the war on the Atlantic—West European battle ground.

Even if the indirect influence of Ultra on the European fronts is not yet assessable, and one does not underestimate the influence of the independent achievements of the Red Army for the outcome of the war, without Ultra the way to the final Allied victory over Hitler-Germany and Japan would have been very much longer and would have taken, in many aspects, a quite different course, and with devastating consequences for victor and vanquished.

To return to the Battle of Britain, let us look at some facts: the intelligence from Ultra and from the Y service.

Hinsley *History of British Intelligence in the Second World War* (Vol. 1 p.177) says:

> 'Enigma gave general warning of the approach of the Battle of Britain . . . AI summed up in a minute of 28 June 1940 the evidence that was coming in. "Reports indicate that the majority of long-range bombers will have completed refitting at home bases by 8 July. In view of one report that a fliegerkorps has been ordered to bring into force new W/T instructions from 2200 on 30 June the opening of the offensive on this country must be anticipated from 1 July onward". From the outset of the battle the fact that Enigma had now been producing intelligence for some months on the GAF's organisation, order of battle and equipment was also of great strategic value.

The intelligence consisted of fragmentary and often disconnected items in the signals of the main users of W/T, the lower-level operational units of the GAF. For AI and GC&CS—which initially undertook the analysis for the help it gave to cryptanalysis and the interception programme, but which soon found that the results were of immense assistance to AI—. . . It was not until 5 August that GC&CS completed its first attempt to compile from Enigma a detailed GAF order of battle. But by the beginning of July the work of identifying and locating the GAF's operational units was sufficiently advanced to enable AI to accept a major revision of its estimate of the GAF's first-line bomber strength. In June it had estimated the first-line strength at more than 4,000 (including 2,500 bombers) and the reserves at 7,000, when actual figures were about 2,000 (including 1,500–1,700 bombers) and 1,000. At the beginning of July AI scaled down the first-line figures drastically, reducing its estimate of bombers likely to be available in the first week of full-scale operations from 2,500 to 1,250 and its estimate of the possible daily bomb load from 4,800 tons to 1,800 tons.

Not least because they were based on the Enigma information which was described as "heaven-sent" and "apparently sure" the new figures enabled the Air Staff to view the situation much more confidently than was possible a month ago.

Valuable as it was the Enigma's order of battle intelligence was of no assistance to AI in its attempt to answer the supreme question—could the RAF outlast the GAF? Because it threw no light on the losses and effective strengths of the GAF units or on the size of their reserves. At the beginning of September, asked to predict how long the GAF could keep up its effort, Air Intelligence calculated that that if German fighter losses continue at the August rate "the German fighter strength will be ineffective in six weeks". In fact the GAF was obliged to go over to night bombing within a week of this reply and to do so because the serviceability of its aircraft had fallen so low. For similar reasons the Enigma was of no help in forecasting the shifts that occurred during the battle in the GAF's methods and objectives. Communications between Berlin and the GAF formations in France went by land-lines, so that strategic decisions were rarely spelled out in W/T signals. From time to time it could be deduced from the decrypts that a change in the GAF's intentions was to be expected but the deductions were of no operational value to the C-in-C Fighter Command. Thus the decrypts made several references to "Adlertag" between 9 and 13 August and it was obvious that some new development must be expected but neither AI nor GC&CS could unravel what the codeword "Adlertag" stood for. For all his major decisions C-in-C Fighter Command accordingly depended on his own strategic judgment with no direct assistance from the Enigma. This may be further illustrated by the events of 15 August, the day on which the GAF sustained the defeat which is sometimes taken as marking the turning point of the Battle of Britain. The GAF attempted on that day to throw Fighter Command off balance by combining diversionary attacks north of the Humber with the main attack against southern England. But there is no evidence in the surviving records that Fighter Command got advance warning of the GAF's intentions either from Enigma or from the GAF's low-grade transmissions; brief forewarning of the two attacks was received, it seems, only from radar.

For all that it was incomplete, and often gave scant warning, if any at all, the Enigma's tactical intelligence could have been put to better use if the organisation for handling operational intelligence had not been defective in one important direction. Before the war the Air Ministry, like the War Office, had built this organisation around the exploitation in the field of low-grade tactical codes. It had thus centred it at Cheadle, where most of the traffic in such codes was intercepted. But because it had not expected the GAF to use high-grade cyphers or at least to use them for operational traffic, it had made no arrangement either for AI to participate in operational intelligence, beyond supplying Cheadle with details about the GAF's order of battle, or for GC&CS to pass high-grade intelligence to Cheadle or the operational commands. When the Enigma began to produce tactical intelligence, that intelligence was distributed only to that section of AI which dealt with the long-term problem of the GAF order of battle, but that section, unlike Cheadle, was not organised or staffed for the exploitation of operational intelligence. The result was separation of the tactical information obtained from the high-grade and the low-grade sources, the former occasionally revealing the GAF's orders and intentions, the latter reporting them as they were carried out, which prevented both sources from being used to the full during 1940 when the GAF effort against the United Kingdom was at its height.

Notwithstanding this defect, AI's rapidly growing understanding of the GAF's organisation and order of battle—which it owed largely to Enigma—was of increasing help to Fighter Command as background for its conduct of operations. By the beginning of the Battle of Britain the interception of this traffic (low-grade codes) on medium and high frequencies was being supplemented by the interception of plain language radio telephony (R/T) on high frequencies at a chain of stations on the east and southeast coasts known as Home Defence Units (HDUs). Manned by German-speaking WAAF and WRNS staff, their activity managed by the RAF centre at Kingsdown, these stations telephoned their intercepts direct to the local RAF command as well as to HQ Fighter Command at Stanmore, where they were co-ordinated with incoming intelligence from Cheadle, the radar chain and the Observer Corps and with the work of the Operations Room.'

Aileen Clayton's book *The Enemy is Listening* was published a year after Vol 1 of Hinsley. It adds considerably to the picture presented to HQ Fighter Command and the Air Ministry, GC&CS and Cheadle.

On 15 June 1940 she was posted to RAF Hawkinge and almost at once to Fairlight, on the cliffs above Hastings to get the longer range on German transmitters afforded by additional height. Six German-speaking WAAF with two Hallicrafters took traffic mainly from recce aircraft and from Ju.87s strafing the French roads where terrified refugees were mingled with retreating troops. Some of these messages gave valuable information to locations of British and French units in retreat from Abbeville to Cherbourg. Several times a day they took messages from recce aircraft giving weather reports and the strength and position of British convoys making their way up the

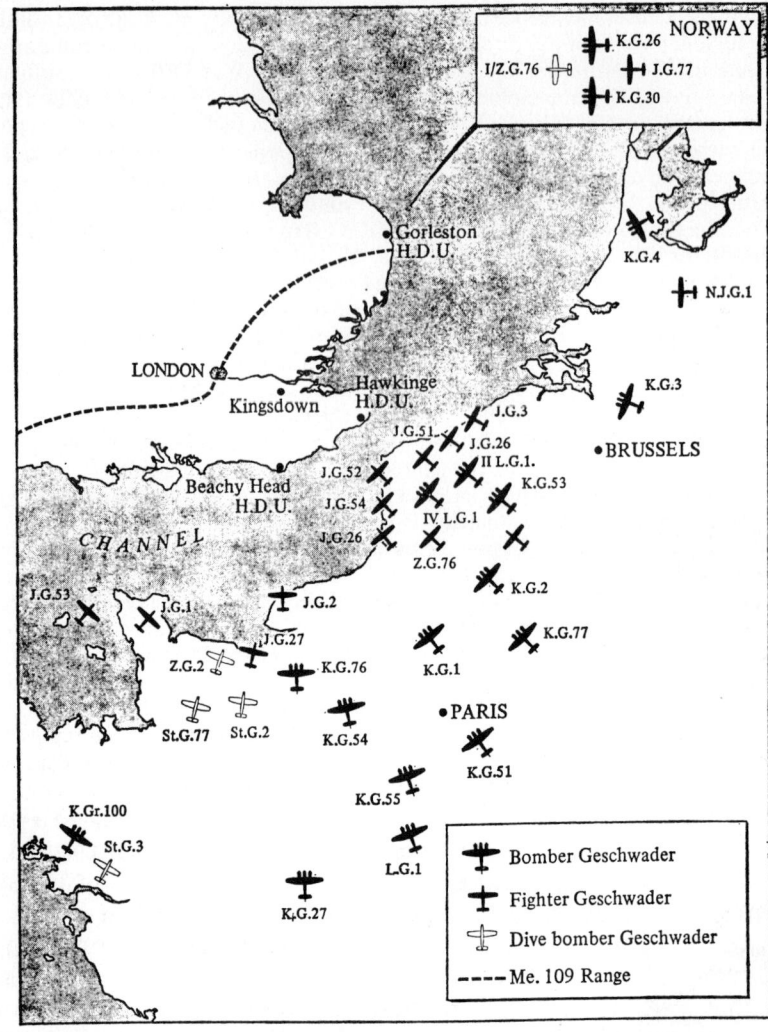

The Battle of Britain, 1940. Distribution of Luftwaffe forces aligned for the onslaught against England, showing the maximum range of the Me. 109 fighters. The strategic position of the monitoring units of Kingsdown, Beachy Head, Gorleston and Hawkinge is clearly indicated. A further HDU was located at Strete in Devon.

Channel. As July began they were pulled back to RAF Hawkinge and joined by another six German-speaking WAAF, several RAF operators and mechanics.

Each day they learned more about the GAF. There were air-to-air instructions between German fighters and fighter-bombers during attacks on airfields and convoys in the southeast corner of England. There were orders from the squadrons' home-bases about landings and twice a day recce aircraft reported on convoys, which they reported to the Navy at Dover and No. 11 Group at Uxbridge. The German High Command had issued orders that all ports and harbours round England were to be destroyed and all British convoys attacked and prevented from reaching their destination. The Admiralty was forced to abandon Dover as an advanced base for anti-invasion destroyers. The neighbouring airfields were attacked almost daily: Hawkinge, Lympne, Manston, West Malling, Biggin Hill, Tangmere were all bombed and shot up. After the airfields it was the radar stations but they were never successful in putting them out of action for long.

After a heavy raid on Hawkinge on 12 August the Y Station was moved back to West Kingsdown, leaving a small party of RAF operators to listen to non-Morse transmissions. They had direct telephone links to No. 11 Group at Uxbridge to the main Y station at Cheadle and to the Air Ministry.

Already before the war the GAF W/T traffic, most of which was enciphered, had been monitored at RAF stations at Cheadle and Chicksands. With a hundred sets and excellent D/F commanding a great range there were few messages transmitted by the GAF in the western theatre which the Y service did not hear. The traffic was of immense value in compiling the German Air Force order of battle—their unit strength, equipment, locations and commanders.

The War Cabinet was fully aware that the odds were seriously against the RAF. Facing them in France and the Low Countries were the two largest German air commands, Luftflotten 2 and 3 commanded by Kesselring and Sperrle, with a combined force of over 1,000 bombers and 900 fighters. To the north in Norway General Stumpff commanded Luftflotte 5 with 100 bombers and 30 long-range fighters. RAF Fighter Command to defend the United Kingdom had rarely more than 600 fighters.

Goering had planned 13 August as his Adlertag and believed he could defeat the RAF in four days. The weather was unfavourable and he had to postpone the main attack until the afternoon, when formations each of fifty or more aircraft swept across the English coast. The records show that the GAF flew more than 1,700 sorties in the 24 hours of 15 August and enemy bombers penetrated as far as London for the first time. An armada of barges was already being assembled at ports in France and the Low Countries for the invasion.

On 5 September an Enigma message, decrypted in 30 minutes, informed the British, according to Col Paillole, of Goering's decision to launch a raid by 300 bombers on the London docks. It was terrible in spite of the measures taken by the British command. On 15 September the capital was the target. Thanks to Enigma the RAF fighters intercepted the most powerful attack as it crossed the English coast. Heavy losses obliged the enemy to withdraw. On 17 September a message signed Hitler ordered the dismantling of the invasion bases.

At Kingsdown they realised the Germans operated an aircraft control system quite different from the RAF's.

'Our fighters were controlled direct from Sector Operations Room. Instructions re height and direction to fly in order to engage enemy formations were fed constantly to the flight leader by the Fighter Controllers, who compiled their instructions from what they saw on the Operations Room tables: the combined information which had been derived from filtered radar plots, Observer Corps and other sources. Unlike the British system of light and instant control the Luftwaffe pilots appeared, from the messages that we heard, to fly on carefully pre-arranged plans, having been given heights and other directions to fly at their flight briefings before setting off on their raids. The advance warning of incoming raids provided by the radar chain was vastly superior to the German radar coverage, and made sure by signals intelligence that every enemy formation had an enthusiastic reception.

Since few of the operators at Cheadle could read German and we were better geared to intercept VHF traffic, we evolved a system where by as soon as their operators picked up a transmission from a bomber they would contact us, giving details of the callsigns heard, the probable units involved and the relevant frequencies. Duly warned we would listen on those VHF frequencies which we now knew were used by the bombers and their home or controlling station. We were then ready to take over monitoring from Cheadle. The interchange monitoring was made easier because the bombers would use phonetically the last letter or letters of their H/F or M/F callsigns. As these were also the unit code frequently painted on the fuselage of the aircraft the Luftwaffe was unwittingly helping us still further to build up details of the Order of Battle . . .

No.61 W.U. at Cheadle had set up a highly efficient D/F network—ours was to come later—which enabled them to pin-point quickly an enemy ground station, and also to locate the exact position of an individual aircraft. Since we now knew where most of the units were based, if we were to hear Vannes control, for instance, communicating with aircraft we could be fairly certain which units were operating even if the aircraft callsign was not given. We were able to advise No.11 Group that the enemy raid approaching Beachy Head was probably made up Me.109s of II/Jg 51 based at St Omer. This would be helpful to the controllers who would then be able to anticipate the probable return route of the enemy aircraft. Even in those early days in the summer of 1940 we could almost certainly confirm the height at which the formations were approaching, and we might also be able to give some indication, from what we were hearing, of their intended action. Obviously a message like 'fly at 5,000 metres and rendezvous with bombers over Dover' had useful tactical value . . .*

By this time the cryptographers at Station X at Bletchley were reading into the Luftwaffe's high-grade machine enciphered Enigma traffic and were producing what came to be classified as Ultra intelligence. This traffic included messages from the German Air Ministry to the Commands as well as between lower formations and provided invaluable information regarding the enemy's strength and movements and even their intentions. We at Kingsdown were not among the privileged few. Amongst the few at that time "in the picture was the Air Officer Commanding Fighter Command, Air Chief Marshal Sir Hugh Dowding. His was the task of deciding how best to use our meagre defence forces against the onslaught of the Luftwaffe. Somehow he had to spread very little butter over a large slice of bread. With the prior knowledge gained from the few Ultra messages which were at that time available, combined with other intelligence information and with the invaluable assistance of the early-warning system he managed to accomplish the impossible.'

Seen in this light Dowding was guided by <u>Ultra and Y</u> and other services, and not by Ultra alone in making his vital decisions.

That is the meaning and significance of Hinsley's 'For all his major decisions C-in-C Fighter Command accordingly depended on his own strategic judgment, with no direct assistance from the Enigma'.

See also Pp 93-96 'The RAF Y Service'

CHAPTER 6

Bletchley Park

The estate belonged to Sir Herbert Leon, who acquired it in 1883 and had the mansion built when he was elected Liberal MP for North Buckinghamshire. It passed to his son Sir George Leon, a wealthy Old Etonian barrister in 1926.

When the head of the SIS Admiral Sinclair had to make plans for the evacuation of his department from London (the third and fourth floors of Broadway Buildings) in view of the approaching war with Germany, he chose this mansion house halfway between Oxford and Cambridge with a good rail link with London. It was to be the home of both SIS and GC&CS from 1939 throughout the war and a home from home for many thousands of young graduates and civil servants during the war years. The story of GCHQ has been fully recorded in detail by Nigel West in his book of the same name and should be studied by all those interested in the subject.

Briefly, in May 1938 a German Section had been formed at Broadway in London by Denniston and a parsimonious Treasury sanctioned an increase of eight civilian graduates. Admiral Sinclair's contingency war plan was authorised with provision for an emergency establishment of sixty 'professor types' and thirty female graduate linguists, and courses in elementary cryptography for potential recruits to GC&CS were begun at Broadway. Almost at once came the Munich crisis in Sep 1938 and a practice evacuation was made from Broadway to Bletchley Park, where some wooden huts in kit-form had been hastily erected to house the overflow from the mansion house. This lasted until 8 October and operations resumed at

Broadway until August 1939 when a permanent move was made and a lot more wooden huts had been erected.

The German Section was increased to cater for all three services. As there was no Army traffic to deal with except during summer exercises, the cryptanalysts in the Army section in Hut 3 had only police traffic; the GAF was being looked at by only a handful of people in the Air sub-section and the Naval section, later Hut 8, began with only one officer and one clerk in 1939. The Army section was headed by Major John Tiltman of the King's Own Scottish Borderers, assisted by Richard Pritchard, a German specialist, Frederick Jacob and Tony Dangerfield.

Until it was bombed, Fort Bridgewoods at Chatham was the Army intercept station. It was a late 19th century hexagonal fort, one of a series protected by deep moats to protect the naval town of Chatham. Headed by Cdr Ellingworth it had a direct landline to Broadway. When evacuated to safety it went to Beaumanor. The Admiralty station was at Flowerdown near Winchester and the main RAF station was at Cheadle. The construction of other stations, at Sandridge near St Albans, Cupar in Fife and Brora in Sutherland, to be manned by Foreign Office personnel, was begun in 1937 according to Nigel West. He also states that GC&CS had known about the Enigma machine since the Admiralty purchased two copies of the commercial version in 1928 and that a study had been conducted by a Whitehall inter-departmental committee since 1926 to find an encrypting machine for the government's most sensitive communications. This committee continued its study until it recommended in Jan 1935 that a cipher machine should be constructed under the supervision of the Air Ministry, based on the commercial Enigma machine but with the addition of a Type X attachment for greater security. This version manufactured by the Creed Teleprinter Coy became known as the Typex machine and was to be used by the Royal Air Force and the War Office.

Parallel to the move of GC&CS to Bletchley Park was the move of the RAF intercept to Chicksands Priory in the same locality in 1939. This beautiful building dates from the 12th century and was the home of the Gilbertine Order, an English monastic order, encompassing both monks and nuns, for centuries. It became the home of the Osborn family in 1576 and in the time of the eighth baronet, Sir Denvers Osborn, became crown property in 1936. A frequent visitor

Above One of the 'Huts' which housed the decrypting machines and the intelligence staff.
Below An aerial photograph of Bletchley Park during the war.

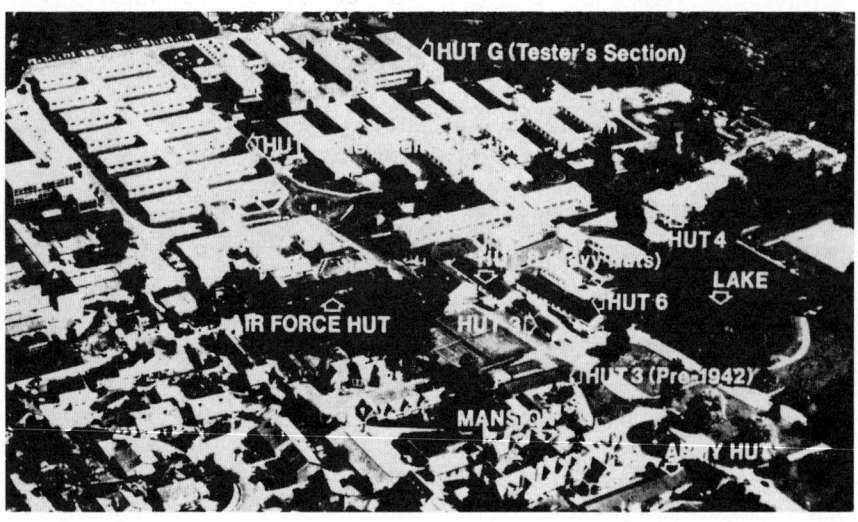

The Typex Mark II derived from the German Enigma machine for the Royal Air Force in 1938. It cost £107.
(Courtesy of James Rusbridger)

had been King James I, and the block housing his bedroom is the King James block. Being seven miles from Ampthill and everywhere else it was ideal for its new purpose and among the 66 rooms were enough bedrooms to put up 30 guests, of which I was one for the month of July 1941. It was known as SYG and had a large intercept with RAF operators controlled by Army officers including Major Jolowicz, under the command of Rear-Admiral Miller. Jolowicz was a professor of Roman Law at University College, London, and I was later to sit at his feet every week from October 1946 to June 1947 when I was reading law. At SYG I was night duty officer relaying instructions to the intercept supervisors from MI 8.

When Gordon Welchman arrived at BP in Sep 1939 he was sent to work in the 'School' which was Elmers School behind the stable-yard and the main building. He knew nothing at all about cryptology or even the German preparations for war. After receiving him on the ground floor of the house overlooking the lake, Cdr Denniston sent him to join Dillwyn Knox who was in charge of the Enigma study programme. He was in a small building in the stableyard which had probably been the coachman's residence and was known as 'The Cottage'. Alan Turing from Kings College Cambridge was already there, working with Knox as was John Jeffreys from Downing College Cambridge.

With some old message pads of Enigma intercept he taught himself log-reading and began work on mathematical formulae to forecast the German call-signs which changed daily at midnight, 0100 hrs in Britain. As already stated Knox kept the information from Warsaw close to his chest and Welchman re-invented the perforated sheets. John Jeffreys set to work on this, set up the Sheet Stacking Room with female staff to punch holes and it was called the Jeffreys apparatus.

Welchman also wondered if the German operators kept to a pattern in selecting the indicator for the day or behaved lazily and the thought that if the operator takes the rotor out from its case and inserts it, it will be almost always in the same position (P. 77). If he adjusts it, as he should, he probably moves it one two or three places forward or backward. He might even use the same three letters for the indicator and the text setting. Welchman called these his 'sillies' or the Cillis.

John Herivel's attention was drawn to a quirk in machine set-up practice. When an Enigma operator was changing the set-up of his

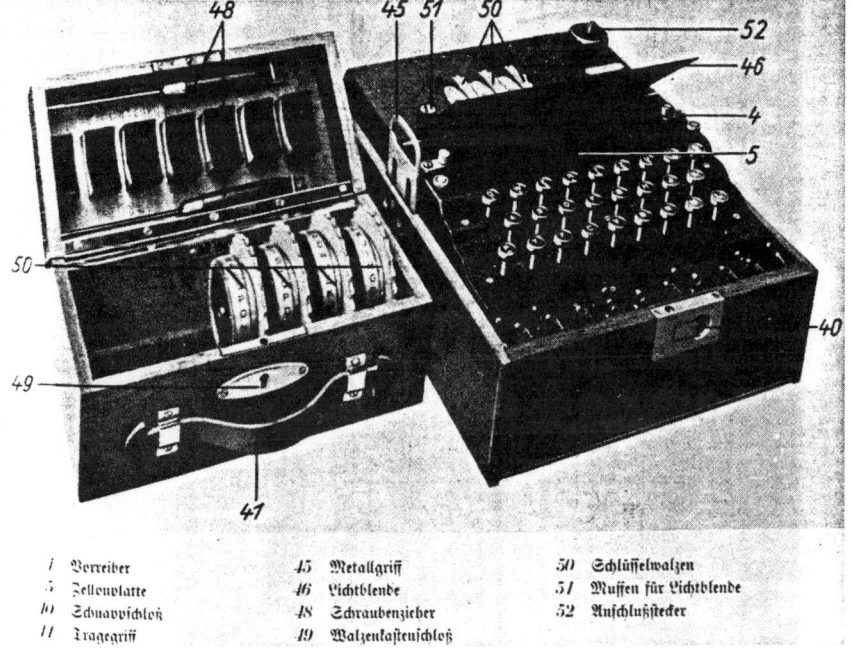

1	Verreiber	45	Metallgriff	50	Schlüsselwalzen
5	Zellenplatte	46	Lichtblende	51	Muffen für Lichtblende
10	Schnappschloß	48	Schraubenzieher	52	Anschlußstecker
11	Tragegriff	49	Walzenkastenschloß		

On the left of Enigma M is the Reserve Rotor-box. Three are in the machine and four in the box ready to interchange
(Courtesy Archiv BfZ)

machine to a new key, he had to choose the correct set of three wheels out of the five available, set the alphabet ring on each wheel, insert the wheels in the machine in the correct order and close the cover. To set an alphabet ring on a wheel he would probably hold the wheel in one hand so that the clip position was facing him and then rotate the ring until the correct letter was opposite the clip position. There the clip would engage. Herivel's contribution was to realise that, when the operator inserted the wheel into the machine the letter determining the ring setting would probably still be facing him, and when he closed the cover it was likely that the three letters appearing in the apertures would be pretty close to the ring settings of the new key. Indeed if the operator was lazy he might leave the wheels in their initial position when he encoded the next setting for his first message of the day. If so, the letters of the indicator setting in the preamble of this message would be pretty close to the ring settings in the new key.

To exploit this habit, the midnight-to-eight a.m. shift of the Machine Room watch, working on the traffic registers, would first identify the discriminants of the Red traffic for the new day. They would then look for the first message on the new key originating from any radio transmitter. The indicator settings of these messages would be entered on a 'Herivel Square' (P. 79). Indicators HDR TKZ JFW etc would be entered by writing the letter R on the square in column H and row D, Z in square TK, W in square JF and so on. Before too long a cluster would appear in the square. On P. 79 the cluster consists of the entries GRI, HSK, GTK and FRJ. The Machine Room would then hazard a guess that the ring settings of the three wheels must be:

Left-hand wheel	F G or H
Middle wheel	B S or T
Right-hand wheel	I J or K

From previous experience they might reckon that the most likely guesses to be tried first on test runs were GRK, GSK, GRJ, GSJ, GRI, GSI. It was as simple as that. The 17,576 possible ring settings had been reduced to 6 probables.

This process was almost certainly discovered by the Poles in 1931 and they too profited from the sloppiness of the German operators in setting up their Enigma machines. But we must be grateful to Gordon Welchman for explaining the process step by step in *The Hut Six Story*. He also explains the Cillis: 'suppose the traffic register showed a three-part message whose indicator settings and indicators were:

First part	QAY MPR
Second part	EDC LIY
Third part	TGB VEA

Having observed the habits of Enigma operators in the traffic that we had decoded, it was not hard to guess what the operator had done, from the arrangement of the Enigma keyboard:

```
Q W E R T Z U I O
 A S D F G H J K
P Y X C V B N M L
```

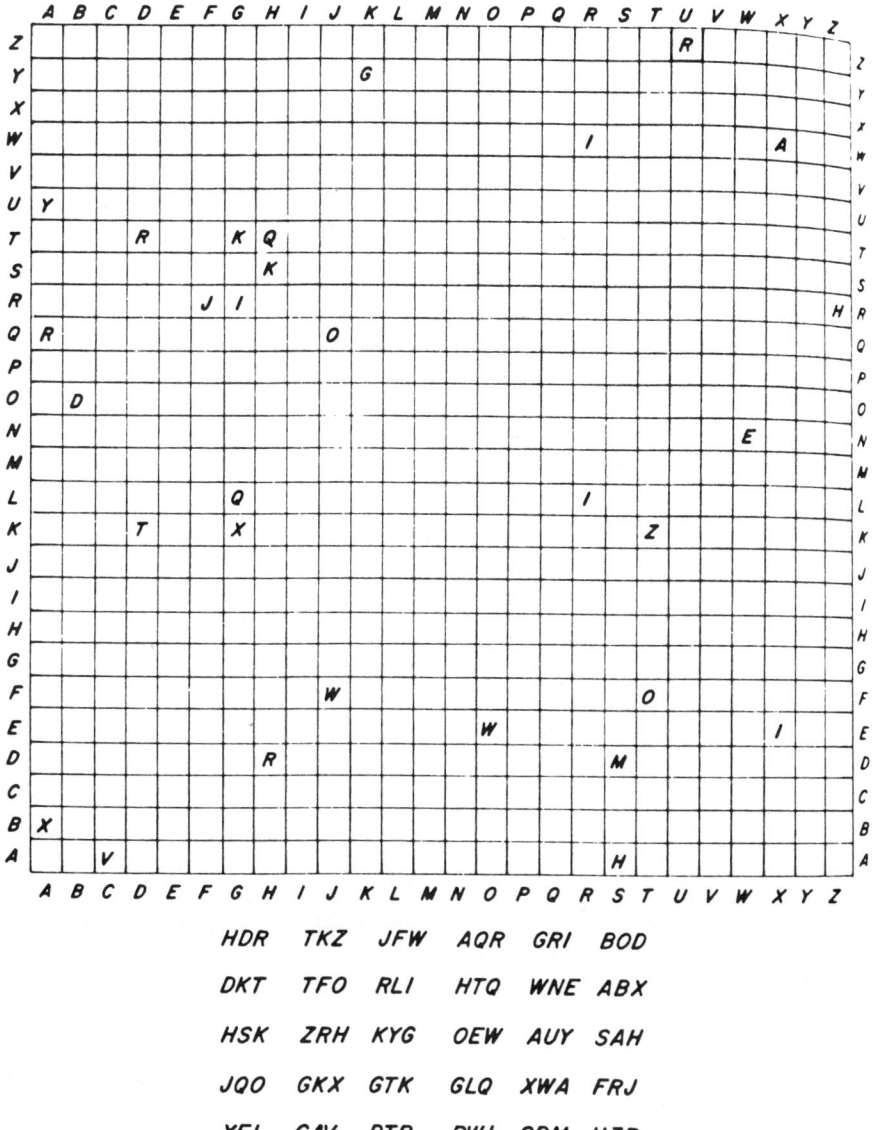

Herivel Square, with entries representing 30 indicator settings

He had obviously chosen as his indicator settings the alternate keyboard diagonals QAY, EDC, and TGB. We would conclude that his text settings would be the alternating diagonals WSX, RFV and ZHN. If the text setting of the first part of the message was WSX, we knew that, with the wheels set to QAY, MPR was the encode of WSX. Similarly at setting EDC, LIY was the encode of RFV and at setting TGB, VFA was the encode of ZHN. Thus this set of three Cillis gave us nine letter pairings. We knew that at the wheel setting following QAY in the scrambler cycle, M and W were paired, that at the next wheel setting P and S were paired, and so on. It was, in fact, a form of crib.

Suppose that, in addition to this three-part message, we could find in the traffic register two single-part messages with indicator settings QWE and QAP. Looking at the keyboard with an eye to pattern and the known habits of individuals we might well guess that the corresponding message settings were ASD and OKL. This would give us six more letter pairings which combined with the Herivel tip would probably enable us to break the Red key for the day. Unbelievable! Yet it actually happened and it went on happening until the bombes came, many months later. Indeed, though I cannot remember when the two prototype bombes arrived, it seems to me we must have been entirely dependent on Herivel tips and Cillis from the Invasion of France to the end of the Battle of Britain, right up to the final crunch on Eagle Day, 15 September, 1940. By then the RAF was near exhaustion, and it appears that Hitler was not prepared to invade until his Luftwaffe had completely knocked them out. Therefore Goering planned a conclusive triumph. Hut 6 Ultra revealed his plans for that critical day, and helped the RAF to make the best use of its remaining capabilities. Goering's attempt to knock out the RAF failed, thanks in part to Hut 6 Ultra. Two days later a Hitler directive, received via Hut 6, made it clear to the intelligence staff at Bletchley that invasion plans had been abandoned . . .

There were other types of Cillis that allowed us to guess a message setting. Occasionally, for example a lazy operator would get in the habit of using the same three letters both for the indicator and for the text setting. This would mean that, having encoded his text setting he would only have to move the right-hand wheel back three places to encode his message. This type of Cilli was JABJAB from the letters used in its first appearance discovered by Babbage. But in JABJAB too our help came primarily from the use of keyboard patterns. If, for example, we found a three-part message in which the indicator settings were QAY, WSX and EDC it would be a good bet that the text settings were the same. It was extremely fortunate that both the Herivel tip and the keyboard Cillis had been discovered before the Germans changed their indicating procedure and defeated our method of breaking Enigma keys with the Jeffreys apparatus. Had we been foiled then, we would not have been breaking at the time of the last Eagle Day and we would have lost the continuity that was to prove so essential later on in our use of cribs.

Whereas the Poles had already done all this in 1931 to enable them to do a much more difficult, well-nigh impossible, job reconstituting the inner works of the rotors in the Enigma machine itself, this independent research in Hut 6 was invaluable when the Germans made a major change on 10 May before the opening of the French campaign, and in May 1944 before the Allied invasion of France. They also coped very quickly and efficiently when the Germans installed a new Umkehrwalze (turn-around disc) to improve security and reconstituted its inner cabling.

Welchman in the early days of Hut 6 was in charge of the Registration Room, Intercept Control Room and the Decoding Room while Jeffreys was in charge of the Machine Room and Sheet-Stacking room. He admits that not many of the girls in the DR (Decoding Room) had a knowledge of German. He could not remember how the bundles of intercepts from various stations were referenced and this must have become quite a problem when not only one key was being broken, but several different keys in one day, with messages arriving from home stations and abroad.

This was revealed in a BBC D-Day broadcast in the 1980s. Mrs Jean Howard (Jean Alington) explained the purpose of 3L—the Liaison Section in Hut 3.

The Liaison Section in Hut 3 (3L)

'The nature of our security system was "the need to know". Each individual working flat out thought that they knew everything. In fact everyone had tunnel vision. Few knew, or had time to know, what the others were working on. Only recently did it become clear how few were "bigoted" i.e. had knowledge of future intentions.

When the tide turned towards victory, the Americans were forced into the war by the Japanese attack on Pearl Harbour, and new Allies were about to join us in the Huts. It became vital that someone should try to liaise between the cryptographers in Hut 6, the intercept stations, Traffic Analysis and the Intelligence officers in Hut 3. Someone had to evaluate the fifty or so ciphers which we were breaking currently. Someone had to read all the German material, published daily in the original, in order to evaluate each individual cipher. Once breaking was a regular occurrence, the Decoding Section in Hut 6 began to fall rapidly into arrears because of the time taken in changing machine settings as each watch came in and changed the instructions of the previous watch. So 3L was set up to give priorities to the Decoding Room and elsewhere. There would have to be a daily meeting attended by delegates from all three services, our American allies, the cryptographers (who needed particular ciphers for cribs, e.g. the Pantelleria weather keys), Traffic Analysis experts, experts from the secret weapons section researching on V1 and V2 cipher, and the Railway cipher experts. This was to be chaired by W/Cdr Oeser, or, if he was overseas on special missions, by one of us, to decide which ciphers should have priority on the Bombes (computers).

So, in early 1943 Sqd/Ldr Oeser set up 3L at the far end of the operational room in Hut 3, behind a map-partition. It was a cold winter, so we were warmed by a paraffin stove which was once knocked over. The ensuing flames nearly put an end to us, our venture and the whole Hut. We built a door to keep others out and Major George Crawford wrote above it in Greek "Let no-one enter here who is not primarily interested in mathematics".

We had blackboards on the walls and F/O Christine Rose WAAF drew on them the German W/T stars which we were most interested in at that time. So that we would not forget that some frequencies might require double banking, we were sent into Hut 6 to familiarise ourselves with the machines working there, we liaised with the Traffic Analysis log-readers; we also made time and study assessments of how to speed up the flow of decodes to the watch, which bore fruit when we moved into Block D and arranged to time-stamp every signal as it passed through. We tried to get better conditions for personnel working in appalling discomfort and we became agony aunts for the miserable and uncomfortable.

We three women graded every German Enigma signal that came into the Hut. These had been bound into approximately 50 separate ciphers covering the German Air Force, the German Army in North Africa, Europe, Balkans, Russian Front, Middle East, Supply ciphers, and specials such as Weather keys, Secret Weapons from Peenemuende, Railway and some diplomatic ciphers. We each prepared a weekly news sheet for Mr Churchill on the areas we were covering. We swapped areas frequently so that we should be competent in all of them. Any extra research—such as "who was killing most Germans in Yugoslavia, Tito or Mihajlović?" "Total forces in Norway for a coverplan invasion" "The new German Intelligence services after the bomb plot, how many and who were running them?" came my way. We were hideously over-worked and extended. Oeser was promoted to Wing Commander and awarded an OBE, George became a Major.

Colonel Telford Taylor USAAF (later Chief Prosecutor at the Nuremberg War Crimes Trial after the retirement of Jackson) recalls that a visiting USAAF officer said of 3L: "Wing Commander and what a Wing!"

As to the question on preparations for D-Day and the value of Bletchley to the invasion campaign I would say from 3L, stressing that it was only one "tunnel", that our main value in preparations for D-Day was:—
1) Our knowledge that the enemy had swallowed the cover plans, believed that the invasion would take place in the Pas de Calais, was still worried about a possible invasion of Yugoslavia and/or Norway.
2) That the Traffic Analysis section had prepared cover for frequencies likely to produce new and so far unused and unbroken ciphers, in that area occupied by German 7th Army which we were going to call Duck.
3) That our knowledge of German Order of Battle, logistics, secret weapons, railway movements, future intentions, remained as always the best we could achieve, and that we expected far more intelligence once bombing had disrupted landlines to OKW—the German High Command.

Naval ciphers, including the U-Boat ciphers, were being broken. The Naval Intelligence was covered in Huts 4 and 8. Shortly after the Battle of Crete we ceased to process Naval Enigma in Hut 3, although we were given access to ZTPG material which had some bearing on the Luftwaffe and German Army'.

This was the efficient well-oiled sophisticated machinery that began with the Welchman Special. When Cdr Ellingworth visited Welchman from Fort Bridgewoods in 1940 they worked out a system giving priority treatment to certain networks. Ellingworth was to teleprint these to BP while the other messages travelled by despatch rider several times a day. Later on a Duty Officer on 8-hour shifts would be attached to the intercept station to relay to the setroom instructions from BP on which frequencies and callsigns to intercept as a priority, but the machinery for passing decodes from the Hut 6 Decoding Room to the Hut 3 watch in an adjacent building was not sophisticated—in fact it was primitive.

'To save the time of valuable personnel it was done with a wooden tray, some string, a broom handle and two hatches. The latter were cut opposite each other in the outer walls of Hut 6 and Hut 3 and the intervening space of six to eight feet was bridged by a flat piece of wood boxed in with wooden sides and a roof to cope with the weather. The procedure was to place the decodes in the tray and shout through the hatches to alert the Hut 3 watch which would then send one of their staff to draw the tray across by the string attached to their side and remove the decodes. When the Hut 6 DR had another load of decodes ready, the wooden tray was retrieved with the string attached to our end and the transfer process was repeated. The purpose of the broom handle was to rouse the Hut 3 watch if shouting failed to do so. It could make quite a loud noise when rammed against the Hut 3 hatch. The broom handle was also used to recover a tray when the string mechanism fouled up'.

By the time I arrived at Hut 3 on D-Day Welchman's team had moved into a new brick building which could now house the Central

Party, as well as Hut 6, Hut 8 and the teleprinters. The transfer of decodes from Hut 6 to Hut 3 was now by an efficient conveyor belt which never stopped. Another conveyor belt brought the raw intercepted messages from the teleprinters to the Hut 6 Registration Room.

The Central Party which moved into Hut 6 in 1942 were log-readers. When the Chatham intercept operators left Fort Bridgewoods for Beaumanor the log-readers moved into the mansion with them and expanded. As RAF Chicksands stn expanded it was seen to be better placed than Beaumanor and the log-readers moved to BP. It was a large organisation of army men and ATS women. Welchman was able to tell them that Enigma was being broken and how this was being done and how their log-reading could help. They were reinforced by a group of US army personnel (male).

Some years after his *The Hut Six Story*, Welchman published in 1986 in 'Intelligence and National Security Journal' a revealing document correcting some misconceptions by himself and Professor Hinsley in 'The History of British Intelligence in the Second World War' about the importance of the bombe. He said in 'From Polish Bomba to British Bombe—The Birth of Ultra':— 'It had its brief day of glory, but was already ineffective when the Poles got us off to a flying start by telling us their secrets in July 1939. It would have been of no use to us as will become apparent after I have discussed Rejewski's brilliant cryptanalytical work . . . the analysis of the radio transmissions started with the intercept operator who recorded all chit-chat and identifications on sheets of a "log". When the German operator had paved the way for the transmission of an Enigma message, this message would be recorded on a separate sheet. The log sheets would go to the MI8 log-reading group, which started in London and moved at first to Harpenden, then to Beaumanor and finally to Bletchley. Except for the time when the group was at Beaumanor, all log sheets reached them by despatch rider. The messages were sent to Hut 6, also by despatch rider, for a good part of the war.

Unfortunately the term "Traffic Analysis" or TA, when applied to war time radio nets carrying Enigma traffic, means different things to different people. To some it means obtaining information from a study of the logs. When I used the term in my book I meant the analysis of enciphered Enigma messages and their preambles. This, from the outset, was done in Hut 6. The log-reading was done by the MI8 group, which ultimately joined forces with Hut 6.

Without going too much into detail I want to show that our method of handling Traffic Analysis, well established in the first year and virtually unchanged throughout the war, mattered a great deal. It was based on the Traffic Register and should perhaps have been called the Message Register. It contained the preamble of each message and the first six letters of enciphered text. This was all we needed in Hut 6 until we decided how we were going to attempt to break a daily key. The Register was sent, page by page, by teleprinter, so there was very little delay between interception of a message and the time at which its preamble reached Hut 6.

In Hut 6 three copies of the Register went to three destinations, to the Registration Room, where the messages were charted, to the cryptological wizards who used them to plan their attempts at breaks, and to Colman's team of intercept co-ordinators, who used them in their constant telephone contacts with Duty Officers at the intercept stations, who had their own copies of the Register pages that they had transmitted. It proved to be a very speedy and efficient system of information exchange between the specialised teams whose contributions were essential to our success. From Jean Howard's research it now seems that the leading people in Hut 3 did not realise how this Traffic Register system reduced the delays involved both in breaking and in giving them the most important decodes. It also seems that Oeser and other leaders in Hut 3 contributed little, but there was probably not much that they could do. When the heyday of Ultra had arrived, Milner-Barry's team of wizards, Colman's team of co-ordinators, the large log-reading effort, and the experienced people at the intercept stations could do a good job on their own. It was extremely important that this group of teams were allowed to collaborate without uninformed outside interference. Indeed the British success in developing and using Hut 6 Ultra was largely due to the early establishment of excellent communication, collaboration and co-operation between many specialised activities.'

Parkerismus

Welchman's team achieved a very real success in forecasting Enigma keys. Reg Parker of Hut 6 Intercept Control Unit, who had kept a comprehensive list of sets of discriminants, wheel orders, ring settings and Steckers of every key they had broken from the beginning, worked out a theory that the German responsible for choosing the monthly keys in advance found the task overwhelming when the number of keys became large. He assumed that the German who had to decide on a list of three-letter discriminants, wheel orders, composed of three of the digits 1 to 5, ring settings and Steckers which specified the pairs of letters of the alphabet to be connected by the double-ended cables, found it difficult to go on month after month using random letters and figures and as the keys proliferated he must have decided to simplify the task for himself. He must have decided to use either the discriminants or the wheel orders or the ring settings or the Steckers for a previous month. This reduced the amount of random fixing he had to do. If he used the discriminants from one month's previous list, the wheel orders from another, the ring settings from a third and the cross-pluggings from a fourth, it would save labour and no one would know. Parker looked at the lists he had kept and he searched for repeats on the first day of the month. Bingo! He found it already in 1942. Sometimes they could set up the complete day's working on the key from Parkerismus. By this means they knew the daily keys Rommel would use for a whole month in the African campaign.

The Bombes

The Polish mathematicians in Warsaw had shown Knox how to link Enigma machines together to create a 'bomba' and the first one was soon in operation at BP in 1940. When the Poles returned from Rumania they went to BP before rejoining Bertrand's intercept at PC Bruno in France. There they assisted Knox and Turing to recreate their six Enigma bomba which Turing further developed. (The Poles called it bomba one day when eating an ice-cream of that name). Welchman believed that the British called it a bombe after the French word for a bomb because it ticked, or rather 'made a noise like a battery of knitting-needles' before it produced its output.

The first two prototypes (called Agnes, whereas production models bore the names of warships and naval shore establishments) went into action in late 1941 and a production line was later set up to produce these in quantity. It was an elaborate piece of equipment which simulated the various operations which were carried out in the

Enigma machine. They were assembled at the BTM factory in Letchworth not far from Bletchley which enabled close co-operation between the makers and the users. Imitating Bertrand's practice in France, (and anticipating Saddam Hussein with the super-gun) for security reasons individual parts were made in different small factories, so that no one knew what they were manufacturing. Some parts, for example, were made in the Spirella corset factory at Baldock which was also making parachutes.

The bombe, mounted on castors, was about four feet long. (P. 100) It was an electro-magnetic series of double-ended scramblers using rotating drums about five inches long instead of wheels, driven on three shafts. It was the design of Doc Keen of BTM. The top middle and bottom drums of each scrambler corresponded to the right-hand, middle and left-hand wheels of an Enigma scrambler unit. All the middle drums were driven together in synchronism, likewise all the top drums and all the bottom drums. The prototypes had ten scramblers each. These were followed by twelve-scrambler production models. A door at the back acted as a frame for a diagonal board, testing devices and other electrical circuitry. It was connected by an enormous 26-fold co-axial cable to the in-out and out-in terminals of the twelve scramblers.

When the war began there was only the Red key to break and then the Blue key. As the war developed on several fronts in N Africa and the Middle East then in Russia new keys appeared as each new command in the Wehrmacht and the Luftwaffe was created in those theatres. New bombes had to be built to deal with these. The Germans changed their operating procedures on 10 May 1940 ready for the invasion of France. They sent the indicator once only instead of repeating it and included it in the preamble. The loss of three letters was catastrophic and the perforated sheets were no longer of any use, but after an interval of ten days BP was back in business.

There were three bombe phases marked by the extension of the war to new theatres. It must be stressed that the bombe did not break the Enigma keys. The bombes were useless without a 'crib'. It was the sheer brilliance of the cryptanalytical methodology of the experts in Hut 6, in using the Cillis and in finding cribs which gave success—almost one day at a time.

The first bombe phase ran from Sep 1940 to the end of 1941. When Rommel began his offensive in North Africa the new keys were

Chaffinch and Light blue for the Army and Air Force respectively and a high-grade key was named Pink. With the invasion of Yugoslavia and Greece and the capture of Crete in May there were new keys and when Hitler attacked Russia in June 1941 the German Air Force was designated by bird names for the keys, e.g. Kestrel and Vulture.

The second phase was the year 1942. There was the invasion of Egypt and El Alamein. On 3 July Sebastopol fell to the Germans and in the summer of 1942 the gigantic pincer movement began towards Iran and the oilfields of the Persian Gulf. The Germans suffered reverses for the first time. The battle for Stalingrad began on 13 Sep and Rommel was defeated and retreated after the second Battle of El Alamein on 23 Oct. Then came the landings of the Allies in French North Africa on 1 Nov 1942 and so the keys multiplied and new bombes were required.

The third phase began early in 1943 and lasted until the end of the war. This third phase was the most difficult. The Germans multiplied their efforts to improve the security of Enigma by modifying the machine itself and by changing procedures. The operators were less careless and Cillis were now rare. They began to reverse the order of the wheels at midday. Two months before D-Day they ceased to use discriminants and in Feb 1945 they were changing all radio frequencies every day and encoding the very call-signs by a method which BP could not break. Nevertheless more than eighteen keys were broken regularly at this time.

The enormous cost of the project, constructing two hundred bombes, had to be faced before the contracts could be continued. The original cost of the prototypes was borne by Secret Service funds but the expansion of the programme had to be financed by the Admiralty. That solved, there was the problem of housing so many units and providing the staff to run them twenty-four hours a day. There were new brick buildings for offices near completion at Stanmore northwest of London and this was a good move as there was ample accommodation for the many WRNS operators. This site had direct teletype and telephone lines to BP. The next site was at nearby Eastcote, Pinner, where there were two new buildings nearly finished and space for a third. This new block went up in six months providing accommodation for eight to nine hundred WRNS. Bombes from Wavendon and Adstock were moved to Stanmore and Eastcote and the few remaining at BP were used for training and demonstration only.

As many of the operations performed by the Wrens, now numbering 2,000, were often repetitive although demanding powers of concentration, it was necessary to maintain their enthusiasm by telling them something about the process they were involved in. A talk was given ten or twelve times a year, invaluable to those joining the establishment, explaining the part played by the Bombes in creating decodes. Snippets of intelligence, fairly harmless from the security point of view, were added to show how their work resulted in real successes in the war.

The naval version of the Enigma was the most complex and the most difficult to break. The first success arose from the sinking of the U-33 on 12 Feb 1940. Divers were able to recover three rotors of its Enigma machine from the wreck and interrogation of survivors ascertained that these were three of eight rotors normally used. But BP now knew that the German Navy used three Enigma keys. Their Home-Waters key was code-named Dolphin and the Distant-Waters key was Pike, which was not broken, and the high-grade Officer Only key called Neptun by the Germans (code-named Barracuda by BP) was used for carrying top-grade messages between Berlin and Admiral Raeder's coastal bases.

On 9 May 1941 the U-110 and another sub attacked a convoy south of Greenland. Brought to the surface by depth charges, the crew having laid the scuttling charges abandoned ship. It took three hours to sink. A prize crew of five ratings and Lieut D. Balme managed to board her while the survivors had been taken below deck on HMS Bulldog. They seized documents and charts. Comdr G. Dodds of Pinner on a later trip carried back an Enigma machine. This was complete with its eight rotors and among the documents were a list of Officer Only keys (code-named Oyster) and a special code-book for the construction of short signals (Kurzsignale) dealing with sightings of enemy ships and weather reports. There were also the Home-Waters keys for April and June and a series of naval grid charts. GC&CS was now able to read all traffic including Officer Only signals for June and July currently. As August began it finally mastered the Home-Waters settings and was able to read the entire traffic for the rest of the war except for occasional days in the second half of 1941 with little delay. The maximum delay was 72 hours and normally only

Die Kriegsmarine verwendete neben dem Maschinenschlüssel „Funkschlüssel M", bei dem man Buchstaben für Buchstaben verschlüsselte, auch einen Code, bei dem ganze Begriffe oder Sätze mit je vier Buchstaben ausgedrückt werden konnten, die in einem Kurzsignalheft – einem Codebuch – festgehalten waren. Hier die Ausgabe 1941.

Geheim!

Nr. 904

Kurzsignalheft 1941

Oberkommando der Kriegsmarine
Berlin 1941

M.Dv.Nr. 96   der Marineleitung

Übersicht über die Schlüsselmittel der Kriegsmarine am 1.1.1943. Die beiden ersten Seiten dieser Zusammenstellung enthalten die wichtigsten Schlüssel M-Bereiche, zu denen auch die auf S. 3 enthaltenen Flottenfunksignale, U-Bootfunksignale, Ortungssignale und Wetterkurzsignale sowie das Funkschlüsselgespräch gehören. Auf den S. 4–8 sind dann 10 Handverfahren, 2 Kenngruppenverfahren und 4 Schlüsselmittel der Versorgungsschiffe in Übersee, sowie je eines für Handelsschiffe, Fischereifahrzeuge und zur Verbindung mit Dienststellen außerhalb der Kriegsmarine verzeichnet. (Vorlagen: Archiv BfZ)

Geheime Kommandosache MDv Nr. 448

Schlüsselmittel der Kriegsmarine

(Stand: 1. Januar 1943.)

1.) Schlüssel M.
(Maschinenverfahren)

a) Funksprüche:

(1) Allgemeines Verfahren: (M Allgemein)
Klartext wird unmittelbar verschlüsselt. Spruchschlüssel wird durch Verschlüsselung der Verfahrenskenngruppe ermittelt.

(2) Offiziersverfahren: (M Offizier und M Stab)
Klartext wird unmittelbar verschlüsselt. Spruchschlüssel wird aus 26 verfügbaren Spruchschlüsseln gewählt. Vor Abgabe als Funkspruch nochmalige Verschlüsselung nach Verfahren M Allgemein.

(3) Verwendung verschiedener Schlüssel (Einstellungen) nebeneinander. Alle mit dem gleichen Schlüssel ausgerüsteten Dienststellen sind zu einem Schlüsselbereich zusammengefaßt.
Es gibt nachstehende Schlüsselbereiche:

Bezeichnung	Verfahren	Wo bzw. wann angewandt	Bemerkungen
M Hydra	Allgemein Offizier Stab	In heimischen Gewässern	Bis 31.12.42 Bezeichnung M Heimische Gewässer
M Aegir	Allgemein Offizier Stab	in außerheimischen Gewässern	Bis 31.12.42 Bezeichnung M Außerheimische Gewässer
M Triton	Allgemein Offizier	bei Front U.Booten	
M Potsdam	Allgemein Offizier	bei Ostland-Unternehmungen	Am 1.1.43 außer Kraft. Wiederinkrafttreten wird von Gruppe Nord befohlen
M Neptun	Allgemein Offizier	bei Unternehmungen Geschichtszeit der Kirchlein	

Anlage 5 zu O.K.M. 1222/43

```
                                              Battle Group
U
 DH (2)
TO: I D 8 G                              ZIP/ZTPG/194876
FROM: N S

5205 KC/S              T OO  1527     T O 1 1500/25/12/43


FROM: ADMIRAL NORTHERN WATERS
   TO:  BATTLE GROUP
        ADMIRAL POLAR COAST

MOST IMMEDIATE

'OSTFRONT' 1700/25/12.

                           will be referred to in Sug Cish
                                as "EPILEPSY."
0025/26/12/43+++EE/FA                Ultra.
```

Ultra played a decisive role in sinking the Scharnhorst. The coded command for the ship to sail—Ostfront—was sent to OIC just after midnight 26 Oct 43 so that the Ultra signal to CinC HomeFleet enabled him to direct the convoy off to the north and send his battle fleet towards the Scharnhorst. Four hours later the doomed ship sent its last signal (below)

```
ADM(1)
TO I D 8 G                              ZIP/ZTPG/195207
FROM N S

2170 KC/S           T 0 0 1945           TOI 1941/26/12/43


F.O. CRUISERS AND C.O. OF 'SCHARNHORST' REPORT AT 1825:

         TO:  THE FUEHRER

             WE SHALL FIGHT TO THE LAST SHELL

         (DEPT. NOTE: COMPARE ZTP/902))


2331/26/12/43+CEL/AM
     E    ENTZIFFERUNG DES LETZTEN FUNKSPRUCHES DER "SCHARNHORST"
```

a few hours. The capture of the naval grid was equally important. Previous to June 1941 the U-boats had given their positions at sea using an irregularly constructed grid. The British had captured parts covering the North Sea and the Baltic and small parts of the N Atlantic area in Dec 1939 and Apr 1940. Now from the U-110 they acquired the part covering the whole of the N Atlantic and most of the Mediterranean. Just as it was being read currently the U-Boat Command complicated matters by giving positions related to fixed points of reference—Franz, Oscar, Herbert, etc, which were chosen arbitrarily and changed frequently. From 16 June a typical Enigma order to a U-Boat now read, according to Hinsley:

> 'If boat is in fit condition for night attacks occupy as attacking area the northern halves of the 162 milesquares (of the naval grid) whose central points lie 306 degrees 220 miles and 290 degrees 380 miles respectively from Point Franz. If boat is not in fit condition report by short signal No.'

This problem which delayed decryption during June was solved in July and on 11 Sep the Germans dropped it as it was cumbersome and causing miscalculations by the U-Boats. The Germans then addressed messages to U-Boat commanders by name instead of using the U-Boat number which was awkward as the commanders frequently changed ship. On 24 Nov 1941 a new problem was introduced by using an imaginary Christian name surname and address to indicate the table which was in use for encoding the larger squares of the grid. Now the U-boat Command could quickly change the grid by giving a new address. This caused problems until a copy of the address book was captured in U-505 in June 1944.

The capture of the naval Enigma machine was stupendous, especially when they came to build a bombe to deal with the German Naval traffic. The first German traffic on the naval Enigma machine was broken on 13 Dec 1942 but it was not due to cryptological expertise on the 'four-rotor' bombe. The U-559 was fired on by HMS Petard 70 miles north of the Nile Delta and the crew abandoned ship. While they swam towards the Petard two of the British crew Lieut Fasson and A.B. Grazier stripped naked dived into the sea and swam to the U-559 sixty yards away. The conning tower was just visible above the waves and they clambered in finding lights still burning. They seized a four-rotor Enigma machine and documents which proved to be the current Shark keys. They were astonished to see outside the conning tower Tommy Brown a 16-year-old NAAFI canteen assistant who had joined them without superior orders. They had just time to pass the Enigma and documents to him which he passed to the whaleboat before the U-559 sank taking with it the two valiant sailors who received posthumous awards of the George Cross while Brown received a George Medal. In Dec 1943 the Scharnhorst was sunk with Enigma help. (P. 90)

The RAF Y Service

On the intercept side the output was vastly increased by the opening of the large RAF Station at Chicksands Priory near Bedford in 1941 with male operators. In August 1942 it was extended with the arrival of WAAF operators and an auxiliary station was opened at Shaftesbury initially with WAAF operators. They became more and more expert in picking up weak signals from distant places in Africa, the Balkans and on the Russian front. By early 1943 there were five widely spaced intercept sites, Beaumanor in Leicestershire, Chatham in Kent (small remnant only), Cheadle in Cheshire, Shaftesbury in Dorset, as well as Chicksands in Bedfordshire.

As Aileen Clayton's book *The Enemy Is Listening* does not cover the campaign in Western Europe the complete story of RAF Y has still to be written. Until then a mention of the structure may be appropriate here. The organisation was based on the Wireless Unit, roughly the size of an Army B-Type Unit. A typical strength return of 382 W U in France was 6 Officers, 1 WO, 3 F.Sgts, 34 Sgts, and 74 ORs. Two or more WUs could constitute a Wing and above them was Group with its Group Control Centre (GCC). No. 380 WU operating in the grounds of Chateau Beraud at Draria near Algiers, built by Napoleon III for his Algerian mistress, intercepted W/T traffic in North Africa including vital Enigma channels. It supervised two large RAF stations, No. 351 at Gibraltar and No. 371 at Freetown, Sierra Leone, liaised with Heliopolis and communicated with Waddon in England by highspeed units through its own Special Liaison Unit. The 276 and 329 Wings had their field units of 200 men across N Africa and the Near East from No. 23 at Cap Bon in Tunisia to No. 3 at Habbaniya in Iraq, with No. 2 at Alexandria, No. 10 at Malta, No. 6 in Aleppo and No. 9 on the island of Kos. After the invasion of Italy No. 25 was set up in Sicily and another at Bitonto.

Ideally the field unit was situated close to the fighter control with Y liaison officer beside the Controller feeding back to the Field Unit information of use to them. WU 380 commanded by F/Lt L. F. C. Turner was close to my 48 WI Section attached to the US 128 Radio Intercept Coy on the same hill-top near Kasserine overlooking Thelepte and Feriana airfields and we exchanged information on frequencies and enemy identifications.

There were also airborne detachments of the Wireless Intelligence Unit at Wyton operating in various theatres and a number of Wellington aircraft tested German radar screens. The RAF also used M Units to 'meacon' enemy beacons. This was subtler than jamming because it re-radiated the enemy signal to destroy its direction-finding activity. It used the same signal with the same modulation and frequency and the ground station could not differentiate between the two signals which emanated from transmitters miles apart. Hence it was impossible to take a bearing on the aircraft.

A look at the operational orders of 382 WU shows how it was equipped and how effective such units were:—

When the unit was formed in 1941 and attached to 83 Group, recommendations were soon made on the establishment. It was agreed to increase the number of Intelligence Officers to seven and Clerks Signals (linguists) to 1 F/Sgt and 29 Sgts. Before moving to an operational site at Folkestone they were supplied with 26 vehicles including a m/c combination and two solo machines. These included an Intercept vehicle and D/F vans and they had a 60 ft mast they could erect. Eventually they organised a four watch cycle for all R/T, W/T and D/F personnel. In every way it resembled an Army B-Type Section but had three times as many linguists. Under command of F/Lt F. H. North their successes in destroying enemy aircraft can be gauged from the following extract from operations records:—

Month ended 30 June 1944

Since the arrival in Normandy, 83 Gp aircraft were in many cases vectored on to German formations entirely on Y and in this respect 382 WU was able to afford information which either entirely or partly resulted in the destruction of 45 German fighters.

Month ended 31 October 1944

The unit moved to Veghel on the 4th in close proximity to the German front line, enclosing the western limits of the Eindhoven-Nijmegen salient which ran within 1,500 yards of the operational site. This was the nearest siting to enemy lines that had been risked by an Air Ministry Y unit. Main Nijmegen road running some 100 yards to the S of site shelled by a German battery which had moved up into woods within 1,200 yards to our NW. A number of attacks on Group 83 airfields by ME 262 aircraft. These a/c indulged in bomb-dropping. Unofficially credited to Y information were 10 German fighters destroyed incl one ME 262 on the 13th near Arnhem and a night fighter on the 29th.

Month ended 30 November 1944

An analysis of credits to Y information supplied operationally to 83 GCC shows that since this Unit arrived on D + 8 at the Beachhead in Normandy the following German fighter aircraft have been destroyed (no record kept of the great number of possibles or probables):

June (25 days)	46	October	10
July	72	November	4
August	42		
September	47	Total	221

The intelligence passed to the GCC and to the CIO of 83 Gp included as much detail as possible of the enemy's presence and movements, his landing grounds, objectives, habits and to a lesser degree his policy.

Month ended 31 December 1944

... Credited to 382 Wireless Unit was the destruction of 30 German fighter a/c, mostly 109s and 190s but a fair sprinkling of ME 262s was included.

Month ended 31 March 1944

The GAF line-up and reshuffle on the Western front preparatory to the Battle of the Rhine disclosed numerous jet units in addition to SEF Geschwader and several ground attack specialists. Our old enemies JGs 26, 27 and 54 were in evidence and led the attack and defence day after day. Sustained attacks on the Remagen bridgehead resulted in copious traffic. Of the a/c destroyed in this area on the 13th 4 were credited to this unit. Between 1550 and 1645 hrs on 28th 83 Gp a/c scored 11-1-5 of which 83 GCC credited this unit with 8 destroyed. At close of play GCC Controller expressed his thanks for excellent gen and cooperation all afternoon.

R/T traffic and excellent bearings were secured on a/c actually over the bridge on several occasions. On the whole Jet a/c were well in the picture . . . the 14th gave us our best 'Jet' day to date. No less than 17 operations were covered, and due warning passed to interested parties. The Rhine was crossed during the early hours of the 24th. Of the German a/c operating over the Cleve-Emmerich area 3 were destroyed by Gp 83 a/c and credited to Y.

Month ended 30 April 1945

. . . On 29th the German Y Service fought for the first time on record with the mask off: we plotted the Hun formations and as the GCC Controller . . . vectored his aircraft to the attack the German H-dienst piped up *in clear*, saying:

'The English controller has warned his aircraft of your position'.
. . . This made us feel that the end was very near for by time-honoured custom the Y service and the H-Dienst of our respective Air Forces surround themselves in secrecy loving the dark. In the May record 'the final score of Hun a/c destroyed in battle as a direct result of Y is 333'.

At GC&CS according to Calvocaressi the most important tool in Hut 3 apart from the decodes themselves was the Air Index. A team of indexers in a large room off the watch room examined each decoded message and underlined key words to be put on cards—names of persons, places, units, weapons, code words, scientific terms and special subjects such as oil. So valuable was this index, thousands of cards, that they were photographed and stored in another location in case Bletchley was bombed. My recollection is of a similar index, many thousands of cards in shoe-boxes along both sides of a long hut which was a growing German–English dictionary. When a new word came up in the message you were translating you looked for it there and if it was not there an indexer put it in with a reference time and date-stamped to the message from which it was taken. When the first-ever jet aircraft was introduced by the Luftwaffe we had an array of neologisms, new types of jet-fuel, machine parts, etc. It was not easy to identify a brand new technical term as these were often garbled words stemming from mistakes by operators or arising in the enciphering process they went through before being sent by high-speed radio from overseas. This was particularly the case when dealing with translations of Fish traffic.

Fish or Geheimschreiber

The sound of the Geheimschreiber had been heard since early in the war and it was concluded that it was a non-Morse emission, a radio teleprinter using the Baudot telegraph code. There were two versions of this machine, one built by Siemens was codenamed Sturgeon and the other by Lorenz called Tunny. The Germans called it Saegefisch or Sawfish from the rasping sound of the machine in operation. They worked at high speed and needed only one operator, and printed a tape, as the Germans had wanted in 1932 for the revamped Enigma, which proved to be a fiasco in campaigns owing to operator errors.

The Geheimschreiber or Secret Writer had a conventional keyboard with 26 letters, 10 figures, punctuation marks and keyshifts and each code-element had five units of equal length, 20 milliseconds. The letter A on the Murray code would be mark, mark, space, space, space punched on a tape. By using the key-setting of the rotors for that day the symbols for A could come out as mark, space, mark, space, mark or Y. Intercepted on an ordinary teleprinter the resulting message would be a meaningless jumble of random letters, figures and punctuation marks. It was intercepted in May 1940 on a land-line from Germany to Occupied Norway in Sweden by a Swedish cryptanalyst Arne Beurling who broke the cipher by hand and had a machine constructed to print out the German plaintext. Fortunately this breakthrough was made before the Germans added the equivalent of a one-time pad in the machine Schluessel-zusatz 40 (SZ40—key addition 40), manufactured by Lorenz, codenamed Tunny by GC&CS, Tunny becoming the generic name for Geheimschreiber traffic and fish names being introduced for the individual links as they developed. Traffic was intercepted on an army link Vienna–Athens in mid-1941 in the Middle East but ceased as Rommel withdrew from El Alamein in November 1942.

There was nothing to intercept when the Fish traffic went by landline but when the Afrika Korps arrived in Tunisia Fish had to cross the sea and the DMG-geraet was used for extra security and the network was extended to Crete and from Pola along the coast of Jugoslavia.

During 1942 another improved machine built by Siemens, the T-52 named Sturgeon, came into use for the Luftwaffe and some Fish traffic was transmitted between the German Navy commands (and names like Shark were used for these links) and by the SS. To decipher these messages known to be a higher grade than Enigma Colossus Mark I was developed and came into use at BP in February 1941 where the Sixta Section was coming to grips with the problem. A new intercept station was built at Knockholt in late 1942 to take Fish which expanded to 600 staff and superseded Denmark Hill and St Albans.

Messages were often very long, 60,000 characters in one case, one character lasting 1/50th of a second, so an undulator tape was used to record the messages reduced at first by manual procedures to a perforated tape and later directly to tape which could be fed in to BP on teleprinter while the manual version and the master-tape were sent by DR to BP for checking.

German technology, far ahead of its rivals, had produced before the war the Dezimeter-Geraet to carry telephone and telegraph communications with maximum security, because being on line of sight, it could not be intercepted by an agent or agency not directly in that line. Hitler was kept informed of the results in the Berlin Olympics in 1936 by the prototype DMG-Geraet later named Olympia. The DMG-3G called Rudolf and the DMG 4 ak Michael were manufactured by Telefunken and used line of sight radio beams at an average distance of 60 km but could operate up to and beyond 100 km in good conditions with aerials mounted on towers or masts 10 metres above the transmitters.

Relay stations of two Rudolfs or Michaels back to back were used to take beams over mountains and round mountains at the seashore. Another advantage in addition to security was that the radio beams were unabsorbed by fog or mist with no reflection from the ionosphere and used less than one watt power to beam messages up to 100 km. Most transmitters had two voice channels and two teleprinter channels but the big Rudolf DMG 3g had nine voice channels and nine teleprinter channels which could be used simultaneously in both directions.

There were two controls—Straussberg (Berlin) for the western front and Anna (Koenigsberg) for the eastern front. When the Germans introduced an additional cryptographic device in February 1942, a Mark II Colossus had to be designed. This incorporated 2,400 valves and came into use on 1 June 1944 just in time to make its vital contribution to the success of Overlord allowing GC&CS to read the army link between Straussberg and Paris, OKH to C-in-C West, the Jellyfish key.

See Appendix 2 for illustrations of "Rudolf" and "Michael".

Geheimschreiber SZ 40 and 42 in case
(By courtesy of Wolfgang Mache)

Geheimschreiber SZ 40 and 42 without case
(By courtesy of Wolfgang Mache)

Geheimschreiber 40–42 interior.
Photographed by W. Mache at Akershus Fortress, Oslo.

SFM T 43 Siemens & Halske 1944. Mechanical model.
(Courtesy Siemens Museum)

T 52 D Military Museum, Dieppe

SFM T 52 e No 53260 Siemens & Halske 1944
Ten-rotors. Five steer the Vernam substitution of the 5-bit Codes and other five control transposition of the 5-bits.
(Courtesy Deutsches Museum, Munich)

SFM T 52 e connected to transmitter.
(Courtesy of Pierre Lorain)

Vehicles for transporting DMG 4 ak (Rudolf). Back to back they beamed messages over 100–200 km and in relays thousands of kms.

See Appendix 2 for illustrations of 'Rudolf' and 'Michael'

At a German Army Intelligence Group conference (Heeresnachrichtenwesen) in mid-April 1943, General Fellgiebel announced that 'before the spring of 1944 an encoding teleprinter will be introduced down to divisional level. It is fairly complicated and only operates in straight lines . . .'

In the autumn of 1943 at a conference with General Thiele, Chief Signals Officer of the OKW, Fellgiebel declared that Enigma was totally secure and as late as June 1944 when the Normandy campaign was already under way, Oberst-leutnant Meyer-Dietring asked Major Laub, von Rundstedt's CSO, if he could believe the enemy had penetrated their ciphers. Laub said it was impossible. The enemy would have to obtain 50,000 five-letter groups to be able to break it, and the cipher was changed every 24 hours.

But it would have been virtually impossible to scrap the Enigma in favour of Geheimschreiber. Unlike Enigma it was bulkier and so less suitable for mobile vehicles. The operator typed his message, which was enciphered by passing the text through ten coding rotors and automatically transmitted at a speed of sixty-two words a minute. The recipient selected the decode switch and decrypted the code automatically which came out on a long paper strip which he cut up and pasted on an ordinary message form.

By great good fortune two Geheimschreibers were captured by the Eighth Army. These were sent to the 'Testery' at BP where Major Tester was in charge of research into the radio teletype machine. A committee had been working on a rotor-type cipher machine which would handle the thirty-two characters of the Baudot code rather than twenty-six letters of the alphabet. On this committee were Welchman, Alan Turing, Alexander, Bayly and the expert Max Newman who was in Major Tester's sub-section. It is to Newman that we owe the Colossus which was designed to break the Baudot code of the Geheimschreiber. Late in 1942 Newman set up his own sub-section the 'Newmanry' and built some complicated electro-mechanical devices known as the Robinsons—they were Robinson, Robinson and Cleaver as well as Heath Robinson (after the cartoonist who drew elaborate machines to perform absurdly simple tasks). They were too unreliable and slow for effective cryptanalytic use and were employed only for research purposes.

It was probably Alan Turing who brought in an old colleague T.H. Flowers, a research engineer with the Post Office who had worked with him at the 'Testery'. Flowers understood that the synchronisation of punched-tape operations need not depend on the mechanical use of sprocket-wheels. He used photo-electric sensing and electronic valves rather than electro-magnetic relays, and did away with the laborious production of fresh tapes. His idea was to store the Fish key-patterns internally and in electronic form. Thus only one tape would be required. The difficulty lay in the fact that internal storage would require a great use of electronic valves. Flowers used 1,500 valves, twice as many as were used in the ACE computer built in England after the war. The director of Dollis Hill research laboratories, Radley, provided the finance for the project refused by BP. Incidentally, at Dollis Hill a deep bunker was constructed for Churchill to use as a war room if he was forced to leave London. Flowers and his group built the Colossus in eleven months and it was installed at BP December 1943. They also had forseen the need for a production line, and were ready when BP requested urgently in March 1944 more Colossi. The photo-electric punched-tape reader operated at a remarkable five thousand characters per second, but by 1944 Colossus was processing five-bit characters on punched tape at twenty five thousand per second. Flowers had also produced a fundamental principle of the post-war digital computer—the use of a clock-tick to synchronise all the operations of his complex machine.

According to Andrew Hodges in his study of Alan Turing *The Enigma Of Intelligence* 'using the new electronic Colossus installed since December 43 Jack Good and Donald Michie had made the marvellous discovery that by making manual changes while it was in operation they could do work that hitherto it had been assumed would have to be done by hand methods in the Testery. The discovery meant that in March 1944 an order had been placed with Dollis Hill for six more Colossi by 1 June. This demand could not possibly be met but with desperate efforts one Mark II Colossus was finished on the night of 31 May, and others followed. The Mark II included technical improvements, was five times faster, and also incorporated 2,400 valves. But the essential point was that it incorporated the means for performing automatically the manual change that Jack Good and Donald Michie had made. The original Colossus, by recognising and counting, was able to produce the best match of a given piece of pattern with the text. The new Colossus by automating the process of varying the piece of pattern was able to work out which

Above: 'Colossus'—the world's first computer
Below: a 'Bombe Room' at Bletchley Park

was the best one to try out. This meant that it performed simple acts of decision which went much further than the 'yes' or 'no' of a bombe. The result of one counting process would determine what the Colossus was to do next. The bombe was merely supplied with a 'menu'; the Colossus was provided with a set of instructions.

This greatly extended the role of the machine in bringing Fish to a state of 'cornucopean abundance'. As with the bombe it was not that the Colossus did everything. It was at the centre of an extremely sophisticated and complex theory, in which far from being 'dull and complex' the mathematics involved was by now at the frontiers of research. There were in fact many ways in which Colossus could be used, exploiting the flexibility offered by its variable instruction table. It took the analyst's work into quite a new realm of enchantment. In one of its main uses, the human and the machine would work together.

The analyst would sit at the typewriter output and call out instructions to a Wren to make changes in the programs. Some of the other uses were eventually reduced to decision trees and were handed over to the machine operators. These 'decision trees' were like the 'trees' of the mechanical chess-playing schemes. It meant that some of the work of the intelligent analyst had been replaced by the electronic hardware of the Colossi: some went into the devising of instructions for them; some went into the 'decision trees' which could be left to uncomprehending 'slaves' and some retained for the human mind. When off duty they had talked about the machines playing chess and taking intelligent decisions automatically. In their work, in this new extraordinary phase, the arbitrary dispensations of the German cryptographic system had brought something like this into being— and even more uncanny for those who did it, a sense of dialogue with the machine. The line between the 'mechanical' and the 'intelligent' was very, very slightly blurred. Whatever its applications to the great surprise that awaited the Germans, they were having a wonderful time in seeing the history of the future.'

The Super-Colossus was completed on 31 May, just in time for D-Day. It was to play an eminent part in the Normandy campaign. The worry at BP had been that the Germans might supersede Enigma with the Geheimschreiber. Now they were ready for the Geheimschreiber.

As this machine was more sophisticated than the Enigma, intended for the messages of Most Secret category, inter-service, echelons above Army level and diplomatic and therefore information at the highest level concerned with the conduct of the war, being of strategic importance, it was not vital if there were delays of a day or two or often longer in decrypting.

It was much heavier than the Enigma machine of twelve kilos, and not easily transportable as it weighed between 100 and 200 kilos according to the model. As originally conceived it was for line transmission, but later models were considered sufficiently secure to be used for transmission by radio. The SZ 40 and 42 built by Lorenz were designed to be coupled to teleprinters (Schluesselzusatz = enciphering addition). In fact a German committee of experts reporting on security of communications on 5 September 1944 advised that SZ 40 and SZ 42 models a and b should be employed only as teleprinters and only model c should be used in radio mode. They were to be employed by the Army and were therefore the most numerous.

The T52

The first studies for this machine date from 1930–32 at the request of the German Navy. According to Gilbert Bloch they are due to the inventor Erhard Rossberg in collaboration with engineers A. Jipp and E. Hettler and all models came from the workshops of Siemens & Halske. The prototypes were all built round the T25 teleprinter then being built by Siemens but later models the T29, T32, T36, etc, were used. The T52 came out in different models:— a (1930), b (1934), c and d (1938), and e (1942–43). More than 1,000 machines were constructed and Model d had the greatest output. At the end of 1944 type f was experimental and two prototypes were destroyed in a bombing raid at Spandau in 1945. Until 1942 the T52 was called Geheimzusatz der Siemens Fernschreibmaschine (secret addition for the Siemens teleprinter) by the Navy and Schluesselzusatz der Siemens Fernschreibmaschine (enciphering addition for the Siemens teleprinter) by the Luftwaffe. On 20 July 1942 the terms were combined as Schluesselfernschreibmaschine T52 (enciphering teleprinter T52) abbreviated to SFM T52. Model T52 e was officially designated 'Geheimschreiber' (secret writer) and the name spread to all other T52s and other similar machines. Models T52 a, b and c were operated only on line and T52 d was the model used for radio.

SFM T43

Described as the most mysterious of the German cipher machines it was said that only ten of these machines were ever built, and only four used regularly by the Air Ministry from 1943 onwards for communications with Luftwaffe HQs in Paris and Warsaw. The system was quite sophisticated with the equivalent of a one-time pad, and the transmitter used decimeter wave-lengths and directional aerials, already described in *Spies of the Airwaves*. (Dipl.Eng. Georg Gluender describes his work with the SFM T43 at the HQ of OKW at Glossen near Berlin in June and July 1944, and the built-in security device in the chapter 'Straight from the Horse's Mouth'). This is probably the type 'Thrasher' which was a link between Luftwaffe HQs which was not broken.

There were 6 links in July 1943, 10 by the autumn and 26 from the first months of 1944. (See Tunnyfish table of links from Prof. Hinsley's History of Intelligence in the Second World War on the front end-papers.)

As often happened when there was a decline in breaking Enigma keys a resurgence of Fish keys bridged the gap. A few days after D-Day there was a big setback when improved security on C-in-C West's link with Berlin (Jellyfish) made it unreadable. But the link between Berlin and C-in-C South West (Bream) had continued to provide valuable intelligence about the battles in Normandy till July 1944, when it, too, failed because of better security measures. In October 1944 BP had solved the problems once again and the output increased with reduced delays in decryption and new links were quickly read until March 1945, when it was higher than in any month of the war.

According to Hinsley (Vol 3 part 2 p.848)

'The most important new links were Army Group B to Berlin (Grilse, broken in June 1944), Army Group H to Berlin (Bleak, first broken in August 1944), Army Group B North and Army Group South (Toadfish, first broken in December 1944), and the link between Army Group B and Army Group H (Triggerfish, first broken in December 1944). There was an important set-back on the Italian front in mid-November when the Enigma key used by the Flivos (Puma), the most important source of operational intelligence for both Army and Luftwaffe order of battle and intentions was read only occasionally. This was a serious setback', according to Hinsley, 'and all the more so because only one army Enigma key in Italy was being read regularly—that which carried traffic between C-in-C South-West and Berlin (Puffin)—and this was little used for communications relating to

```
                    Fernspruch - Fernschreiben - Funkspruch - Blinkspruch
   Nacht-Stelle          Nr.                            Befördert
                                         an    Tag   Zeit   durch   Rolle
    Anna              044904
 -- ABSCHRIFT FUER HERRN OBERST  H A H N --
      Angenommen oder aufgenommen
    von      Tag    Zeit    durch
   HOSF      27/6   1152   /Oktdt/

   Abgang     + -SSD- HMEX/FF 002080 2716 0100
   Tag:
   Zeit:        (DG GHCSF .006209) =
   Dringlichkeit
   Vermerk     -- GEHEIME KOMMANDOSACHE --

   -- L A G E B E U R T E I L U N G  DURCH O B WEST FUER DIE
   ZEIT VOM 19. - 25.6.44:-- .-
   1) -- F E I N D L A G E :-- .-
   A) -- WESTKUESTENFRONT:-- .=
   FEINDTAETIGKEIT IN DER BERICHTSZEIT ZEIGT 2 SCHWERPUNKTE
   AUF:
   1) DIE KAMPFHANDLUNGEN ZUR GEWINNUNG DES HAFENS CHERBOURG,
   DIE KURZ VOR IHREM ENDE STEHEN, .-
   2) DEN ANGRIFFSBEGINN DES ROEM 30. ENGL KORPS BEI TILLY AM
   25.6. ZUR ERWEITERUNG DES BRUECKENKOPFES IN SUEDOSTA
   RICHTUNG. .-
```

The Fish message from Hitler's HQ ANNA giving the sitrep of OB West for the period 19–25 June 44 shows they were still counting on the fictitious US Army Group arriving in greater strength than Montgomery's forces ashore, three weeks after D-Day (Source Rohwer's *Die Rolle des Funkaufklaerung im 2. Weltkrieg*)

```
   O B WEST BEURTEILT LAGE IM GROSZEN WIE FOLGT:
   NOCH HAT DER FEIND DIE IN SUEDOSTENGLAND BEREITGESTELLTE,
   ABSPRUNGBEREITE AMERIK H GR NICHT EINGESETZT. SIE IST
   KRAEFTEMAESZIG STAERKER ALS DIE H GR MONTGOMERY, SIE WIRD
   DURCH ZURUECKGEZOGENE TEILE KAMPFERPROBTER LUFTLANDETRUPPEN
   NOCH EINEN ZUSCHUSZ ZU DEN BEREITGESTELLTEN
   LUFTLANDEKRAEFTEN ERHALTEN, VIELLEICHT AUCH DURCH
   KAMPFERPROBTE STAEMME AUS DER NORMANDIE DURCHSETZT WERDEN.
   IM ZUSAMMENHANG MIT DEN SICH ABZEICHNENDEN FEINDLAGESICHTEN
   IN DER NORMANDIE ZUR GEWINNUNG EINER OPERATIONSBASIS
   RICHTUNG PARIS KOENNTE DIE AMERIK H GR ZEITLICH GESTAFFELT
   -- EINER LANDUNG VON BEIDERSEITS DER SOMME BIS ZUR SEINE
   ..GESETZT WERDEN MIT DEM ZIEL, DEN GROSZHAFEN LE HAVRE
   ....SCHLIESZEN UND ZU FALL ZU BRINGEN, IM UEBRIGEN ABER
```

the Italian front after the invasion of Normandy. The keys of Fourteenth Army (Kingfisher) and Tenth Army (Albatross) which had rarely yielded decrypts of great operational importance had ceased to be read regularly in August for lack of priority. But the situation was saved by the recovery of C-in-C South-West's Fish link (Bream). Bream had been lost following its adoption of improved security measures in July 1944: but GC&CS began to produce solutions in October. From then until the end of the war Bream decrypts regularly supplied a large volume of intelligence which, consisting as it did of signals exchanged between enemy commands at the highest level, lost little of its value from the fact that the decrypts were now obtained with delays of a week or even more.

From the autumn of 1944, moreover, the Fish decrypts were supplemented by the fact that despite the resort by the German Army to improved security measures, GC&CS recovered some Army keys. The Y key in Italy (Sparrow) was broken again from November after a gap since July, and read regularly until February 1945. Albatross was again read regularly from the beginning of November, and in the last two months of the war it was heavily used and carried for the first time decrypts of great operational value. Another key in use in Northern Italy (Shrike) still yielded from time to time important intelligence about the movements of German reinforcements and reserves. The main Naval key in the Mediterranean (Porpoise) which was read currently throughout, increasingly provided additional information about the ground fighting as the German Armies retreated.'

On the eastern front, already in 1943 when no Army Enigma keys and few of the Luftwaffe keys were broken, Fish supplied essential intelligence. The greatest land battle of the war at Kursk ended in failure for Germany and the Russian counter-attack against Army Group South early in August took the Germans by surprise. (It was for the intelligence given by 'the Fifth Man' Cairncross, working at BP, supplied to the Russians on the German order of battle, especially tanks and air power, that he was awarded the Red Banner by Stalin—information already supplied no doubt officially by Edward Crankshaw, 'our man in Moscow'). By May 1943 BP was reading the Fish links with Army Group South (Squid) with Army Group A and the Seventeenth Army (Octopus) with the Air Force Mission in Rumania (Tarpon), the German authorities in Memel (Trout) and the link with Army Group Centre (Perch) which was broken in August.

As the German armies withdrew often in disorder, in 1944, commands were closed down and amalgamated and there were frequent changes of keys and even of W/T networks. By the end of June only the key of Fliegerkorps 1 (Ermine) was being read outside the Balkans and even the profitable keys like Gadfly declined as the Germans withdrew their Luftwaffe from the Balkans. A new key for the Luftwaffe Y service (Mustard II) produced a large volume from June till the end of 1944 and Fliegerfuehrer Croatia (Yak) right into 1945. A new key, introduced in September for Luftflotte 4 in Hungary and all areas to the south (Gorilla) was read till the end of the war.

Avocet, formerly Vulture, became the key for use between OKH and Army Group North, between Army Groups North and Centre and between Army Groups and their subordinate armies. Eventually it was used by most of the remaining active units and was read regularly until the end of the war. Various other Army keys were read until they disappeared by the end of 1944. A new Balkan key (Quail, broken in September, 1944) for Army group E's remaining formations was broken regularly until the end of the war. The decline in Enigma was off-set by the success against Fish links. Most of the links between Berlin and the eastern Army Commands had been broken before the middle of 1944 but new ones were broken for Army Group E (Gurnard) and for Army Group Courland (Whiting) from June, and for Army Group Vistula (Crooner) from February 1945. They all carried an enormous amount of signals throughout the German retreat and though there was some falling off in the number of links and volume of traffic after March, 1945, the decrypts kept the western Allies well informed about the main developments, if not about the day-to-day fighting on every front.

During this period from June 1944 until June 1945 I was engaged in translating German especially Fish emanating from the Russian front and from the Balkans at a time when we did not know whether we were supporting Tito or Mihailovich. I kept the German order of battle map for the eastern front up-to-date with a variety of pins showing German army Divisions, Corps, Army and Army Group HQs and red pins for Russian formations and other colours for Tito and Mihailović.

Another deep-seated worry was whether the German intelligence had been able to break Bertrand who had been a prisoner in Paris for nearly a week being interrogated. Had he been tortured and made a bargain with them? Had he died and not revealed the Ultra secret? How much had the Germans learned? Would everything be lost at the vital time of D-Day? To appreciate the gravity of this situation it is necessary to describe Bertrand's predicament in his own words.

CHAPTER 7

The Ordeal

1. *At the 'Bureau' 101 Avenue Henri-Martin.*
On the first floor the doorway gives on to a fairly large hall, round which are three doors: semi-darkness reigns there. No military personnel, only civilians come and go, staring at me with rivalry as if trying to recognise me, but I know none of them.

Suddenly, a certain ripple of movement: the Chief is arriving. Young looking, unbearded, close shaven, scarlet shirt and black tie, wearing a bibbed apron in black rubber and mottled beige trousers. He eyes me up and down with consideration it seems to me! He will tell me later by my appearance he had realised I bore no resemblance to the mass of arrested 'spies'. That's always a pleasure to hear.

I am searched fairly brutally and all I possess is taken away, then they examine in detail all the contents of my pockets. Attention is immediately directed at my identity documents (identity card in the name of Georges Baudin, work permit, demob certificate, driving licence); all are recognised to be false including the driving licence which they opine to have been printed in London which was true. There was also a photo of Mary.

As for my notebook it had been emptied of its contents up to the first blank page—as was my wont each time I went to meet an agent—but unfortunately this time on one of the following pages had been inscribed at random in abbreviated form two compromising references—the imponderable—which they inevitably found. Besides, there was also in my pocket a half-price railway season—for all classes—which told my interrogator that I travelled a lot: he even claimed to have met me several times between Paris and Vichy, which was not impossible for I had been to Paris twenty-five times, on 'special missions', between Dec 1940 and Dec 1943.

He added that I was carrying on me an abnormal quantity of toilet paper as any individual who travels a lot and who is sure—at that time—of not finding any in trains or hotels! But my overcoat had been forgotten. In one of the pockets I had inadvertently left a list of radio call-signs of the Gestapo that an agent had handed to me the previous evening—which was naturally discovered under my very nose and labelled immediately as a 'secret document', and proof of espionage. Finally my ration card and the monthly sheet of corresponding tickets—they were astonished that I did not have several like all those who live with a false identity—a sum of 20,000 francs and my clothing card: all this was purloined at once by a Frenchman who seemed to be part of the HQ—as well as my purse. I begged them to give me back my purse: general stupefaction, what cheek!

They are all of them, ten at least, standing around me. I then explain that my rosary to which I am much attached is in it. Sneers from some, shock from others. The Chief opens my purse and from a distance throws me my rosary which I just catch in flight, because of the handcuffs encircling both my wrists and I have the impression that on its way the rosary burned the Chief's fingers for he rubs them one against the other as if . . .! It is in these conditions that I am going to face the interrogation.

2. *From the 'Bureau' to the Hotel Continental.*
We proceed into one of the rooms giving on to the hall, the one at the back on the right: the Chief followed by another man—the very one who had recently thrown himself on my effects with uncommon rapacity, and myself, while the 'guardian angels' remained in the hall.

The room, large and well furnished, is an office. At once the Chief said to me: 'You are very lucky in your life, you have been arrested by the Abwehr the German military counter-espionage—and not by the Gestapo which consists of nothing but a "band of brutes" '!

He named himself: it was Masuy, a name still unknown to me: he introduced his deputy Humbert, a lieutenant in the French Reserve! Before putting any questions my attention was drawn to Article 8, para 2 of the KSSVO which stipulates:

'He is a spy who consciously in the German Military Zone—any territory occupied in war-time is part of this—secretly or under cover receives or transmits—or tries to receive or transmit—any information relating to the conduct of the war, principally information of a military nature with the intention of communicating this directly to the enemy. In so far as he exercises any intelligence activity he is "guilty". The question of knowing whether or not he has acted as an accomplice does not enter into it".

And also that: "from the fact that I a Frenchman had been taken red-handed in relations with the British Intelligence Service that is" spying for the profit of a foreign power in time of war (because the ciphered telegrams addressed to Paul, intercepted and deciphered by the Abwehr mentioned that it was about "a Friend of the Chief") "and from the fact that a German secret document had been found on me. I was here and now condemned to death and would be "shot" with the least delay according to the law in force'.

Then, presumably to impress me, three individuals were made to file past in front of me chained to each other, real living dead who did not recognise me for the good reason that I did not recognise them: one of them, it appears, was Ferdinand. It is possible that the other two were Poles as they were introduced to me, without being named, and it was considered strange that I did not recognise them since I was in relations with the Poles, which I denied energetically: how were they to know that unless it was deduced from the word 'Polack' written on the same page as my rendezvous in Paul's red notebook.

Scarcely had the group passed the threshold of the 'Bureau' to withdraw than Humbert hustled me and added: 'A good piece of advice, hurry up and sit down . . . otherwise it's the bathtub for you!' I replied coldly that I refused to be interrogated by or in the presence of a French officer, and Masuy ejected Lt Humbert: he was replaced by the chauffeur Bernard. But the tone heightened immediately. Pressed with questions in a yelling tone and under the incessant threat of an automatic pistol (they were lying on all the articles of furniture!) and unwilling to be executed under a false identity—so that France would know!—I gave my true identity: at the same time I had to give my address as well as the one where I had stayed in Paris where Mary was staying. I was then invited to telephone her 'as discreetly as possible so that she would not give the alarm' and fix a rendezvous at the Café des Sports (Porte Maillot) at 11 a.m. where I would wait with a friend for her: during this conversation the chief had the earpiece at his ear and the parabellum at the ready. As soon as I had revealed my true identity the tone changed quickly to become now even more threatening, now more accommodating, for they had rediscovered in me the 'Technical-Commander of the 2e Bureau' whose name was in the corresponding clandestine organisation and they deduced very quickly that I must be the commander.

Moreover, Paul (whose arrest was admitted for the first time) had said of me: 'I believe he is the commander'. Finally, certain allusions on the part of my interrogator had let it become obvious that my real function was known to him. With doubt uppermost and fearing they would prove the contrary to me only too quickly I decided to confess. (Indeed, when the German troops arrived in Paris the very next day two officers had presented themselves to my concierge and had asked to see me. The concierge, dumbfounded, told them I had not been there for a long time . . . which was exact—without managing however to convince them. He offered to conduct them to my flat to prove it but they refused: 'No use, we have the plan of the seventh storey, staircase C, first door on the right leaving the lift . . .' which they presented to him.) It is true that I had not waited for the Resistance to give myself up to research for intelligence and for ten years already I was known to them. I was then invited to explain how I had been brought to this rendezvous and my connection with it. So I then launched into a story completely concocted and which I thought I would be able to carry off: but it was not to be, for it is always rash to launch into lying stories especially when you are not left time for reflection. I did not have the impression that it was 'sticking'. Then I was asked if I had had any other rendezvous during the day: I replied in the negative certifying that I had come to Paris just for that matter—when I had six others—but nothing betrayed it.

In this atmosphere of hot and cold shower-baths in which yelling followed the devilish smiling of my interrogator I felt mysef weakening physically and morally, which was all the more vexatious for me as I had always counted myself among the strongest, but one has to go through that to make a healthy judgement. It may be that he realised that, for at this precise moment the interrogation was cut short to give way to an exposé of different tortures which might be inflicted on me if I did not talk, that's to say:

— *those peculiar to the Abwehr*, of which the most efficacious, combined with prolonged fasting, are—'general anaesthetics' and the 'bathtub job' which, cold and calculated, consist mostly in

'depressing the individual without killing him and which till now even the most hardened have not resisted for more than three days' unless we have been obliged to 'hand them back' to the Gestapo.
— *those peculiar to the Gestapo*, i.e. 'the works' which 'immediate and savage' rarely last longer than twenty-four hours (for there are too many people to be made to talk and not a minute to lose) and always bring you to co-operation: They do not always allow them to obtain desirable details for 'these executioners are brutes who understand nothing of anything'. And the Chief finished on this note of 'if the cap fits wear it!' If I was acquiescent. But this short interlude permitted me to prophesy the future.

Then I was interrogated on my past activity for my name had appeared in a 'pre-war history' in which I had been mixed up: indeed my best 'supplier' in Berlin, Asche, had been shot after confessing everything. He had met me nineteen times in various parts of Europe bringing me each time what I had ordered on the previous occasion.

It concerned others as well, which allowed me to sidetrack the interrogation for quite a few moments and to reflect. But how difficult it is to reflect in duplex.

Finally we came to the crunch and still in this atmosphere in which the electricity grew by the minute I was called upon to say exactly:
— what was the complete scheme of the organisation in the metropolis, as well as my dependence with regard to Algiers and London, not forgetting the names of the respective chiefs and of all the officers known to me.
— where were the funds held which allowed me to function and what was the actual amount, where did they come from and who held them.
— where did the radio function and who was in control as well as all details relative to its personnel and equipment
— where were the ciphered codes in use and who ciphered them as well as the nature of the intelligence transmitted.

All the questions I would have asked if I had been in his place!

Offers of collaboration were made to me simultaneously: It was about being a 'Double agent' and 'the lives of all my collaborators saved' if I ensured that my Organisation was paralysed, for the Abwehr unlike the Gestapo found no pleasure in shooting Frenchmen for the pleasure of killing but aimed solely at suppressing any intelligence agency working against Germany'.

More tired than ever, and anxious to consider calmly the future, I requested a few moments rest before replying: a cigarette was offered which I refused. Now the situation appeared to me to contain only two issues:
— on the one hand, to decide to remain silent while the imminent torture, possibly even a vulgar anaesthesia, might make me run the risk of talking much more and without being in control of myself.
— on the other hand, at the price of a bone to gnaw, still to be able to play another role, being henceforward almost sure of saving, in sufficient time, all that I could deliver and perhaps even to escape if this role became beyond my means, for I had felt the chief's interest growing that he attached to my person and from which he was hoping to be able to profit, all the more because this chief intended to act 'prudently' so as to cause no upset, therefore through me.

And I opted for the second way out certain of having the approval of my Chiefs as I had always had in the course of the fourteen years spent in the 'Service' but the game promised to be tight.

And so I insisted first of all at length on the poverty of the means at my disposal (in personnel and equipment) which did not surprise the chief, then I would give up to him some names of people who had cover or whom I thought I would be able to warn in time, and none of whom has ever been worried moreover.

As for the kind of intelligence transmitted, I made it clear that it was keeping up to date the Order of Battle.

I was then asked if I was in contact with 'Organisations of Resistance or Terrorism' or even with the 'Maquis': I showed I was offended and denied it energetically, which was exact moreover.

As for the funds the chief envisaged that I should draft a note for the person who had them or even to play the game of the 'false inspectors' to make it seem more normal.

The address given for the radio station was false: the cipher documents did change places constantly . . . like the radio itself, without reports being made to me. As far as London was concerned I certified that the radio link that I maintained was only the consequence of a 'technical link' of the war, insisting heavily on the fact that my present chiefs knew nothing about it for it was purely personal (which was admitted without difficulty, but will be exploited on a large scale later on for the 'double agency!)

My Chief was in Algiers. I was the head of the organisation. No minute of this interrogation was kept, the Chief having the appearance of taking 'personal notes' now and then which the future will moreover come to confirm. 'You are a unique capture' he concluded.

This first interrogation finished in this way while the Chief decided to go to the Café des Sports to pick up Mary and take us both to a 'safe house' because he was very keen essentially to keep us away from the Gestapo which risked being alerted any minute and demanding we be handed over to them. In fact a commissar of the Gestapo was a member of the group which arrested me: in reality the Chief was keen on the affair not getting out of his hands. This is normal with all the Police Forces in the world!

To 'avoid any distress to my wife' in frail health, the handcuffs I was wearing were removed momentarily while the inner lining of my overcoat pockets was widely slit to allow my arms to pass under it, which was buttoned over it as soon as the handcuffs were replaced: a tactful touch leaving Mary to believe I was keeping my hands normally in my pockets because of the cold, which was in fact the impression she had. Masuy got out of the car in front of the Café des Sports while I stayed alone with the driver, a certain Bernard, with whom I shall later make a greater acquaintance.

He came back very quickly with Mary who was practically alone in the Café—not without gallantly offering her a coffee which she did not accept, of course. From there we were taken to a sumptuous villa in the Bois de Boulogne—7, rue Adolphe-Yvon—where we were left alone in a large drawing-room, largely equipped with microphones to judge from the wires trailing on the floor, for a few minutes which I used to tell Mary that:
— I had certified that she knew nothing.
— my real name, alone was concerned.
— the compromised address was my mother's.
Then we waited on someone to take care of Mary and to take her to a 'safe house' and we parted, looking at each other like beings who are not sure of seeing each other again on earth and we embraced, stoically without tears on the first step of the marble staircase . . . which caused one of the witnesses to say 'Er liebt seine Frau' (he loves his wife).

Meanwhile there had appeared for a few seconds only a personage who to all appearances had just recognised my face. And, having recognised the person, I asked to speak with him and I was placed beside him in the car which was going to take me to the Hotel Continental.

I reminded Otto, for I had formally identified him, of the past events lasting an hour at Lille that 'I had saved his life' because of his correct attitude, which made him start and call me by my real name which he had heard pronounced by an officer that day and which he had remembered. He had not recognised me just then for at Lille I was in military uniform but it was indeed me whom he had come to try to recognise.

And so it was that Otto (Otto Brandl, Head of the German Purchasing Office in France, brother-in-law of Goering—by his first wife—Head of the Abwehr in Brussels but camouflaged in the German Embassy staff) held out his hand to me expressing his gratitude and assuring me he was going to do everything to 'save my life' in his turn. He added besides that if I had not got him out of that mess he would not have been able to save the life of the Chief (Masuy) whom he had delivered shortly after Lille from a French prison (Caen) the night before his execution by the French. Could this be the Good Samaritan?

Truly I felt I was on familiar ground and hope was growing. As I thanked the good Lord, the car arrived at the Hotel Continental and was about to go through into the inner courtyard when it bumped into the changing of the guard which it had to let pass. The relief guard in field-grey preceded by an officer on horse-back went under the porch and lined up in the inner courtyard in front of the old guard: Commands, howls rather, goose-step, relief of the sentries, exchange of passwords, the usual procedure in use in all the armies in the world. How many times, on request from London, had I counted the numbers of this entire guard, that is to say, including the naval section which went to the Navy Ministry, because they wanted to have it machine-gunned by aircraft on the Champs-Elysées!

3. *At the Hotel Continental.*

Masuy and Otto lead me to a well heated room, washhand basin with hot and cold water with two beds and red carpet Empire style, WCs en suite and with comfortable but scanty living space.

An NCO comes first while they are still there to offer me his services to procure anything I would wish, for payment of course, 'as for

Lemoine', of whom I was a friend, they told him. But I haven't a sou in my wallet for all I had possessed was filched at 101 and the NCO looks grieved all the more because Lemoine paid him well.

Then the two acolytes remove my fetters and hand me over to an armed sentry on guard in front of my bedroom door who is made responsible for any eventual move on my part.

A little later a guard brings me with many bows and heel clicks the guard-room menu: I don't touch it. Oh, only because my stomach refuses it. I refresh myself with the half litre of good red ordinaire which is part of my ration. We must 'have a lasting life' as the admirable nun said who cared for my father throughout his cruel illness which consisted of keeping going by any means.

A little later Masuy returned to request me to put in writing 'what I had done since my entry in the service in 1929 (he had certainly just consulted the yearbook)—this in two copies, one very detailed 'for himself alone' and the other 'very general' for the Colonel Head of the Abwehr. He announced moreover the visit of this personage for the evening.

In addition he asked me when would be the next meeting in Vichy so as to take me there 'so that all would seem normal': 'Next day the 6th at the arrival time of the Paris train 15h08'.

I filled without delay a 'vague' form corresponding to what anyone could check and Masuy showed himself satisfied. I had to certify that my people had no stocks of weapons and that I was affiliated to no Resistance movement.

'A last question: can you continue to maintain for the Germans your radio link with London and without anyone suspecting?' Reply in the affirmative for already I felt able to sabotage the contact by making myself understood to the Intelligence Service even if it were only by 'tutoying' my correspondent. In the evening Masuy came back to remind me to be very circumspect with the Head of the Abwher, and especially 'say nothing more than you have put in writing!' He had brought me a pack of sandwiches (foie gras, sausage, ham) and a good bottle 'to supplement the menu of the guard-room'.

About 8 p.m. an unknown appears introducing himself as 'Deputy Chief of the Abwehr' who asks me if I accept to meet the Chief of the Abwehr: I showed I was very honoured and the Chief arrived shortly afterwards. The latter, very well dressed in mufti, of the best parachuted English cloth and of a certain distinction, came towards me, clicked his heels and called me 'Major' as he did throughout the conversation: He spoke fluent French. He introduced himself 'Colonel Rudolf, Chief of the Abwehr in France, on direct orders from Admiral Canaris'. He started a discussion with me on Communism, the merits and sacrifices of Germany in face of the 'Russian peril': and asked me to help them 'in this struggle against a common enemy to safeguard Europe'.

He handed me the V card. I acquiesced. Then he added that he could not understand that Frenchmen could still go astray to the point of lining up with the Allies, to which I replied that as a true French officer I had followed the way of my Chiefs which was necessarily that of Honour . . . which appeared to satisfy him. He insisted at length on the 'double game' with London and on the result obtained by decryption of ciphered German wireless messages: I confirmed all the possibilities I had in that direction on condition of course of being able to be on the spot. Finally he asked me if I was ready to 'collaborate sincerely', given that it was understood in advance that nothing would be asked of me against my country: I assured him of that. Visibly satisfied the Chief took from his pocket a silver tastevin which, according to him, 'was becoming once more historic' and requested the deputy to fetch him 'a bottle of very old brandy'. Unfortunately scarcely had the latter risen from his chair than the neck of the bottle was already coming through the door which had just opened. What a good microphone! He asked if I would accept to drink 'as comrades' that is to say 'to the same symbol'. I the first, he the second and the deputy last, which was done in full measure.

Then he left me saying he 'would communicate his decision in the course of the night after the dinner-conference given to this end by General Oberg, the Higher SS and Police Chief in the military command of France', and shook my hand not without adding: 'Major, I hope that this whole story is true: besides if you disappear never forget that we shall always find you, wherever you may be in France, Spain and even in North Africa or England where we have our agents'. This was the first hint of scepticism to appear! Shortly after, the field-grey brought me my evening rations certainly more pleasant than this share of sandwiches streaming with butter: I offered them to him and he did not need to be asked twice. Then I took some food, for hunger was beginning to make itself felt: I despatched the 'good bottle' keeping the coarse red of the guardroom for the night. It was then I found myself terribly alone.

I try to put myself at my ease, slump in an armchair, and pray . . . and pray . . . and try to sleep. At each movement I make the sentry on guard outside my bedroom door jerks simultaneously into action and manifests his presence. Without any doubt I am well guarded, no possibility of escape! I am assailed by memories, by remorse, by entreaties to God . . . what a comfort, what a means of 'holding on' is this rosary, as in the hour that precedes the final departure! I doze off into a complete nightmare; visions of war pursue me—in the Dardanelles, among the 'manure of the dead' in Belgium, in the sand dunes of the North Sea forty metres from the enemy, in real hell, in Bulgaria at the time of the great offensive, the danse macabre among the dead and wounded under the glare of the enemy's dazzling flares, for we have to advance at whatever the cost . . . it is hard to give one's life, even for one's country, and even if that is the finest fate, the one worthy of the greatest envy, I thought once more. Then comes the film of my life which always precedes death (again, I realise) and I waken . . . have I really been dreaming? I get up and pad round my room . . . poor field-grey who by induction cannot stay in one spot, a real mechanical toy. I force myself to envisage the questions which seem must be put to me and the answers to be given, but the film scenario keeps interfering incessantly, it's enough to make you lose your reason! I struggle, as in the war, against this invincibly invasive fear which only leaves me in my colloquy with God, thanks to this rosary which is all my hope. 'How pleasant it must be for God to see us hoping against all hope', as Saint Alfonso de Liguri would say. From inside the Continental, presumably from the guard room, an obsessive music rises, interspersed with morsels of the last Christmas. O Tanenbaum . . . stille Nacht heilige Nacht . . . It's the refrain from the 'Blue Angel'

                    Jonny, wenn Du Geburtstag hast,
                    Bin ich bei Dir zu Gast
                    Die ganze Nacht!

and especially Lill Marlene with 'all its melancholy, its sadness, its smokey' images, all the verses with refrain go on and on! (These are the accents which became the favourite song of the British Eighth Army in the desert and which will be quoted one day in the Daily Herald that 'the British are mad on this tune and they wait impatiently for the end of the day to play it on their gramophones; deeply moved by the beauty of this song the homesick British burst into tears at its first chords'. And the Daily Herald concludes: 'It is perhaps not the secret weapon but something must be done to make them forget this song which seduces the British soldiers in the desert!'

The hours sound on the belfry of a nearby church. The pulsations of silence are making me mad. I pray incessantly stringing the beads on my rosary which, in my pocket, has been the witness of every act of my existence and which is henceforth my only consolation.

Where is Mary at this moment, my companion of 22 years already who suffers the anguishes of all my espionage missions and who is now mixed up in this one, the hundred and first and, perhaps, the last? Shall I ever see her again? My brother who, not seeing me at the rendezvous of 11 o'clock to which he was equally invited, and must be looking for me following up every bit of gossip? My old mother who, under the Riviera's blue sky hasn't a clue to all my activities? My friends and even my rare enemies? During this long journey around my room, I see again as if in a dream the principal phases of my existence and the projection is extra-clear. Ah memories, at the final hour, what an obsession!

For a man judges himself before appearing before the Supreme Judge. I hum quietly with desperate gaiety old tunes of long ago. All the past comes back to me mixed up in a horrible hotch-potch with, as background music, the Hitler hymn, the Horst-Wessel-lied and the Marseillaise, at the place of execution!

But fatigue wins the day, I am going to try to sleep: no washing facilities are there. A towel, supplied by the hotel, that's all. I rinse my teeth with my right index finger as an ad hoc tooth-brush. I refresh my face, but not my ideas. At last I stretch out on my bed, half-dressed to appear when they will signify my sentence in the course of the night, but my greatest regret is at not being able to shave to make my entrance in death as into a drawing-room. The field-grey has stopped his comings and goings, he must have discerned the noise that the springs in my mattress made when a weight of eighty kilos has collapsed heavily on it and he is going off at last to be able to take a rest.

23h50. I waken, the sleep has not been a long one! And then I am off round my room again varying the itinerary this time for there is a passage between the two beds. I do the round, now in one direction and now in the other. No sound in the night apart from the squeaking of springs in a metallic mattress in the neighbouring room, a guest like me perhaps whose last night it is as well.

The same tour of the past invades me again and adds itself to an uncertain future still completely unknown to me. The Chief of the Abwehr does not come often! There is an evening. Will there be a morning or a terrifying tomorrow?

'From the depths of the abyss I call to you Lord! Lord! Hear my prayer!' I again manage to fall asleep. In my sleep I dream. The execution is taking place! There I am at the stake, head uplifted, I have all the courage, I look at death in the face and regret still not having shaved to present myself 'smartly' to it—as at the front each time I went off on the attack. The NCO lowers his sword, the salvo hits me. I die for my country! At the moment when the officer designated to give the traditional coup de grace draws near . . . I leap up jump at his throat and deliver the real coup de grace to him.

I feel I am hallucinating. I wake up: it is 4.30. Fortunately they have left me my watch . . . a sequence of life around me 'it's the time I have left to me!' I perceive the first street sounds, the dust-bins, the milk baskets, the noise of people whose life is normal! I pray again and incessantly. 'Do not abandon me, Lord my God! Do not leave me! Hasten to succour me, Lord, who are my strength and my salvation!' The man from the Abwehr has not come yet. What does that mean? However, the dinner-conference must have finished some time ago; they do not wish to disturb me on my last night . . . for they would have otherwise reassured me, Lord, Your Will be done! 6 o'clock! Someone comes in without knocking, standing inside—coffee! It's a field-grey of the guard bringing me a bowl of black liquid. Salute! Salute again! About turn! A backside that calls for the boot! Wait and hope! About 10 o'clock Masuy and Otto arrive. They come to deliver me and tell me: 'You are free!' I cannot believe my ears and with good reason, for this means: 'Your life has been saved by Otto; as for liberty, it is subordinate to the conditions that will be imposed on you for your collaboration!'

We go downstairs together. Leaving the Continental, Otto asks me to speak with him for a few moments in his car, a magnificent black Mercedes parked outside in the Rue des Pyramides. He said to me: 'In my turn I have saved your life and henceforth we are quits: work for them or not, do what you wish, I do not give a damn!' We shake hands vigorously and we leave each other . . . Never to meet again!

But Masuy picks me up and takes me to his home where Mary is waiting, but not without making a short stop at the 'Bureau' to hand me back my papers, with the exception of my clothing coupons and the sum of 20,000 francs retained for the purchase of black market petrol, following the house custom.

On the way he explains to me that relations between the Abwehr and the Gestapo are limited to those prescribed by regulations 'their means being so different: and so horrified are the military by the brutes'. Nevertheless the Abwehr cannot proceed with arrests without the presence of a representative of the Gestapo or more exactly the SD (the Sicherheitsdienst-Security Service). For the Gestapo exists only in German territory, as its name indicates—<u>Geheim Staatspolizei</u> or Secret State Police). Whereby there is a certain dependence which displeases him in sovereign fashion. So it is that the Abwehr has frequently recourse to Sonderkommando Masuy to 'liquidate' its affairs alone. And it is why he is taking me to his home to sequestrate me and Mary from the Gestapo.

4. *At Masuy's home—146 Boulevard Bineau, Neuilly*
There I found Mary who had been received the day before for lunch, dinner and breakfast—in princely style—and I was introduced to Madame Masuy: then a wash, bath, breakfast. In the course of these operations I was able to learn from Mary that she had destroyed all the sheets of notes still in our home thus avoiding an immeasurable catastrophe with regard to all the names, addresses and rendezvous figuring in them, because she had been able to return to her sister's. Indeed after our separation at the Rue Adolphe-Yvon, Mary was taken into care by a rather old person of unsympathetic aspect called Jan (a doddery old Belgian from Brussels) speaking bad German and who took her on foot to the 'Bureau', the same one where I had been taken on my arrest (101, Avenue Henri-Martin). After a short stay there she had to leave again, this time accompanied by Jan and one of the Wiasewsky sisters, nicknamed Moussia, to go still on foot and in the Metro, for there was no car available) to 25 bis, Rue de Constantine where she was to wait; so on foot to the Trocadero Stn direct Metro to la Motte-Picquet and from there still on foot to the Rue de Constantine, bordering on the Esplanade des Invalides.

As they left the Metro Lamotte-Picquet a gentleman stopped, a little too long, to look at Mary and her escort, for he must have understood. Jan, maddened, asked Mary if she knew him. On her negative reply they walked fast while Jan was mulling over the idea of having him arrested. She waited a long time at No 25 until Masuy came to fetch her, this time in a car, to take her to his home. As soon as they arrived, introduction to Madame Masuy and straight to the table for lunch: there was one guest . . . Humbert. The conversation at first of a general nature came round fairly quickly to centre on me; Mary, imbued with what I had been able to tell her about Otto reacted coldly until Masuy considered it necessary to insist on the gravity of the fault and to declare 'that he could still not be answerable for the future!'

It was thus that he announced to her that I was 'condemned to death for espionage against Germany', that a 'secret document' had been found on me, that I had confessed to my real identity and thus opened up a compromising past, but that 'having saved the life of a German colonel in 1940' there would seemingly be an attenuating circumstance there in my case.

Mary, having decided to observe the strict instructions I had given her, showed herself naturally utterly crushed then burst into tears, which permitted Masuy to realise that she was telling the truth and to shower her with words of consolation aided in that by his wife and Humbert. Moreover in the course of the lunch, they thought they had recognised 'English origins' in her, (by her face, her appearance and her manner of speaking) and they had insisted strongly to make her admit to that. Then Masuy authorised Mary to go to any hotel of her choice and to reside there 'freely' on condition only that she should communicate the address by telephone.

He demanded nevertheless that no word of the truth should be communicated to anyone whatsoever so as not to alert anyone in the Service; he requested therefore that she should tell any tale whatever to expain the different phases of the morning. Then he proposed to accompany her to a Metro station. Madame Masuy left with them, by car, and it seems they talked about Mary, because before arriving at their destination, Masuy declared having thought it over he preferred to keep her at home where she would be in greater safety and where she could pass the time with the children by way of distraction. Consequently it would be sufficient just to pick up her case and mine at the address where we had stayed (at her sister's) and he gave her a rendezvous for 6 p.m. at No 25 *bis* Rue de Constantine. At the Trocadero Metro, he left her with these words 'There is a chance that your husband may be saved, on the other hand the slightest indiscretion on your part can compromise everything!'. And so she went to her sister's where they were anxiously waiting for news, for a family lunch was to bring together that day some relatives and friends. She told them a hastily fabricated story and they did not insist. She packed her suitcases, destroyed all compromising documents and in good time took the road to the Rue de Constantine. At the time fixed she presented herself to Masuy who was waiting and he took her in the car with her cases. He made his apologies for not attending the evening meal as he had to go to a 'big dinner' (probably the Abwehr Chief's dinner-conference) where the fate of her husband would be decided. Otto was to be there as well.

Dinner tête-à-tête with Madame Masuy who showed her an incomparable kindness and understanding—then she was shown her room. The decor at Masuy's is worthy of a description. A real Thousand And One Nights background in a private mansion in Neuilly (belonging to a 'Rumanian Jew deported to Germany', very richly furnished and marvellously heated, illuminated without the least concern for restrictions in force, maintained by an imposing and stylish body of domestics (French personnel): everywhere infinite comfort and ceaselessly a standard of living of rare quality.

In this setting a lady elegantly dressed, of charming friendliness, an accomplished mother and three little girls (Helen, Loulou and Christiane aged respectively three, two and one year old) evolving among flowers which literally proliferated. One shadow only marred the picture! Wherever your glance fell appeared a parabellum or a revolver of a smaller calibre (with two or three extra magazines beside them): they were everywhere, on the furniture and even on the mantelpieces.

On the first floor, in the bathroom the window of which looked over the external entry passage, you could see a real arsenal of all calibres even three big American machine guns. Early next day Masuy came to tell Mary her husband was free 'He had not dared waken her in the night to tell her' and so I arrived about 11 a.m. with Masuy at 146 Boulevard Bineau. After our ablutions and breakfast, departure by car for Vichy, while Mary would wait at the Masuy's in the company of his wife and three little girls where she would be in complete safety.

In fact Masuy had decided at the Continental to take me to Vichy 'so that everything remained normal vis-a-vis my own personnel' at the nearest date to the one fixed for my return (6 January—15h08)—and to supply me with the opportunity of a short stay to encipher a message destined for London, which would contain a new rendezvous to take delivery of equipment and by the same token, allow them to arrest a new IS agent and perhaps identify a new organisation: not daft, the Wasp! And so we set off at 13h in the company of Bernard, the chauffeur and the Captain (Wiegand) Deputy Chief of the Abwehr, the real one this time for the one who had appeared at the Continental seems to have been only an interpreter or a simple witness. Briefly, in front, Bernard and Masuy and behind, myself and Wiegand.

Right from the start Wiegand explained that he was only there 'to regularise this mission of the Abwehr' and it was he in fact who carried the mission's orders and showed them on the way to the Field-gendarmerie 'so that the Chief would not put in an appearance'. On board, a choice armament (4 parabellums and an American machine-gun not to mention the personal weapons carried on each: Masuy claimed always 'to have three revolvers on him' put there by the French servant) arriving at Vichy after midnight after a very difficult journey (hoar-frost, black ice, etc.). And how morally painful in spite of the friendship of these gentlemen! For en route we had dined at Nemours (and dined in the Relais Gastronomique of Saint-Pierre-le-Moutier (Allier) a meal in the course of which I had to affect a certain devotion to the cause and was 'tutoyéd' by Masuy from time to time while confidence seemed to mount by the hour . . . ah! What a frightful role to play! But I was trying to play the game to be able, if the opportunity arose, to escape from their clutches. Leaving this dinner, heavily laced with wine, Masuy declared to me forthwith clapping me heavily on the shoulder: 'Truly we were made to understand each other, the two of us, we shall do great things!' At Vichy, Wiegand was delegated by the Gestapo to procure billeting forms, which was not easy, apparently, for the Gestapo Chief was very discontented that the Abwehr had come to 'hunt on his preserves'. Masuy, Bernard and I were lodged in the Hotel des Lilas, without filling in forms, and Wiegand at the Hotel Astoria. Masuy addressed Wiegand as 'my dear captain' and Wiegand addressed

Masuy as 'my dear Sonderfuehrer' while I was addressed as 'Major' and from time to time 'tutoyéd' by Masuy but never by Wiegand.

5. At Vichy

The next morning at 8 a.m. I went out alone, after making sure that nobody was following me: to be still surer I went beforehand to greet the Chief and Bernard in their beds, which allowed me to confirm, in each bedroom, that the bedside table was covered with automatic pistols, parabellums, magazines, etc.

The previous evening, Masuy had given me a rendezvous for today at 11 a.m. in front of the railway station. I paid a visit to my own people, normally, despatched current business and enciphered the telegram foreseen for London, giving for the rendezvous a date as far off as possible so as to be able to cancel it in time and in an unusual style which my correspondent could detect as transmitted under enemy threats: I handed it for transmission by my radio operator and took a copy both of this cipher and the detail of the operations of the encipherment for Masuy, without any importance besides given the system of encipherment in usage, strictly hermetic because it was changed with each telegram.

I made no reference to anything with my subordinates, being henceforward assured of controlling events and to avoid any panic: with the result that when I set off again for my rendezvous everything was normal. At the appointed hour, in front of the railway station, I presented myself to my new chief who welcomed me with a satisfied air with these words: 'It's a great thing, confidence' to which I replied 'Especially when it is well placed'. And then I handed him a copy of the message transmitted to London . . . But what a burden on my shoulders! Then we took the homeward route to arrive back in Paris about 10 p.m.—after dining once more at Saint-Pierre-du-Moutier and several times pushing the car—a 15-HP Citroen—after a succession of breakdowns: chauffeur at the wheel and the three acolytes as beasts of burden!

On the way, Wiegand was dropped at the Lutétia, HQ of the Abwehr. At Masuy's own home, where we were awaited with some anxiety (because of the serious delay in our time-table) a sumptuous dinner was served: champagne, family conversation at the fireside until very late in the evening. It was during this feast, well laced with wine, and after putting the question to him, that I learned from

Masuy's own lips what the 'bathtub' treatment consisted of. But let's leave the word to him:

'The patient, entirely naked, his feet bound together and wrists bound behind his back, is presented opposite a bath-tub filled with cold water and which will be used all day, in spite of the patient's excrement which is carefully retained in it. From time to time his chest will be splashed with a glass of water with some first unpleasant reactions (especially in winter) following which the question of confidence is put to him: if he does not want to talk, it goes on. He is then projected into the bath, by means of the belt round his feet, his belly against the bottom of the bath; his head is kept under water making sure, however, that he can breathe. And again a further interrogation while they turn him over so that he can reply and draw breath for a few moments out of the water.

If he persists in saying nothing his feet are bent back to his forehead (quite literally bending him in two whatever his age) while his head passes usually under water and so on for hours until he consents to reveal all he knows.' A radical process, it appears.

They also spoke of Bernard: 'chauffeur' is his official function, in reality 'executioner of the Sonderkommando'. I then told Masuy that I recognised him as one of the group which arrested me . . . reply in the affirmative! During the lunch at Nemours Bernard will tell me willingly that he had reached 'his 22nd clandestine execution without leaving any traces' that is to say followed by 'incineration at Père-Lachaise' as Masuy pointed out. At that moment I expressed the hope of not being the 23rd victim, to which the reply was silence and a very thinly sketched smile.

On the way, placed at Wiegand's left, in the back of the sumptuous car, as I was all the way, I had had the opportunity of conversing at my ease and at length with him: he had introduced himself in the German manner as Hauptmann Wiegand, deputy to the Chief of the Abwehr; as soon as he got into the car at the Lutétia, and immediately after this introduction Wiegand had said to me: 'It is clearly understood that what we shall ask of you, my chief and I, will be solely directed against the British and especially the Russians, for we are well aware that from a sense of honour a senior officer such as you cannot accept to work against his country!'

It was thus that I learned that, sold by Rex and others, I had been known to the Abwehr for a long time, as 'Technical commander of the Deuxième Bureau': And as I asked him why he had not arrested me sooner Wiegand replied that it was fruitless for they knew 'I was continuing to work' and by this token it was inevitable that I would fall one day or another into the hands of the Abwehr'.

The conversation becoming friendly, for Wiegand was of a different kidney from Masuy, it was a question of 'numerous pieces of knowledge held in common' which will permit me to give useful information to my counter-espionage: you have to think of everything and see far ahead. Finally I was able to hear from Wiegand who made clear that, for a Frenchman, spying for the profit of Algiers was simply punished by deportation to Germany (civil internment) while spying on behalf of London (thus, a foreign power) was normally punished by the death penalty. But my case was different.

Naturally I had not opened up to Masuy especially because Wiegand was a factor in the course of this memorable dinner. We got back to our rooms at 2 a.m. with rendezvous for 10 a.m. for breakfast . . . and then to talk business so as to decide the future! At dawn on 8 January the barometer was already very high!

6. *Temporary Liberty*

The next morning, Saturday as foreseen a long conversation, 11 a.m. to 2 p.m. consisting especially of examining my possibilities concerning London. It was an obsession with Masuy. It appeared more and more clear that Algiers, much less interesting than London, would see its metropolitan network reduced to nothing. 'Thanks to my good offices'.

A true 'golden bridge' was being built for me already, a 'brilliant' situation in Paris where I would reside as soon as the liquidation of my net-work permitted and also to be nearer my 'Chief'. Indeed having asked me what my salary amounted to, I had told him 6,800 francs . . . the chief replied it was ' a porter's tip'.

At breakfast-time nothing positive worked out except the conversation would resume after rest and reflection on Monday, for it was necessary to act quickly. Lunch, still en famille, one of the best selected menus, wines of the best crus, champagne and with a concluding toast 'to our success'! After breakfast Masuy went up to his room to change (hunting costume) and requested me to accompany him: he undressed completely even presenting himself in Adam's costume, but I was watchful.

In confident vein he showed me the Abwehr map in France, as well as the file on all the organisations 'destroyed' or 'to be destroyed'; on French territory and with a corresponding sketch drawn up in French. I assumed an absent-minded look and refused to look at it 'out of discretion' but I squinted as much as I could nevertheless. And so I realised that this Abwehr network in France comprised 750 representatives, following a well established pattern. It was then that I learned that Masuy was actually the chief of a Sonderkommando or 'Flying team for special missions' on behalf of the Abwehr. He admitted to me that he frequently changed domicile 'according to the threats received' and that the identity card he possessed showed him as 'civil servant of the German Embassy in Paris'. Then a hunting trip was proposed to me, an invitation that I declined. At last Mary and I were left 'free' with the only condition that I should turn up on Monday morning at 11 a.m. at the Metro station Concorde (Rue de Rivoli entrance) where Masuy would meet me with his car. He took us in his car to the Pont-de-Neuilly Metro and on leaving us I gave him a telephone number where he could contact us: it was preferable to be correct and to be not over-hasty.

There was no surveillance to be seen around the address in question, nobody took any notice of us—neither Saturday nor Sunday—no telephone calls were made even on a checking basis: it looked as if confidence reigned!

7. *Conditions for Collaboration*

I was punctual at the agreed rendezvous and got into Masuy's car (a luxurious Talbot convertible saloon, grey this time) and we went to the Bois de Boulogne to an absolutely deserted spot to 'talk quietly'. The Chief was nervous and immediately declared he was ready to accelerate events saying he had decided to cut great swathes in my Organisation and take me back to Vichy the next day to help me 'to act quickly' for as he had to leave urgently for Spain he wanted the radio link with London to be operating before his departure. Moreover he was also anxious, before his departure, that the Chief of the Abwehr should prevail with the OKW (the German GHQ in France) in taking possession of the codes of French Intelligence Service and thus of controlling its communications with Algiers and London, waiting to deliver an offensive camouflage (deception) on a grand level to deceive the adversary. This was a new one without any doubt!

But rested physically and morally I had taken a new grip on myself and was decided to dominate him and especially to leave on my own. Masuy had to realise this for he made the excuse of fatigue 'having stayed up all night to interrogate new clients' and went to have a rest as I had strongly advised him, giving me a rendezvous for 5 p.m. at a new address this time, 25 bis Rue de Constantine, the address of the free people where Mary had had to wait a long time for him.

The evening rendezvous did not last much longer than a half hour, around a monumental fireplace and a big wood fire. I had beforehand swallowed nearly a bowl of pure rum, to dope myself and to dominate the situation. That's what happened! I accepted in general all the conditions for collaboration which were presented to me, but with the caveat that I 'should leave alone', in default of which I declared I would be incapable of fulfilling them. Indeed, I did not wish at any price that the slightest imponderable should occur to make me suspect in the eyes of my comrades or of my subordinates, because I risked being liquidated by the Frenchmen. Finally, setting down a new rendezvous fairly soon (about 48 hours) 'I could be judged by my actions'. I had calculated that 36 hours would be sufficient to get to safety. The chief accepted. The match was won! The match certainly seemed to be won, to take to flight, but I would wonder up to the last moment if I could not sustain a game so full of interest—the taste for the struggle was still working in me! Even so the separation from Algiers, where my Chief was, and the peace-time example, when my Chief was next door and when a decision was so difficult to obtain in any matter were enough to prove to me I would very quickly find it impossible to continue, without mentioning the inevitable vindication of those who would be so quickly turned to judge me badly. And so I had engaged myself to deliver to my 'Chief' on Thursday 13 January at the Café Terminus in Vichy from 12 noon till 12h30 and from 7 p.m. till 7.30 . . . and in case of delay, the next day as well so as to immobilise the team for at least 48 hours:

— all the funds of the Organisation, about one and a half million which would be shared with me,
— the current codes with London and Algiers or photocopies of them,
— all the addresses of officers 'collaborating with the Organisation or forming part of it',
— the exact locations of all transmitting points as well as all radio

call-signs and frequencies corresponding to these links 'so as to facilitate the work of the radio-Abwehr',

— to ensure that a radio operator should be detached from Paris urgently, to be at my disposal, 'quite normally'.

Then my return to Paris was foreseen to operate with extreme urgency the radio link with London to which I had engaged myself to return with the shortest possible delay in order to:

— receive the final instructions relating to the envisaged disembarkation (The Allied invasion of France),

— verify what other German enciphered texts were being read by the British,

— prepare the passage of a German agent who would be established there, and in all possible measure to make contact with agents who were already there,

— eventually the same mission with Algiers,

— later the Bertrand Organisation having been dissolved, to succeed in having all the radio equipment stocked in one place where a police operation, skilfully launched would take delivery of it,

— consequently at last, to make every effort to procure at any price files on interrogations of German agents arrested by the French.

In exchange Masuy would guarantee their lives saved 'for everyone'.

As for me, a 'heated' bungalow was reserved for me at Neuilly with the servants of my choice, a car (as much petrol as desired) and a fixed salary of 200,000 francs plus a percentage on the profits of the Sonderkommando, not to say food supplies on the black market and 'intercepted parachute drops'.

Finally my card as a member of the Abwehr 'making me untouchable even with regard to the Gestapo' would be handed to me at Vichy at the time of delivery. There were it so happens two passport photos in my wallet, which I had just had done on the eve of my arrest with a view to having my card as a French citizen issued.

He took me back to the 'Pompe' and when I was raising my hat to greet him, Masuy said to me: 'Keep your hat on, I beg of you, it is I who owe respect to you!'

With these words we took leave of each other.

8. *The Escape.*

We left Paris 11 January on the 8h25 to Vichy in the most normal way in the world: we were expecting Masuy to come and greet us at our departure were it only to identify us to some 'guardian angel' but nothing happened and nobody bothered about us as far as we could observe anyway! At the German military control at Moulins, nothing abnormal either. The evening before we had a very beautiful rich plant, cactus type, delivered to the Masuys, acquired at a well known florist on the corner of Rue Auber and Rue Caumartin, on the left as you go towards the Opera—for 2,800 francs—and some picture albums for the little girls. All accompanied by a card expressing gratitude and thanks.

With each revolution of the wheels it seemed to us we were drawing nearer to Liberty . . . but the plexus was submitted in each of us to a harsh test—the obsession with the flight! In the next compartment a German general and his Chief of Staff probably, in the rank of colonel, had unfolded maps and plans on both seats and seemed to be discussing tactics: I quiver, and regret that I am not alone . . . what a fine coup! I pass and re-pass in front of this compartment which conceals what operational plan, perhaps vital for the future of the war, but it is not the moment to draw attention to oneself!

On arrival in Vichy we had to book in at the hotel so as not to compromise anyone: very fortunately there was a room available in the hotel opposite the railway station and the regulation form was completed in the name of my false identity card, which Masuy would have been able to verify in consequence. I made enquiries to find my own people and to give, with extreme urgency, all the appropriate warning orders, because there remained about 48 hours to save everyone, at least those who risked being compromised: liaison agents went out to them. Next I enciphered a telegram for London to cancel the rendezvous of the 15th and to update everything: in parallel my deputy reported to Algiers on my behalf.

Finally I hand over control of the Network to my second in command, Lucien, and restore to him the capital fund I had, which Mary, alone, has to withdraw from a safe-deposit in the Societé Générale along with the personal cipher code which I utilised with London and divers compromising and secret papers. In the night we leave Vichy for Brioude where we reach our clandestine flat used before 'the hundred and first mission': still nobody behind us!

The next morning I had the good fortune to meet the Head of French Counter-espionage who often came here (I knew where) and dictated some precautionary measures concerning first of all about radio and the despatch of clandestine mail (intercepted pick-ups): all intelligence which I had just gathered in from Masuy was given to him, including all details relating to the various planned rendezvous. And so if he had wanted, the French Head of Counter-espionage could have set up an operation to have the whole of the Masuy band arrested or killed, at the arranged rendezvous. But I had the strong impression that he did not feel deeply about it, and yet . . . what sport! And so, after a late dinner we were leaving Brioude for the unknown. A commisioner of police, a friend of the counter-espionage whom Providence had put in our way, travelled beside us incognito to Saint Georges d'Aurac . . . ready to intervene. Nothing happened.

On Thursday 13 January while the chief was waiting for me at the Café Terminus at Vichy, everybody had been alerted and saved, while there was no risk of anything falling into the hands of the Germans. Honour being safe I did my best to disappear and find shelter with Mary.

At Nimes first of all in the clandestine command post in which my deputy resided at 14 Rue de la Lampèze, not far from the walls of the Central prison which gave you a foretaste of the future . . . but not for long however for the spot could be known! Escape is not easy: You feel torn between the hope of freedom to come and the anguish of the present. There is over all an atrocious anguish—a panic fear that takes possession of the mind and never leaves it, for you think that everything reeks of the enemy.

And yet, we had to take cover as quickly as possible, because fear invaded me and paralysed me—I saw everywhere those who are coming looking for me—fortunately Mary stood the strain. We found asylum, providentially, with secure friends the P. of Chateau-Gombert who did not hesitate to hide us, far from Vichy and far from Nimes. In such misfortune rare are those who have the courage to accept such a heavy responsibility, for at this time in cases of discovery the death penalty was assured.

Now all was due to terminate at Vichy at the latest on the evening of the 14th, in principle. If he did not see me at the rendezvous Masuy had to wait 24 hours longer, as I would have done myself, and he came back to Paris on the 16th for that day he telephoned my sister-in-law to ask her:

— Is Monsieur Baudin there?	There is no Monsieur Baudin here. You must have made a mistake.
— Yes indeed I am mistaken. Your brother-in-law Monsieur Bertrand?	No, he has gone.
— Where has he gone?	To Vichy.
— When will he be back?	Certainly not before Easter

— I wish to speak to your husband.

My brother-in-law then confirmed all that had just been said and assured him he would tell me of this call as soon as he saw me. A few days later another call from Masuy to find out if they had any news of us and especially if anything had happened to us. Meanwhile other phone-calls, to people who had been threatened, revealed no action had been undertaken, by the Germans, on elements known to them . . . Mystery?

But Masuy must have been rigid when the BBC announced in broadcasts of 27 and 28 January among 'personal messages' this one:

'The Bertrands have arrived safely in London!' Which was evidently false. Did he believe it? Or else, did he promise to wait for me at a cunningly prepared 'mouse-trap' of which he had the secret moreover from the elements whom he detained? No one will ever know.

9. *In the Shadows*

From now until he was lifted with Mary in a Lysander sent by General Menzies in London in June 1945 Bertrand was a hunted man, moving from town to town, from house to house, with the Abwehr or Gestapo sometimes getting very close and still keeping open his radio link with London. This was the man who could tell the Germans the whole story of the huge success of the Poles in reconstituting the military Enigma machines from the plans purchased by him from 'Asche' (Hans-Thilo Schmidt) between 1931 and 1939, and the complete success in decrypting Enigma messages by the Anglo-French experts since the beginning of the war. Not Winterbotham nor anyone else at BP, not Colonel Langer nor any Polish expert knew the intricate story in detail as he did. He was the architect of the Allied secret weapon against Germany. He was decorated by the French, by General de Gaulle himself, by the United States, by Poland and received a DSO from Great Britain.

When Sir Winston Churchill presented General Menzies to King George VI he said: 'It was thanks to the secret weapon of General Menzies put into service on all fronts, that we won the war'. 'C' got the credit but it was Bertrand who began the job in 1931 against all discouragement from Great Britain and France, and carried on the war at the front, 1939–40, and in the midst of the enemy in his own occupied country right till the end, maintaining his intercept stations and keeping up the flow of intelligence back to London and BP.

On the run from January till June 1944 he knew that the Abwehr had caught Lemoine (Rex) who first recruited Asche in 1931, and 'entertained' him at the Hotel Continental from 1 March until 18 November 1943 where he eventually betrayed Asche who was arrested on 21 March 1943 and died on 16 September 1943 having probably taken poison concealed in his hernia belt. Without revealing the betrayal of the Enigma secrets to Bertrand. Lemoine had been careful not to talk about Enigma and the Poles, only about the military intelligence supplied by Asche, obtained from his brother Colonel-General Rudolf Schmidt, to the French.

Lemoine had been interrogated by the same Captain Wiegand whom Bertrand had met at the Hotel Continental and was now in Paris busy in the black market and living the good life. Bertrand knew that Colonel Langer, Major Ciezki and three other members of his Polish intercept section had been arrested on 13 March 43 trying to reach London via Spain, then imprisoned in Perpignan, interned in Front-Stalag 122 in Compiègne (they were to be deported to Czechoslovakia on 9 September).

With Ultra well established as the highest priority intelligence about the war, the only event which could disturb this happy circumstance would be the capture and interrogation of Bertrand. He and Mary have to change their identity and resort to disguise. He has new identity cards established by one of his double agents at Toulon and they have to travel by car as the surveillance of trains is very good. An attempt to find a safe house at Theouile failed where the mayor was scared of the Gestapo and said that he had no faith in the Resistance and its cortege of bandits' so they made a hurried departure from there. At Aubagne it was a baby clinic. Why should Mary not be expecting and he a male nurse? But without ration cards they were about to starve and they needed new identity cards and a marriage certificate in the new identities. His deputy brought them ration cards and new identities but in the name of Gaudefroy which did not fit the letter B embroidered on his shirts and handkerchiefs, for the first time. In the street and at the restaurant where they had to go once a day they were rubbing shoulders with the field-greys (German soldiers) but they were more worried by the 'sbires' (officious policemen in mufti) who were easy to spot. He was becoming restless, impatient to get back into harness because his successor had not yet been appointed and there were some in his network who were not 'hard men', that is they might be got at. He decided to use his radio and his two codes (for Algiers and London) to get their help to escape from France.

They then took the train at Marseilles on 1st February for Nimes where his deputy was waiting to take them to a small place called Ventabren which seemed ideal as their room on the first floor had an external escape into the fields. They had some frights especially when the Abwehr cordoned off the market when he was there and he was able to escape and get on his bicycle. Then the SS-Division Hohenstaufen occupied the town and the region and a regiment was in barracks not far from Ventabren. Shortly afterwards they saw people who had been hanged at the entrance to a cinema and under the railway bridge.

There were two possibilities of escape:
— the less dangerous, but the longest—across the Spanish frontier at the mercy of a Spanish guide more or less in the pay of the Germans. In his mind the fate of his Equipe Z (Polish section captured in that way) was ever-present. In this way he could get to Algiers. His Chief in Algiers recommended this method.
— the more dangerous but shorter way, go to London by special shift, as was proposed by his colleague in the IS Bill . . . one night . . . in a field . . . in the moonlight.

In agreement with Mary and having informed Algiers he chose this method but it was to take a long time. Bertrand was at Nimes and the transmitter at Clermont-Ferrand so he had to go back and forth risking the German military control each time in the train. On 27

April he was advised by London that 'Fafa would be in front of the main Post Office at Nimes every day after the arrival of the train from Paris—12h30—on 30 April, 1 May and 2 May. Fafa was not known to him but he was given some recognition signs. But Fafa did not appear on these dates. What was up?

Not until 8 May did London come through to say that Fafa had been prevented at the last moment. Was it possible that he had been arrested? The new rendezvous was Orleans on the 8, 9, 10, 11 May in front of the cathedral and the password: 'The Nimes train has arrived'. So they set off by train for Orleans on the 9 May at 14h50 arriving Orleans at 0630 and their carriage was invaded by German parachutists. At noon Mary is on one pavement facing the cathedral and Bertrand on the other. Then Fafa appears carrying the newspaper in his right hand. Two men in grey-green raincoats—Gestapo—standing beside Bertrand nudge each other indicating Fafa. Beside Mary a young blonde woman—of the 'blonde de Gestapo' type—is talking to a neighbour about the train from Nimes, which must have arrived! Then a stranger speaks to Bertrand and asks if he has come from Nimes to which Bertrand says 'No'. The situation has a bad smell. They talk together and then discuss what they have seen and heard and walk slowly away but round the first corner they scarper. They lunch and dine at the Restaurant des Cigognes near to their hotel, the Hotel de Bordeaux. Next day at noon Bertrand is on the same spot and there is nobody about when Fafa arrives, calling out before parking his bicycle: 'The Nimes train has arrived'. Fafa had thought he and Mary were Gestapo just as they thought the strangers were Gestapo. The pick-ups are finished until the next moon and everybody has gone. They had lunch with Fafa and his wife at the 'Petit Hotel de la Rue Bannier'. And Fafa gives them rendezvous for lunch at the same place next day when all the team will be present. On the way back to the Hotel de Bordeaux they saw Masuy at the wheel of his car which grazed the pavement they were standing on . . . without recognising them. They run down the next street sharply but wonder if he had been tipped off or was it just coincidence!

And so next day they are introduced to three men of the 'Gestapo' and the 'blonde de la Gestapo' and they have a happy lunch together. But it is the last day of the operations and they will have to come back and repeat it all on the 26th as operations resume on the 28th. At 20h30 they leave Orleans for Vichy. The German military control at

Moulins is tight but the certificate from the German Navy wharf at Toulon is good and the officer clicks his heels. At Vichy reunions and lunch at the Floride and dinner at the Athénée with Lucien and his wife and back to Ventabren in the night.

On 23 May they leave Ventabren for good, their luggage limited to three kilos each, and they carry mail from the network, a full case, via Vichy where they spend the day and reach Orleans at 10h00 on 26 May. They breathe freely as there is no German control on the train but cannot make Orleans because the town and station have been bombed. With a taxi they thread their way through the hordes of refugees carrying their belongings and furniture and reach Orleans and the Hotel de Bordeaux.

When they go to the Rue Bannier in pleasant anticipation at 3 p.m. they discover to their dismay that the Petit Hotel has been razed to the ground. Bertrand thought there might be a message in the debris as he would have left one in the circumstances but Mary is sceptical. However, on a slate is a message in white chalk: 'The friends of Pierrot have to report to the cobbler opposite'. The cobbler fetches Pierrot who brings the team. Pierrot announces they will leave next day for Beaugency where they will stay in hiding until the departure. Emile will go with them and take the next room . . . 'In case . . . you never know'.

It is the eve of Pentecost and they stay at the Hotel Saint-Firmin taking meals in the courtyard along with some German officers. In the evening the atmosphere is enlivened by a grand banquet for German NCOs, Sunday and Monday are spent pleasantly. On Tuesday back to Orleans to the Hotel de Bordeaux to wait for final instructions probably on the morrow. It is D-Day, 31 May and they leave at 6 p.m. for an unknown destination. On the way they learn that the message 'Les lilas blancs sont fleuris' has been passed at 12.30 and will be repeated twice more at 19.30 and 21h30. The first time it means 'We intend to come' the second 'It's on' and the third 'We are coming' and the operation will take place as planned. The van is full—with Philippe, the Chief, André, Pierrot, Bernard (a flying officer) and the 'Polish courier'. Bertrand is carrying the mail from the network and is worried in case they should be arrested. They stop at Charmont, 15 km NE of Pithiviers for an aperitif and rest and Bernard drops the bottle of Armagnac destined for the Lysander pilot. Bad luck? They pick up a Jesuit at La Grange who is also going to London and start for Lilas on foot, Indian file, across the fields, the team in front with a trolley carrying the mail . . . and luggage on a trolley behind a bicycle.

They take turns in pulling the trolley and they pray all along the 4 km of muddy path that they will not meet a German patrol. At 10 p.m. they are told to lie down in a field of lucerne and have to wait till 1 a.m. The team spread out to place themselves as sentries, to keep guard and protect them if necessary. At the time foreseen the sound of an aircraft engine is heard and they light the landing place as agreed. Seen more closely it is a Messerschmidt and they hope he had not seen the lights. At 3.30 the Lysander not having appeared they trudge back to La Grange, and their shoes full of mud go flop-flop across the fields. Bertrand gives his spare pair of woollen socks to Pierrot who cannot walk any further. They fall down exhausted and sleep. About 6 a.m. the van arrives from the farm to take them back with the trolley to the farm. A wash and they sleep till 4 p.m. They are joined by the radio operator Janot but he has no news. The departure will not be that night for the message did not come through at 12.30. It's a bonus, a real night's sleep in peace, perhaps the last night. Next day 2 June the message, the same one, is transmitted at the fixed times by the BBC. They have to stay in their room as agricultural workers, vehicles, and buyers go back and forth incessantly in the courtyard. Lunch and dinner are taken upstairs 'sur le pouce' and Philippe enciphers messages with a key from Ave Maria, while Mary rearranges the 3 kilos of luggage and Bertrand polishes his crocodile leather shoes scale by scale. It's long waiting.

At last at 10.30 p.m. departure again by van this time by a different route, to the same landing ground to avoid the trip through the fields and for safety's sake, as someone might have seen the traces of their journey and the flattened grass near the landing ground where they had lain. There is nevertheless a way to go on foot but much shorter than before. The moonlight is magnificent; morale is excellent—at least so it appears. They cross the wheatfields and finally arrive at the Lilas lucerne fields and take up their combat positions, with the mail in the middle.

In the distance the air base at Chateaudun is being bombed. The sky is all streaked with tracer bullets and they count eight bombers crashing in flames. About 1 a.m. another bombardment lighting up Lilas as if it were broad daylight, and there is a German post only

10 km away. 'Lord have pity on us!' prays Bertrand, because all this is in the direction from where the rescue plane must come. Then half an hour later an engine is heard and a plane approaches. The lights in the shape of an arrow pointing to where the wind is blowing from are shown with torches and the plane replies by putting on its landing lights. It settles like a dragon-fly and turns and stops level with the group, the engine still running and the lights still on. Luggage is quickly unloaded. An unknown passenger gets out and three passengers including Bertrand and Mary get in, thanks all round, full throttle—and they are off. The change-over had taken three minutes but the RAF pilot had told them what to do—'keep watching the heavens, if you see a Messerschmidt on the left press the green button—if he is on the right, the black button' and Bertrand asked what will you do then as you have no guns? The pilot said he would do acrobatics to escape the fighter and Bertrand ruefully confirms they are not strapped in.

The plane was a Lysander III, maximum speed 333 kph, (208 mph) with a normal crew of two. There were four of them plus cargo! The Polish courier, a Jesuit priest and Bertrand stood with their backs to the pilot watching the heavens. Mary had to lie flat in the luggage compartment in the tail, swimming among luggage and sacks of mail. They had to fly at 1,000 metres because of the weight and in full moonlight. Reaching the coast they saw German searchlight beams probing the surface of the sea but not the air—and the Channel sparkling in the moonlight and then the land . . . They flew over eight aerodromes lit up for returning bomber squadrons and landed at the unlit ninth. Bertrand made the Sign of the Cross as he set foot on terra firma and gave the traditional bottle of Armagnac to the pilot. The flight had lasted four hours. Then RAF personnel ran towards them and they were taken to a hut on the edge of the field and given drinks—gin for Mary and whisky for Bertrand. They were quite deaf and stupefied as the Lysander engines had no silencers and they had not yet taken in how kind Providence had been. After reception by Mrs Bart and Group-Capt. Sophianu—a rest till 10 a.m. They had a good breakfast and left the aerodrome near Cambridge for London. What a funny feeling still to be alive!

10. *London.*

Along the roads they saw convoys of military vehicles with the white star of SHAEF going to embarkation ports for Normandy. Met by Bill and Uncle Tom, the two chiefs of the special operations at Caxton Street who showered them with congratulations, Bertrand handed over his account of his arrest and escape. It was given over to a photographer to be copied and returned by 5.30 p.m. when Head of French counter espionage, Colonel Paillole would be going to see Bertrand at Bill's office.

After lunch they were installed in St Ermin's Hotel and later taken to see General Menzies, head of the IS whom Bertrand had known for some years (he had handed over the first Polish Enigma machine to him at Victoria Station in Aug 1939) and who had organised their escape from France. He told them the first Lysander they had expected had been shot down by a mobile anti-aircraft battery, and in the evening BBC broadcast three times the message 'Michel has shaved his moustache' to let their friends in France and everybody know that they had arrived safely in the UK. Paillole advised Bertrand not to communicate his personal report to the British as they must not have knowledge of it.

After an up and downer with Colonel Passy of the French Resistance in London who accused him of having worked only for the British IS and not for France, Bertrand pointed out that all his written reports went to Algiers and he had only a radio link with London and believed that Algiers had sent everything to the Allies in London, including Col. Passy. He learned that apparently Algiers and London did not get on well together.

On 25 June he went out to Boxmoor to meet his old team, the Polish section of PC Bruno (Equipe Z), the ones who had managed to slip through the German net into Spain. He was delighted to get news of the Enigma traffic in which the Poles were again fully engaged. They enjoyed the quiet away from the flying bombs in the London area and decided to move out to Boxmoor, an hour in the train from Euston, and to take up residence in the 'The Old Fishery House' out in the country. They were disquieted by a scrap of a message from the Equipe Philippe, which had seen them off from Lilas. In clear the message read: 'SOS—Philippe captured . . . Pierrette . . . Papa . . . QSL?' It must have been about Philippe of course and Pierrot and perhaps Fafa. As the message was in clear it meant the operator was cut off from his codes. QSL means 'Have you received me?' He could not transmit any more but could he receive? In fact no more was ever heard from Philippe's radio after the SOS. Not only was the Lysander in front of them shot down, so was the following Lysander. They had indeed been lucky.

Bertrand was authorised to collect together his intercept team and resume operations in France. On 28 September he took off from near Cambridge again in a Lysander and flew back to Paris landing at Le Bourget. Three senior RAF officers were waiting to return in the Lysander. Introductions . . . some kind words and it flew off. It disappeared without trace into the sea!

Bertrand collected together the survivors of Equipe D (Spanish) and Equipe Z (Polish) with additional personnel from London and Algiers, and recovered all his Enigma machines and archive material scattered in many areas, hidden from the Germans who never found any of it during the occupation and Source Z (the French Y Service) resumed operations on 1 January 1945 with the armies and at the rear. They worked up till the end of hostilities on 8 May 1945 and the occupation of Germany.

Making regular visits to the former occupied zone of France he found two eminent cryptologists of the German Forschungsamt (Asche's German intercept organisation) and recruited them for his team in Paris, with their families to follow, and found the German intercept centre in Stuttgart which specialised in France. Then to the concentration camps to try to recover old comrades or to find out what had happened to them. They were brought back to hospitals or to the Lutetia Hotel which had become a Welcome Centre. Every day Bertrand paid a visit looking for comrades—for Philippe. One day in June 1945 he and Mary attended a memorial service in Paris of Philippe Keun, captain in the British army who had been executed on 9 Sep 44 at Buchenwald. A British subject he had joined the Foreign Legion to fight in France and was captured in June 1940. When he was escaping his younger brother who had become a fighter pilot was killed and their mother living in New York thinking she had lost both her sons committed suicide. The cause of her death had been concealed from Philippe who, after hiding some time in Paris, regained England and was commissioned in the British Army. He was sent over to France to head the Jade-Amicol group, returning to England sometimes by air and sometimes by submarine. Dr Odic, a member of his network was captured along with other members in Paris by the notorious Masuy and was in Buchenwald when Phillippe arrived.

'Do you remember' he wrote to Bertrand, 'that little group that joined us in a special convoy at Buchenwald about mid-August 1944? About twenty-five British officers and some French, one of whom was the racing car driver Benoit. They were immediately locked up in Hut 17, behind barbed wire. I was doctor of the quarter and as such I was permitted to cross the barbed wire which surrounded Hut 17. Philippe had a fracture of the spine from a parachute drop but said it would need more than that to keep him down. He was betrayed by one of his agents at Orleans and taken while asleep with four comrades on 29 June 1944 in the Sologne. You remember what happened at Buchenwald. A fortnight after they arrived the crime which is engraved in our memories took place.'

In August 1944 forty-three British, French, Belgian and Canadian officers and agents coming from Neue-Bremen were incarcerated in Block 17, the death block. At the beginning of September sixteen of them were hanged in the crematorium. On 5 October eighteen others were shot. Two were executed the next day and one was hanged a few days later. Thanks to a very risky substitution of names, numbers and files, only one of the officers, Colonel Thomas, thanks to Kogun, escaped death. It is written somewhere that the day before their execution the Germans distributed to them, Philippe and his companions, British uniforms which they had to put on—in view of their hanging.

France paid its share in blood and mourning in the cause of liberty and independence. Out of 238,000 deportees only 27,000 were to know the exalting hours of liberation and return. Hundreds of thousands of widows and orphans wept for a dear departed one. Some figures were to be learned later:—

Auschwitz	4,000,000 dead
Buechenwald	56,000
Dachau	70,000
Maidanek	2,000,000
Mauthausen	123,000
Ravensbrueck	92,000
Sobibor	300,000
Stutthof	53,000
Treblinka	over 300,000

There were two columns of German espionage in France—Otto and Masuy. What became of them?

Hermann Brandl, called Otto, was the most important head of the Purchasing Office in Paris created to organise the black market methodically for the profit of the state, buying from French industrialists the products that official requisitions could not deliver in sufficient quantity. All payments were without bills and in banknotes. Otto was the great chief who moved everything out of France, Belgium and Holland, the most formidable organisation of looting that ever existed. Every day he sent to the Reichsbank a bill for about 400 million francs corresponding to the 'occupation costs' and reserved a commission of 5% for his 'office expenses' and 'diverse expenses'. Arrested by the Americans in Germany on 6 August, 1946, he hanged himself the same evening in his cell.

All Masuy's former collaborators had already been arrested. Among them were Cavalry Lieut Humbert, the Wiazewski sisters, Bernard Fallot, Raymond Fresnoy and others totalling 26 traitors. Masuy alone was able to escape to Spain. He had some problems with the Gestapo there who delivered him to the Spanish police who transferred him to the Americans who had him sent to Stuttgart. Detained in Fortress Asperg, then in Camp 74 Ludwigsburg, he was transferred to Dachau and held by the French authorities. That was his statement. From his two interrogations at his trial Bertrand extracted only what concerned him:—

> 'For some time I had been watching the traffic of a Polish radio network and through it I heard of a rendezvous at Notre-Dame. I had the radio operator arrested along with an individual whom I found later to be Major Bertrand of the French Deuxième Bureau. I seized on him German call-signs that he was proposing to have under surveillance by receivers of the PTT. He did not wish to give me the composition of his unit. He asked to be brought together with Otto whom he knew to be in Paris. He explained to me that he had saved Otto's life in 1940 in Lille. I put him in contact with Otto. Otto decided to keep him away from the Gestapo and to avoid his arrest. Because of these circumstances I did not interrogate Bertrand. The Radio Abwehr wanted to take him over. I opposed it, installed him and his wife at my house. I tried to obtain from him details of his organisation but he was not willing to tell me. He simply promised not to continue working. I accompanied him to Vichy to see that he could deliver his codes and equipment to me, in reality to allow him to put his organisation in safety. We returned to Paris and after a few days, thanks to the liberty that I left him he disappeared after sending flowers to my wife'.

The Masuy trial, which took place in July 1947, had 22 hearings.

There were 14 charged, Masuy and 13 accomplices. The jury needed three hours to reply to the 43 charges against Masuy and his accomplices. The death sentence was pronounced on Masuy, Fallot, Fresnoy and Charbonnier. Humbert was given life and the others varying sentences from twenty years hard labour down to six months in prison. All their possessions were confiscated. Those condemned to death were shot on 2 October, 1947.

CHAPTER 8

Straight from the Horse's Mouth

A Wireless Operator and Geheimschreiber Operator in the War 1941-1945.
by Georg Gluender

(German-French translation by Gilbert Bloch, English by H.Skillen)

Foreword

The reader will find in this text more personal souvenirs than historically useful technical details. There is a simple explanation: I cannot remember in detail events of more than 40 years ago. Moreover, everything was, at that time, 'secret', and I have made neither notes nor any sketches, but while I was examining the Siemens Geheimschreiber exhibited in the Deutsches Museum I met a colleague to whom I mentioned that during the war I worked on these machines (including those manufactured by Lorenz).

This colleague asked me for some details because the cryptographic techniques and their importance for their operations were his pet subject his . . . (violon d'Ingres). That was the origin of the present article.

PREFACE
by Wolfgang Mache.

I met Dipl Eng Georg Gluender on 5 May 1989 in the exhibition hall of the 'Deutsches Museum' devoted to enciphering machines which was inaugurated on 7 May, 1988.

I had gone back to this room after being present at the inauguration of an extension devoted to MICRO ELECTRONICS I was examining the block of key-rotors belonging to the entry mechanism of the 'G.Zusatz SZ 42' of the firm S.Lorenz, the model on exhibition being the only surviving one in our country. This machine had been deposited at the Museum on the evening of 29 November 1988 by Herr Zeidler, representing 'Standard Electric Lorenz'. The Director of the Museum, Dr Otto Mayr, assisted by Professor F.L.Bauer Professor of Mathematics and Information at the Technical University of Munich (and responsible to the Museum for the setting up of the historic collection of technical trail-blazers) took custody of it on behalf of the Museum. I knew that the research until then had been in vain, to recover witnesses capable of bringing details concerning the 'complementary apparatus of encipherment' elaborated by the firm Lorenz for its radio teleprinters used by the German Army in the course of the Second World War.

It was at this moment that an older colleague, Herr Gluender, whom I had known in the 50s at the Central Communications Laboratory of the firm Siemens & Halske entered the hall. I greeted him and introduced myself and soon, in front of the showcase of the SZ 42, questions and answers were exchanged. When my colleague revealed that he had used the radio enciphering machine SFM T.43, the very memory of which had till then completely disappeared, it seemed to me imperative that Dipl Eng Gluender should commit to writing his souvenirs of his adventures in the G-Kommando in the course of his military career. The following retrospective was not long in forthcoming. It is a rare commentary on the experience of a signals NCO attached to highest levels of command, and at the same time an example of the capacity for reconstructing the past.

1. A Radio Operator fresh out of the school of instruction goes to 'ANNA'

Conscripted at the age of 19 on 2 April 1941 I passed through the gates of the barracks at Potsdam where the 3rd Company of the Signals Instruction Detachment 3 was going to take over my training. After just two months my training was judged to be sufficient for me to be posted to the GHQ of the Land Army (OKH). In morse I could maintain—receiving—a speed of 100 letters a minute and, in sending, a speed of 60 (although my touch was passably nervous). That would suffice.

'ANNA'—the Fuehrer's HQ near Angerburg (East Prussia) was going to bring my training up to perfection. I was happy to escape the foot-drill squads in the barracks courtyard. Radio operators worked in teams: six hours on duty followed by twelve given over to admin and sleep. Little free time. For wireless reception we used the 'Portable signals apparatus b' (Tornisterfunkgeraet b), a short-wave receiver, very simple: in this way we intercepted the signals of our correspondents in uncluttered frequencies. Only a few days after my arrival I took part in a romp that sowed confusion and chaos among the novices of the Radio Service: by manipulating the aerial circuit of their receiving sets tuned in I succeeded in making them intercept messages en clair . . .

2. ENIGMA

The sending of clear texts was strictly forbidden—as was the prank in which we had participated. To encipher radio messages we used the ENIGMA machine—best known to all the secret services. It is common knowledge today that the British succeeded very early in penetrating our enciphering procedures and in decrypting our messages. The ciphered messages were transmitted in groups of five letters and their plain text reconstituted on the ENIGMA by a team of three: the first spelt out the text of the message; the second tapped the letters on the machine's keyboard and the third read off on the latter the letters which lit up. Of course they proceeded in this reading by using the usual alphabetical code (for example for the word TON they would say THEODOR, OTTO, NORDPOL). For a certain time the reading of the plain text was carried out by a Berliner and we were astonished by the number of messages couched in Berlin jargon (in Berlin the sentence 'A good roast goose is a good gift of God' becomes 'eene jut jebratne jans is'ne jute jabe jottes'. The problem was resolved when we noticed that instead of 'GUSTAV' our Berliner pronounced 'JUSTAV' transcribed naturally as 'J' by the operator taking down the plain text . . .

In the same way before they were sent the messages were enciphered on the ENIGMA. At the head of each message, the starting position of the rotors used for the encipherment of the key of the message was indicated en clair (indicator); this constituted certainly one of the reasons which permitted the decryption. Each night at midnight it was necessary, in accordance with the instructions contained in a top secret sheet of tables, to set up the machine according to the arrangement for the day (the discriminant): choice of rotors, arranging the 'crowns' on these mobile connector plugs. This was an unpleasant chore. The arrangement for the day determined, according to the position of the rotors which advanced by one click at the striking of each letter of the plaintext message, the corresponding letter of the enciphered text: a single error was sufficient to prevent encipherment or decryption.

At 'Anna' every possible type of transmitter on short-wave was used; their power varied from 50 to 800 watts. In addition to German sets, radio sets—mostly French sets resulting from war-booty—were used. We very much admired the French jobs whose handles, controls and ornaments were splendidly chromed. Unfortunately they were difficult to tune accurately to the required frequency which bothered us greatly when we had multiple changes of frequency. The majority of our radio traffic was directed towards the East for we had excellent liaison channels towards the West. Soon liaison channels were also established towards the East and the work load at 'ANNA' diminished somewhat.

3. Experience in the Ukraine (1942)

The above quoted development involved the sending to Russia of a part of the Signals personnel of the OKH so that the indispensable liaisons with the different armies could be guaranteed in the best possible conditions. The result was that I was posted to Gomel for some weeks and in 1942 for a year to Winnitza, an important town in the Ukraine. We lived there in a very pleasant manner, for our group of twenty persons was considered a complete company and we were able to enjoy a mess as varied as it was copious. The local population was also fairly well disposed towards us although, unfortunately, the Jews were executed, some of them near our billet. I made a protest to our section leader but he threatened me with the most severe penalties if I brought the matter up again. This section leader was a sports fanatic who used every minute of our free time to drag us to the stadium. A little dodge delivered us from this chore: a female Signals auxiliary willingly performed this service for us. She accepted to become acquainted with him: she was very nice but also very absorbing: Our leader had to devote a great deal of his time to her.

4. Military Radio Teleprinter 1943
('Saegefisch' = 'Saw-fish')

In the domain of wireless communications as in much else, Stalingrad constitutes a turning-point. The wireless communications—whose capacity was limited by the slowness of the transmission of messages—could no longer compensate for the destruction of the network. The Army therefore adopted the system already tried out by the Luftwaffe: the wireless tele-enciphering system called 'Saegefisch' (Saw-fish). The Saegefisch system used modulated emissions which gave on short-wave a sound in the form of the teeth of a saw. The reception was made with superheterodyne receivers of excellent quality. For many reasons it was essential to secure excellent transmission conditions. The distances were considerable. The modulated senders delivered a lower power than the morse sets and the impulses corresponding to the signals were shorter. As the signals were enciphered it was absolutely essential to receive the 7 'phases' corresponding to each sign, otherwise one obtained instead of a plain text an incomprehensible gibberish. We used to say 'the machine has swallowed the key . . .'

5. A technique for reception on short waves in diverse fashion

At the beginning we worked with linear aerials. Very rapidly so as to avoid too many incidents wasting precious time we used lozenge shaped aerials so as to guarantee an exact directional emission. To save space we used two aerials one behind the other, and the three channels of a special telegraphic installation of current carriers (WTK) were used in parallel, so as to limit the fading effect. As we were all experienced operators we wore ear-pieces constantly which permitted us to control constantly the quality of reception and to make timely wave changes. We had—in addition to fading—to take into account foreign interference. War time does not recognise international allocation of frequencies.

Our communications were always effected in duplex and we were in consequence able to propose to our correspondent a different wavelength when reception was unduly affected. But this change had to be accompanied always by a modification of the enciphering key. Moreover, the new wave-length chosen was rarely free and it was necessary to 'liberate' it. To do so we always had handy an automatic sender reading a perforated tape utilising a chain of 'RY' characters and the terrific resulting din spoiled the transmission of the other sender. In the beginning many of our long-distance transmissions were still being sent by manual key but soon we too were using perforated tapes. These could be prepared in advance and were moreover more difficult to spoil, as the transmission was continuous. If our addressee lost control momentarily of the transmission it was easy to re-wind the tape for the necessary length to permit him to recover the message in its entirety.

6. The Key Additions ('Schluesselzusaetze' SZ of the firm C.Lorenz)

The strictest precautions were enjoined upon us in the use of these sets. The same text must never be sent twice even if the key had been changed between the two transmissions. Similarly it was forbidden to use twice the same enciphering configuration: to shackle us to this last stricture we used tables supplying a complete list—with a code-number for each one of the start-positions of the twelve key rotors. We ourselves and the addressee were the only possessors of these tables, sent by courier. Another source indicated the juxtaposition of the cogs of the key-rotors, a juxtaposition which had to be modified at midnight . . . but the key-rotors of the 'Schluesselzusatz' carried more cogs than the rotors of the Enigma machine . . . Consequently we appreciated still less being members of the night-shift. As we had sometimes six lines of communications to cover we had to adjust on each 'Schluesselzusatz' (there were 8 of them including spare machines in reserve) about 500 'ergots' (Wheel ridge nuts).

These 'G-Zusaetze' were presented in the shape of 50-cm-sided cubes and weighed with their framework more than half a cwt. On the electric circuit they were interposed between the teleprinter and the WTK installation. The 5 phases corresponding to the transmission of a sign were enciphered by five of the 12 key-rotors furnished with cogs. These cogs determined by the intermediary of a two-positional relay if the 'phase' in use should be transmitted as such or inverted. The cogs on the seven other key-rotors commanded the movement of the key-rotors (each one influencing the movement of the others). In practice the G-Zusatz engendered a ciphering key whose effect was the equivalent of a contingent perforated tape. The purpose sought was to deny at all times to the enemy the intercept of any 'recoveries'.

It was therefore necessary to obtain an enciphering key that was as long as possible. That poses no problem today thanks to electronics but at that time it could only be carried out with much difficulty.

7. Introduction of the 'Autoclave' (plain text function KTF')

Meanwhile, it had finally been considered that the Allies would probably have been able to decrypt some Enigma ciphers: that is why one fine day we introduced into the 'G-Zusatz' a 'plaintext function' (Autoclave). To familiarise me with this secret at the source—and with some others—I was sent to Berlin for a fortnight to my great pleasure, for I found myself at home. As I had in the meantime been appointed radio mechanic I was able to procure from the Army ordinance service a very important stock of DIY material which was subsequently very useful for me. I was especially given in this year of 1943 the opportunity of learning so many things that my comrades treated me jokingly as a 'war profiteer'.

But to come back to the 'Autoclave'. It was the perfect refinement by which the enciphering key engendered by the machine became dependent on the plaintext of the message. The value of the fifth phase of each sign of plaintext, acting in some way as a 13th rotor, influenced the movement of the 12 others. But how could the addressee be informed of the value of the fifth phase since he was receiving a ciphertext? The solution is simple: to influence the movement of the rotor-keys, the autokey does not use the sign in course of transmission, but the one preceding it by three positions. In this way the machine of the addressee has already begun decryption, and the position of the rotor-keys can coincide with that of the rotor-keys of the sender.

8. Routine work and the 'recovery of the key' dodge

In the army we were so well accustomed to using teleprinters that we soon had a lot of work on our hands. The machines were rarely at rest—even during the night—and at times of great movements of troops or when there were problems of supply, each member of our teams finished his stint in a state of complete exhaustion. As instrument mechanic I was responsible for maintaining all the machines in good condition. I had to give them regular maintenance and supervise their correct installation. Essentially it was the synchronisation of the machines and the setting of the receiving equipment which claimed constant attention. The operators helped me to diagnose in time the weaknesses and failings. For my part I made an effort to make their task easier by some small technical clever dodges. One of these dodges was the 'recovery of the key dodge'. It was a Morse key, a brief tap on which allowed the return to the preceding position of the rotors and hence to 're-cover' a transmission error committed on a single sign. One could thus correct the bad position of the rotor-keys and avoid the wastage of time that would have been incurred by a return to a new start-position. Save when it was a question of enciphered texts one could dispense with the lost sign. Unfortunately this procedure became mostly inoperable with the introduction of the 'Autoclave' as the information relating to the fifth phase was indispensable for the proper function of the rotor-keys. We never asked our superiors if this 'dodge' was authorised as it would probably have been forbidden. I had also to take care of the transmitters and receivers for which the indispensable documentation was missing. It was therefore by painfully multiplying the attempts that I succeeded in mastering the breakdowns. But little by little in this way I acquired the technique—and the practical knowledge. Thus it was that I was once dragged from sleep during a violent storm, because the operators could only work with their feet detached from the floor. As soon as they rested them on the concrete floor sparks shot from the sets, which I had forgotten to earth in the correct manner! Once when I was paying a visit to the operations room of a signals company adjacent to ours, I was surprised to discover in the modulation cable of our 800-watt transmitter that there was contact between the modulation of the transmitter and the telephone circuit. It was the partisans who provoked such contacts by pouring copper sulphate into the connections of our 4-strand cable. In the radio station that I was visiting the smokers had got into the habit of lighting their cigarettes by causing a high-frequency spark which such a contact provoked: but this contact had another effect: between the aerial of their disconnected transmitter but regulated by the sending frequency and ours it made our own modulation audible. At the exact moment when I was there this contact gave me the opportunity of hearing, not the sound of the 'Saegefisch', but the conversation between the radio operator and his colleague busy writing out the message. In other words the plain text was audible to the intercept service . . . . It was the abomination of wretchedness.

9. The tribulations of a telephone exchange

For the establishment of telephonic communications we had at our disposal an exchange of an old type which obviously allowed us to listen to all conversations. Our superiors did not appreciate this situation because these conversations were in part secret and in part banal or quite simply private . . . That is why towards the end of the war, a high-grade officer gave us orders to replace the old exchange with plugs for an automatic exchange. I had arranged that the new installation could serve simultaneously only 10 'subscribers' while the old one serviced 50 (and we could as before listen to the conversations on the ear-piece!). The officer in question had to suffer particularly long and embarrassing delays to establish his communications . . . two weeks later, the old exchange was put back in operation. During the critical period which followed Stalingrad we were always well informed. In spite of prohibitions, important news was immediately circulated to all our group. It was thus that we were the first to hear the following information: the Crimea was now encircled and the 17th Army stationed there was demanding the installation of an important transmission centre.

10. Towards the encircled Crimea—by JU 52 and with the Saegefisch

On 1st November 1943 in the company of a detachment specialised in long-distance communications, I made on a good old JU 52 the journey that had led us to the capital of the Crimea, Simferopol. The pilot of the aircraft—a Sergeant-major, white-skinned under the harness, had declared to us by way of encouragement that he had previously brought safe and sound our comrades into beleaguered Stalingrad. That seemed rather macabre to us because they had not come out again. The 17th Army had prepared a good billet for us for they realised full well the important role we could play in avoiding a second Stalingrad for them. We had to install two links: the first towards GHQ Army Group A, in the Ukraine, and the second for the communications with GHQ of OKH in East Prussia. Transmitting and receiving stations were installed outside the city because we needed room for our aerials. After only a few days we were ready to cope adequately with the traffic. We had a sufficiency of equipment at our disposal: 2 G-Zusaetze and 3 radio teleprinters, 2 tape perforators, 5 receivers and two senders, and I had with me all the necessary DIY material.

Our stay in Simferopol began well. For 5 months the Russians—except for the partisans who continually attacked our cables and sometimes the personnel at our transmitting and receiving stations—did not bother with us. The city was overflown from time to time by a reconnaissance aircraft but there was no destruction of property and no one was injured. I had been provided with a big revolver, because in case of breakdowns I had to go out, even by night, to transmitting and receiving stations by motorcycle. I wondered if that was enough to afford me protection but fortunately I did not have to experience any difficulty. As I was the only person conversant with all the equipment I had a private telephone installed near my bedside. It was in this way that I was often summoned to the exploitation room which was near our billet. It was there that most incidents happened. During the day I worked in a small workshop which I had installed for my own use because constantly there were teleprinters and enciphering equipment waiting or in need of repair. The enemy was not to be allowed to learn anything about our installations and consequently we had not taken with us the instruction manuals. I could rely on my own memory. This situation, after dismantling and re-assembling equipment, resulted in me often having a few extra screws over! I was very proud finally after a few more fumblings to manage to put everything back in perfect condition.

11. A special relay to change the key

We used of course all the tricks we had learned at 'ANNA'. After the 'dodge to recover the key' came another dodge. As the HQ of Army Group A installed in the Ukraine often experienced difficulties in contacting the GHQ (OKH) it was arranged that its communications by radio-teleprinter (with OKH) should pass through us. To begin with we used on this occasion, in conformity with orders, two different enciphering keys for the same plain text transmitted on the two routes. In fact this twisted the rule according to which the same plain text should never be transmitted with two different keys. But following the introduction of the 'Autoclave' this practice was tolerated. Nevertheless my comrades in the exploitation room saw their burden heavily increased by the duplication of the enciphering operations. To mitigate this inconvenience I built a relay permitting us to re-transmit on our sender towards East Prussia the enciphered text received from Army Group A without any alteration. It was not as simple as you might think, for the WTK installations (4 of these installations now came into operation instead of 2) caused distortions.

Moreover, it often happened that the mechanical parts of the receiver functions of the G-Zusaetze and the teleprinters broke down in the middle of the operation and we used to put our own machines into use, acting as Control, and in this way were able to know very quickly what our superior command (the Army Group) was discussing with OKH. As we always informed our general of the content of transmissions he allowed us to continue this practice although it was formally forbidden.

12. Construction and exploitation of radio station Simferopol

The distortions caused by the WTK installations gave us considerable worries. Our sets contained amplifiers of continuous current the purpose of which was to ensure sufficient power for the receiver relays. These amplifiers which at this date were still equipped with valves had to be re-aligned and balanced every few days, so as to minimise distortions. In the end I suppressed the amplifiers and coupled the reception relay directly to the WTK. The distortions were appreciably diminished and the re-alignment became superfluous. From then on we worked constantly with this simplified montage, although here again it was probably a forbidden practice. To ensure the good transmission of the messages towards East Prussia we installed with particular care an aerial of lozenge shape in that direction. On this occasion as radio mechanic I had some disagreements with the signals officer on the correction necessary to take account of magnetic declination: my practical experience as an old hand assured me victory. At that time we found ourselves in the middle of a desolate former battle-field full of rocks. We looked for some means of marking the future site of our 8 aerial masts. All round there were skeletons of the victims of former combats. It was with heaps of bones that we marked out our sites . . . What else could we do? Soon we had our aerial masts installed and were delivered of the sight of our sacrilege. The masts were gigantic—over 20 metres high— thick at the base but so fine at the top that it was impossible to climb up there with a single pair of crampons. It was necessary to change crampons half-way up . . . not so easy for someone who was untrained. The task completed I had won the reputation of being so capable at installing aerials that during my free time I had to walk on many a roof. I do not know if my employers, thanks to my aerials, listened only to German broadcasts. We ourselves did not do so with our service receivers. But beware: listening to enemy stations was strictly forbidden: anyone caught at it was surely sent to discipline companies which was equivalent in most cases to condemnation to death.

13. Postal agency towards the distant Fatherland— Telegraph Office

The HQ officers and soldiers at Simferopol realised quickly the possibilities that our signals detachment offered to send their news to Germany. We agreed with our colleagues at 'ANNA' to send during quiet periods private telegrams which they transmitted to Germany through the Army Post Office. In exchange we received compensation in kind. During the whole of the winter of 1943–1944 the Crimea remained accessible by sea and was well provisioned in food. A great food depot of the Navy was in a shed adjacent to our billet. It was heavily guarded on the outside but we discovered it could be reached from our place by the roof without being seen. Thanks to ropes and our habit of climbing we were able to extract supplementary provisions. As it was to be feared that, at the beginning of 1944, the Russians would undertake the re-conquest of the Crimea, we used to say to each other that it would be necessary to blow up the dump at any rate. Our consciences were thus tranquilised.

14. Under the pressure of the Red Army

That finally happened in April. We were obliged to evacuate the 'pocket' of Simferopol. An enormous amount of traffic encumbered the only vehicular road in the Crimea, leading to Sebastopol. We approached this gigantic fortified place in the south-eastern part of the peninsula. Our troops had occupied it in 1941/42 after hard combats and it was now to serve as a retreat, as orderly as possible, for the way to the Black sea remained open. We were proud of having helped our general through our installations to persuade the OKW of the need for evacuation: he would sit down 'at the machine for conversations by radio-teleprinter' with the highest officers of GHQ. We were then to leave him alone in the signals room. But it was necessary to let in the mechanic in case of breakdown. It was therefore not concealed from us that the maximum number of soldiers was to be saved and evacuated from this trap. We suffered no air attacks during our falling back to Sebastopol although Russian aircraft flew continuously overhead. Probably they did not want to damage the only tarred road in the Crimea.

Sebastopol was nothing but a gigantic heap of concrete fragments unusable as a defence position but supplying a refuge for the great numbers of wounded who were moving into the city and for whom makeshift hospitals were being installed. In this environment they allocated a 'Bunker' to us in which we succeeded for another month to maintain links with East Prussia. We succeeded in a few days in establishing two linear aerials of sufficient height to allow us also to correspond with Army Group A, but the wireless traffic was often disturbed, as much by failures of supply as by bombs and shells. We had very often to repair our aerials and the cuts in current became more and more frequent.

15. The enciphering rotor-keys thrown into the sea

When the enemy had reduced the surface of our 'pocket' to about 25 square metres we received orders to dismantle our installations and to destroy our cipher equipment. This destruction had to be effected in two stages. We had first of all to throw into the sea—as far out as possible—rotor-keys. The three photos which illustrate the present text are taken from my album: in the first, I am smashing in pieces the entry cage of an SZ 42; in the second we are carrying towards the rocks on the coast the rotor-keys and finally, in the third, we are throwing them into the Black Sea. The second phase consisted in blowing up our two G-Zusaetze but no one had told us how to do it. Finally our detachment leader gave me 2 kilos of explosives and some metres of Bickford fuse.

The cipher machines were placed in an area used for detonating bombs and I received the orders for destruction. I placed the two machines sloping them one towards the other so that the upper portions of the casings were touching and in the triangular cavity thus formed between the two machines I placed the explosive charge, joined the fuse to the charge and I took up my position, holding the other end of the fuse, in another site for detonating bombs. Then I lit the wick. But I had no idea of the speed of combustion of the fuse and the waiting time was very long. As we were at this time under machine-gun fire from Russian aircraft I had to emerge several times to prevent soldiers sheltering in the site where the explosion was to take place. This finally occurred scattering afar the debris from our equipment.

16. From Sebastopol to Constanza

Where to next? I was first sent to the 'Saegefisch' station of the Luftwaffe. Might they still need the rest of our equipment? But they still had sufficient teleprinters and our equipment could not be of use to them: they were using Siemens equipment incompatible with Lorenz. As for the radio equipment, their aerials were destroyed, their accumulators empty. What remained for them to do? To be evacuated like us but they had not yet received authorisation to do so.

Our lieutenant had the imperative order to get us out of Sebastopol. With regard to our knowledge we must not fall (alive) into enemy hands. For this evacuation our lieutenant had indeed received from OKH the necessary papers but the few ships which, despite the bombs and shells, succeeded in reaching the embarkation points were taken by assault by numerous soldiers some of whom were seriously wounded. The majority of the comrades in my section had shortly before been killed by a discharge of weapons from an aircraft which had dived in unexpectedly. With his revolver in his fist our lieutenant cut a way for the four survivors towards an already overloaded ferry for no one respected his papers any longer! Although our ferry received several machine-gunnings and bombing en route we arrived on 12 May 1944 at Constanza in Rumania. From there we went by air via Vienna to East Prussia.

17. 'Saegefisch' 1944 in Berlin—the 'SFM T 43'

With the continuous withdrawal of the front line we were transferred to the neighbourhood of Berlin. The new signals station at a great distance from Army GHQ (OKH) was installed in the little village of Golssen, this time with directional aerials beamed towards the Groups of Armies in all directions. We then used eight linear aerials arranged in the form of a star, which an aerial and frequency coupler allowed us to link with the senders and receivers of the ten or so existing lines.

In the exploitation room, lodged in an unpretentious hut, the machines were tightly packed against each other: the shortage of trained personnel for teleprinters obliged us to deploy all the resources of our technique. I installed for each operator a system allowing him to be linked to each of the senders and receivers. During an inspection of the entire installation the specialists of the Equipment Branch (whom we had never seen in Russia) were offended more by the blue colour of the systems than by our technique. In their opinion such a civilian colour could not be tolerated in such a hard war. Naturally the possibility of commuting between the sets would have served no purpose, if we had continued to work as before with the G-Zusaetze, whose enciphering arrangements were affected in a fixed manner to the different links. But we had meanwhile taken delivery of the first radio-teleprinter-encoders T43 whose handling was of an astonishing simplicity. They were presented as ordinary teleprinters furnished with a device for reading perforated tapes. One placed in the reader a tape whose perforations corresponded to a risky key: the addressee had possession of a copy of this tape. On this tape were displayed at determined intervals the numbers corresponding to the start-positions to be used (the latter had to be transmitted in the beginning of the message). In fact that was not necessary for we always took the start position situated immediately after the one we had just used. It was agreed to be economical with these perforated tapes. To each sign of plain text was mixed a sign of the key inscribed on the tape (by adding without remainder) and the used portion of the latter was automatically destroyed so as not to be capable of re-use. We were told that the random keys inscribed on the tapes were manufactured by machines creating random effect, so that they presented no possibility of recurrence. We were congratulating each other on this solution regretting only that the engineers had not thought of it sooner.

18. The 20th July at the Army GHQ (Zossen)

Came the 20th July 1944. It had for us operators at OKH a quite particular significance. On the one hand the Supreme Chief of Signal, General Fellgiebel was found to be implicated in the conspiracy. On the other hand at this moment all links between East Prussia (where the attempted assassination had taken place) and Berlin (where other conspirators were anxious) took on a great importance. Radio-teleprinters were immediately focused on Zossen where the replacement of GHQ of OKH was in session in a concrete emplacement six storeys underground. And we found ourselves henceforth under the strictest surveillance by the SS. Naturally, down there I also had to take care of the machines and radio apparatus: with no car, I have often done the journey of 30 km on a bicycle.

The front line was approaching Berlin. We realised that a growing number of 'Sonderfuehrer' were arriving to seek refuge in the safe shelter offered by the 'Bunker'. These 'Sonderfuehrer' technicians wearing officers' uniforms thought they were entitled to tell the little NCO that I was what had to be done. They had to justify their presence although they knew nothing at all of signals procedure. At these times of excitement some arguments with these 'Sonderfuehrer' almost brought me before the Council of War. The accusation of 'sabotage' was easily and rapidly proffered. Fortunately my company commander, First Lieutenant Rudolph Zoeckler, has always saved me in those perilous situations. In 1950 at Siemens we became colleagues and good friends. He has unfortunately died too soon. But for many reasons I wanted to recall a memory of him here.

19. A Radio-teleprinter station in the Alpine Redoubt

In the Autumn of 1944 I was sent into the Alpine Redoubt in a place situated between Surheim, Saaldorf and Freilassing. There we constructed from zero installations similar to those in Golssen but much more primitive in some respects. As we could not depend upon the network for our provisioning in electricity we alimented our apparatus on accumulators and with electrogenic groups driven by diesel. We had serious problems when one brand-new group refused to supply us with current. I remembered then that Werner von Siemens used retentive magnetism to animate his generators. With the help of a pocket-lamp battery I made the current pass through the windings. And so the magnetism, thus replaced resulting from that, exercised its action and the situation was saved.

20. Under the machine-guns of Allied aircraft. End of the War

We were more and more often caught under the fire from weapons on board US Air Force fighter-bombers. Sure, our station was in a forest and therefore to some extent camouflaged, but a railway line passed quite close and it was not seldom that bombs fell in our vicinity. Every day we had to repair the aerials. At the beginning of 1945 no one could any longer be unaware of the approach of the end. The teleprinters were on their last legs. We only hoped that the Americans would arrive before the Russians.

We had begun to bury the precious material, essentially some hundreds of RV 12P 2000 valves in the hope of being able to recover them later and turn them into cash. In fact we eventually found our hiding place was empty.

On 4th May, 1945, four days before the capitulation, our company commander Zockler went to meet the Americans who had then reached Salzburg and made us prisoners without any resistance. What would we have been able to fight with against tanks? And why? We did not need to blow up our G-Zusaetze since we were using the tele-encoder T 43. They did not justify such luxury. We were happy with this result.

I still have my army paybook in my possession. It is from the beginning of this document that I have been able to reconstruct the time scale of these events. I showed this army paybook to the Americans; the mention 'Unit with G-Zusaetze' figures in it. Although at the end of the war American specialists researched feverishly for intelligence in this domain no one interrogated me on the subject of the G-Zusaetze and the enciphering processes. Perhaps the function of human communication also carries within itself a wild perforated tape . . .

CHAPTER 9

The Impact of Ultra on the Conduct of the War

Ultra intelligence about German military actions and intentions during the Second World War—was derived from decryptions of Enigma and of the Geheimschreiber (Secret Writer). The Poles were already decrypting Enigma from 1932 and passed their expertise to the French and British in 1939 when they were about to be overrun by the Germans.

In the French campaign of 1939-40 Major Bertrand had been the lynch-pin, first of all buying the Germans' secrets from Berlin and passing them to the British (who at first, and for eight years, refused them) and the French (who would not accept his gift) united the refugee Poles with his Spanish and French teams in the intercept station PC Bruno. He supplied the French GHQ and the Allied GHQ with the battlefield intelligence derived from his decrypts of Enigma on the Polish reconstructions of the German military Enigma machines. The British sent No 1 Special Wireless Group with its HQ section at Army HQ and three B-type sections at Corps HQs with the BEF to France and deployed its D/F (direction-finding) stations eastwards and southwards close to the Maginot line to take bearings on enemy radio transmitters and intercepted Enigma which they sent back to Bletchley Park.

At Chatham and BP the operators were busy taking Enigma, especially Luftwaffe signals which were more powerful, during the Battle of France. They intercepted Enigma during the Norwegian campaign and had just managed to read the same day's traffic when the phoney war ended and the shooting war began in Flanders. The extracts of the military and air traffic decryted by Major Bertrand's PC Bruno in conjunction with BP are extensive, although they are only examples of some of the thousands of messages taken by Bertrand and recorded in his book 'Enigma' (1973), translated and published in my *Spies Of The Airwaves*. The top secret intelligence derived from these, later known as Ultra was transmitted to the GHQ of the French army and to the commander of the BEF but because of the chaos of their retreat it could not be used by the disorganised armies.

After Dunkirk, the defence of Great Britain was greatly facilitated by Ultra, and Air Marshal Dowding was able to make the maximum use of his small and dwindling fighter squadrons to defeat the might of the Luftwaffe, as he knew the order of battle and when and whence the Luftwaffe was coming.

In the war at sea it was different. The German Navy had a more sophisticated Enigma machine with a choice of eight rotors instead of five, and map grids to conceal map-references, and special sighting codes for Allied ships they were hunting to destruction. Being underwater the submarines could not be detected at that time by radar or sonar and they were able to destroy many thousands of tons of merchant shipping weekly until Britain was on the verge of starvation. It was only after the capture of naval Enigma machines and map-grids and other documents from U.33 and U.155 that the balance of the sea-war turned in our favour. As their naval telegrams resisted more strongly to our cryptographers it was the use of Y, the identification of the 'fist' of an operator and then radar, which enabled the Royal Navy to identify and destroy the larger German battleships, even when they could not read their Enigma.

The expertise of our Y service in building up the Bird-book—with the call signs of Luftwaffe units and, later, the Elephant book, containing the Army and especially Panzer unit call-signs, enabled our intercept services quickly to identify the enemy transmitters very soon after they changed their callsigns at midnight. Having identified the enemy unit or headquarters they could concentrate the available services on the formations or links for which they could read the appropriate Enigma key.

In addition to intercepting Enigma for immediate transmission back to Cairo or BP, the field units, Army and RAF, could break the low-grade codes and supply immediate tactical intelligence to their commanders in the field. The A-type sections at Army or Army Group level were equipped with a crypto team to break middle-grade ciphers, and all sections had their own D/F platoons to locate enemy transmitters in the field.

Bertrand warned London that he was repatriating his British liaison officer 'Pinky' Macfarlan on the last RAF plane out of Cazaux to which Bertrand drove him, and moved his unit south in twelve vehicles preceded by an autobus. He went in four bounds via La Ferté-Saint-Aubin, where they worked their Enigma machines until 14 June, then to Vensat on 15 June, Larches on 17 June, and on 19 June to Agen, where they stayed in the Grand Séminaire de Bon-Encontre until the 5e Bureau was dissolved (10–15 July). All these movements over crowded roads filled with refugees and soldiers separated from their units—the chaos which Bertrand said was best translated by the English SNAFU (situation normal etc).

He had now to save his Equipes D and Z. He placed the archives in a safe place, and considered sending Équipe D from Marseilles to Algiers by hydroplane to avoid overflying Spain but finally obtained three aircraft from the Air HQ of the 3e Bureau and left Toulouse with both teams and their equipment for Algiers on 24 July.

Already from 8 July he had been planning a new location in the Unoccupied Zone and made reconnaissance trips to find the Chateau de Fouze near Uzès which he purchased with the special authority of Gen Weygand in the name of Monsieur Barsac. There were difficulties and delays in getting authority for the Polish section Equipe Z to work for the French (Vichy). And it was 1 October before Luc brought the team to PC Cadix to join Bertrand and Equipe D. Bertrand had lost his own French personnel, either demobilised or scattered. The full story of their operations has been told in *Spies Of The Airwaves*.

No. 2 Special Wireless Group went to Egypt in March 1941, located at Heliopolis with No. 7 Intelligence School in control. A mobile section was formed and went forward first to Alexandria, while 101 SW Section went into the desert attached to the Western Desert force which later became the Eighth Army. As this unit was withdrawn to go to Greece, along with No. 4 Australian SW Section which it had trained, 103 SW Section took its place and an Armoured Div SW

Section was formed, operating in armoured cars, to assist 7 Armoured Division especially. By the time the shattered 101 SW Section came back from Crete without vehicles and equipment new sections were joining No 2 SW Group in Egypt, namely, 105 and 106 SW Sections.

The accompanying Wireless Intelligence sections were able to decode and translate both German and Italian, and from time to time a section was relieved from duty in the line to intercept strategic traffic on Enigma links. In this way 103 Section, which had just relieved 101 SWS in August had a 'stonking' by a dive-bomber on 1 Sep 1942, in which three men were killed and five injured and the setvans damaged, and was put on mainly Enigma while static. They were able to intercept German traffic in South Russia (Vulture 1 and Vulture 2) as well as Mallard (German Army Rome admin key) and Robin, and covered the Russian front until the surrender of Stalingrad, until 2 Feb 43 when Gen Paulus was captured with 90,000 of his troops. They then went over to cover the Balkan traffic as well as Italian links.

Vital intelligence was not always acted upon by the General Staff. My first experience was when given command of the newly formed 48 WI section attached to 109 SW Section to begin training at Chertsey in Jan 1942. On 11 Feb a network in France began to build up with scores of aircraft signalling take-off and landing times every half-hour all day and night. These reports went off at regular intervals by DR to GHQ Home Forces in London and the GSO 1, Lt Col Wallace, rang up to ask for more details especially the wavelength. RAF Cheadle and other stations were unable to pick this up and we learned later that the coastal intercept and radar stations had been blacked-out by German jammers. We were receiving no intelligence summaries at Chertsey but at GHQ they had the Admiralty Appreciation of 2 February that the pocket battle-ships Gneisenau and Scharnhorst were preparing to leave Brest with a large escort. The traffic, which was from an umbrella of fighter aircraft flying over this large convoy moving slowly up the Channel from bases in France, Belgium, Denmark and Norway, lasted three days and nights. It was not until 11.25 on 12 February that the convoy was spotted within twenty miles of Boulogne and attacked by ancient Swordfish one of which was able to damage the rudder of one capital ship, further slowing down the convoy which did not reach sanctuary in the Norwegian fiords to join the Bismarck until three days after leaving Brest. No other intercept unit had taken these signals. It was a fluke but if acted upon could have given a wonderful target to the British Navy and finished off the German Navy.

By this time the British generals were confident about Ultra and used the intelligence well. The Americans were now coming into the war and when Generals Fredendall, Bradley and Patton commanded the US II Corps they relied greatly on the intelligence supplied by its US 128 RI Coy and its British 55 Wireless Intell. Section although they were not privy to Ultra which was reserved for Montgomery. The heyday of the Special Wireless Sections was in the desert before, during and after El Alamein. The full story has been told in *Spies Of The Airwaves* (1989) and the history continued across Sicily and Italy up to the end of the war with the augmented No 2 SW Group which supplied sections to the US Army and even to the Brazilian contingent.

An important part of this organisation was the MERS or Middle East Radio Security which was the radio security service for the whole region including Italy and like the RSS in the UK under the control of Brigadier Sir Richard Gambier-Parry. The SCUs (Special Communications Units) derived from MERS, in addition to distributing Ultra to overseas Commands, were involved also in intercept and D/F duty especially SCUs 3, 4 and 10.

It was not until December 1942 that GC&CS broke the Shark key of the four-wheel Marine Enigma. The U-boats had been taking a fearful toll of Allied shipping as the German Navy increased its submarine stock. At the end of 1942 they had 249 commissioned and 91 operational. The average number active in the Atlantic each day rose from 22 in January to 61 in May and 86 in August. The tonnage sunk went up from 327,000 in January 1942 to 721,000 in November 1942 which was the highest monthly total ever reached in the war. In August, September, October and November the Allies lost 50, 29, 29 and 29 ships respectively in convoy and the Germans lost on average 7 U-boats each month while 249 ships sailing independently in these months were lost.

This was especially worrying as the great armadas of ships were preparing to sail from the USA and Britain to carry their armies to Morocco, Algeria and Tunisia for the D-Day landings of Operation Torch on 8 November. Before the break in Shark on 13 December the

Admiralty had used evasive routing of convoys to avoid the U-boat packs and this was successful until the German intercept service broke the 'Convoy Cypher'. The contents of the decrypts of Shark were comprehensive—the times of departure and return of U-boats, the dispositions and movements of their patrol groups and their operational orders. Returning U-boats signalled their TOA, and every outgoing U-boat reported when it cleared the Bay of Biscay, or if leaving from Norway or the Baltic the time of crossing latitude 60 degrees North, and reported when it was beginning its return journey. No U-boat could deviate from its orders or begin its return journey without requesting and receiving permission. It had to append its fuel state and give its position.

Professor Sir Harry Hinsley gives a typical example in Vol. 2 of his *History of British Intelligence in the Second World War*:

Von Schulze:
QU 8852 1 DAMPFER, 1 TANKER WAHRSCHEINLICH. AM 15.10 TANKER FACKEL. STEHE 8967 69 CBM 2 PLUS 1 AALE SW 3 BIS 4 996 MB PLUS 21.
AN BEF UBTE.

FROM SCHULZE (U 432).
TO ADMIRAL COMMANDING U-BOATS:
IN SQUARE 8852 HAVE SUNK ONE STEAMSHIP (FOR CERTAIN) AND ONE TANKER PROBABLY. SET ONE TANKER ON FIRE ON OCTOBER 15TH.
MY PRESENT POSITION IS SQUARE 8967. HAVE 69 CUBIC METRES OF FUEL OIL LEFT. HAVE TWO (AIR) AND ONE (ELECTRIC) TORPEDOES LEFT. WIND SOUTH-WEST, FORCE 3 TO 4. PRESSURE 996 MILLIBARS.
TEMPERATURE 21 DEGREES (ABOVE FREEZING POINT).

The OIC (Operations Intelligence Centre) at the Admiralty and in Washington had their Tracking rooms and were joined later by one in Ottawa when Canada became fully briefed. A special series of telegrams called the 'Sunset' Series was despatched daily to Washington via 'C'. The enemy increased the average daily number of operational U-boats to 116 in February 1943 and sank 34 ships against 19 in December and 15 in January. There was a hiatus in March with the Shark breaks. They were interrupted from 10–19 March and in the previous ten days there was a longer than average delay in breaking on seven of these ten days. When the Germans broke the 'Convoy Cypher', losses shot up to 72 in March after averaging only 16 in December 1942 and January 1943 when the armadas of ships were transporting armies and their supplies to North Africa, which entailed the suspension of the Arctic convoys. The capture of the 'Convoy Cypher' meant that the German Navy HQ directed their U-boats towards their targets until June 1943.

Decrypts from the German Navy and Air Force enabled the British to interfere seriously with the supplies for Rommel in North Africa. On 17 April forty transports going to supply the Axis were brought down. Towards the end of the campaign in Tunisia, when the great Germano-Italian armies were being penned in round Tunis, desperate attempts were made to carry petrol by sea and air. Of a convoy of five ships due in Tunisia on 6 April a tanker carrying 2,000 tons of fuel was sunk before the convoy assembled, a second was torpedoed after the convoy started, two others were blown up off Bizerta and the single arrival was delayed until 17 April, ten days after the British assault on Akarit. Only four ships of above 3,000 tons succeeded in reaching Tunisia and the enemy had to rely on air transport. The British mounted Operation Flax to attack the heavily escorted air convoys and attack the transport aircraft on the ground in Sicily and Tunisia. The decrypts from Enigma gave details of cargoes, variation of routes, flight cancellations, and the RAF Y Sections intercepted the tactical signals of the air transport systems of the German and Italian air forces which gave the Allies the points of arrival and departure, the time taken to unload and turn round, and the normal routes and the strength of the escorts. When Operation Flax began on 5 April the Luftwaffe had 263 transport aircraft and by 27 April they had lost 137 of these. Altogether, with the Italian Air Fleet, they lost an estimated 432 aircraft which, along with the heavy losses at Stalingrad, crippled the German air transport system for the rest of the war.

The naval key Porpoise, used by the German Naval Command in Tunisia, came into use at this time to help evaluate the supply position, very opportunely as there were long delays in decrypting Army Enigma.

The Germans were still heavily reinforcing their armies, and Italian destroyers were running the gauntlet laden with troops. By 29 April when Army Enigma came back on stream some units reported to HQ

Army Group Africa that they had petrol for only 37 miles and in one case for 6 miles and GAF Enigma announced they had not 35 gallons a day needed to operate their radar. Warned by Ultra, the British destroyers sank the Campo Basso near Cap Bon and the US Air Force sank the San Antonio near Sicily on its way to Tunis on 4 May. They were the last merchant ships to try to reach Tunisia and the Germans were planning to take petrol and supplies by submarine when the end came on 8 May. The German public was prepared by radio broadcasts for a Dunkirk-style evacuation in small boats but a fleet of ten destroyers patrolled the seas, able to avoid minefields by decrypts from Italian Navy ciphers. Nearly 250,000 were taken prisoner, and only 632 officers and men were evacuated by air and sea, among them some divisional commanders of Rommel's army who went back to reform their divisions, for example 10. Pz Div, for the campaign in Russia and later in Normandy.

The detailed intelligence supplied by Army Y sections to commanders in the field in the Western Desert, Tunisia Sicily, Italy and Normandy which supplemented the Ultra intelligence pouring forth in great spate, was revealed in *Spies Of The Airwaves* and in it was described the failures of the Allies to block the great German Armies in the Ardennes in 1940 and 1944, the former from sure intelligence straight from the lips of the Panzer commander above Rommel, and the second forewarned by Ultra decodes in plenty. These were not screened out from the mass of information pouring out daily from BP for Montgomery's British and Bradley's American staff officers.

To sum up, the theatres where Ultra is known to have played a decisive role were:
— The Battle of Britain 1940–1941, when the Luftwaffe was seen off by the RAF, and BP had decrypted the Enigma controlling the U-boats.
— The Battle of Libya in which three Panzer Divisions were destroyed by Montgomery and the Germano-Italian Army there totally destroyed.
— The Battle of Normandy in which many engagements were won by decrypts beginning with the Americans being warned in time to resist the savage counter-offensive by the Germans at Mortain.
— The Battle of Alsace when the American Command was given from 1 January 1945 the German plans of attack in the north of the Vosges and on newly liberated Strasbourg.

— Battles in the Pacific area especially on 4 June 1942 at Midway and many others which have not yet been recorded.

The battle for which we have the least information about Ultra is the Battle of Britain. The decrypts of the signals sent to fighter commands warning them of the departure from bases on the continent and the targets of the attacking enemy formations have not been released and perhaps never will be, having been destroyed. One thing is certain, that is at the beginning of July 1940 Enigma supplied essential data. Until then the British had largely over-estimated the strength of the Luftwaffe attributing to it 5,000 first-line aircraft (of which 2,500 were bombers) with 7,000 in reserve, whereas then the actual figures were 2,500 first-line and 1,000 reserve. On 6 July the British were able to make a more accurate estimate from Enigma decrypts. They then knew that they had to combat 1,250 bombers, 800 single-engined fighters (Me 109), and 300 twin-engined fighters Me 110), their order of battle and more important their rate of replacement. Dowding knew that the battle for these islands was not already lost. He knew that the Me 109s had only a quarter-hour's flying time over London whereas the Hurricanes and Spitfires had three-quarters of an hour, and with the help of radar could make the best use of that time.

To all this must be added the inestimable quantity and quality of the information on the rise of the Nazi party from 1932, the organisation of the German Army and Air Force, in particular of the development of the Panzer divisions and their close co-operation with dive-bombing aircraft taking over the role of forward artillery of devastating accuracy, and the training of forward Engineer battalions in bridging rivers. There was also the development of the administration of all the services—High Command, Police SS, Abwehr (counter-intelligence), derived from Asche's brother General Rudolf Schmidt, who also provided Asche and the Allies with Hitler's successive campaign plans before the war, in the re-occupation of the Rhineland, the invasions of Austria, Sudetenland, Czechoslovakia, Poland and the Netherlands including the dates and plans and even of the breakthrough in the Ardennes, which took the Allies by surprise, because they did not believe it possible and sealed the fate of France in June 1940—all this from one secret agent, as has been revealed in detail in *Spies Of The Airwaves*.

Professor Juergen Rohwer, summing up after the international conference in Nov 1978 in Germany, took the view that 'Ultra had the effect of not alone deciding the issue but at least of shortening the war on the Atlantic-Westeuropean battle ground'.

Professor Sir Harry Hinsley in the Liddel-Hart Lecture at King's College London on 18 February 1992 said: 'The Allies would not have lost the war even if Ultra had not given them supremacy. But the end of the war was three-and-a-half years away. It shortened the war, but by how much if Ultra had not existed? The loss of Egypt would have set back the conquest of Africa to at least the summer of 1944. The Allies might have cancelled the Northwest landings and ignored the Mediterranean. What would have been the prospects for the cross-Channel operation if the U-boats had not been prevented by Ultra? The Allies would have prevailed in the end but not in time for the Overlord landings—it would have been impossible until 1946. Even if it had been delayed only until 1945 other events would have come into play. The Overlord Operation would have failed without Ultra's Order of Battle. In 1945 it would have failed more certainly because Germany's V-weapon campaign would have been in full swing. From early 1943 she had been preparing the introduction of new super U-boats, rocket and jetplanes for 1945. Unless the Allies had succeeded by doubling Ultra, Germany would not have had to disperse her forces in the Mediterranean. Who can say what strategy the Allies could have pursued? In Russia? What about the A-Bomb? No conscientious historian could answer these questions.

But there is another imponderable. Britain would have been starved into submission in a few months unless the capture of naval Enigma machines and their extra rotors, sighting codes and map grids had enabled Bletchley in 1941 to defeat the U-Boat threat. Without Ultra at that moment Britain was defeated. There were no signs of military victories—only disasters. Russia was not yet in the war—until June 1941—and we stood alone against Germany and its conquered territories, Italy and Japan. Worse was to come with the loss of Singapore, its base and 100,000 prisoners including 17,000 Australians, which decided Australia to withdraw its troops from the Middle East to defend the homeland. There was no sign of the United States becoming involved.

Churchill might well have been forced out of office as we reached the nadir of our despair and there were others very ready to make an accommodation with Hitler and Mussolini.

APPENDIX 1

Commentary in French by Gilbert Bloch transcribed by Jean and Thérèse Scoffoni

Vous avez devant vous un exemplaire de la machine Enigma du type utilisé par les forces armées allemandes du ler juin, 1930—donc bien avant l'arrivée d'Hitler au pouvoir—jusqu'à la fin de la guerre en mai, 1945.

Je vais vous expliquer à quoi servait cette machine, comment elle est née et a été developée et comment elle fonctionne. L'Enigma est une machine à chiffrer et à déchiffrer. Concrètement cela signifie que l'on rentre dans cette machine le texte clair d'un message; on le rentre en tapant sur ce clavier, que vous voyez ici devant vous. Le texte chiffré de ce message va apparaître lettre à lettre sur des voyants qui se trouvent ici, je vous le montre. Vous voyez que ces voyants sont exactement de la même disposition que le clavier d'entrée. Chacun de ces voyants représente une lettre et peut être éclairé par une petite lampe qui se trouve en dessous et que vous verrez tout à l'heure. Le texte clair est rentré ici le texte chiffré apparaît lettre à lettre sur ces voyants; mais inversement, si dans la même disposition des organes de cette machine, c'est à dire dans la même configuration de cette machine—vous verrez tout à l'heure ce que cela signifie—on frappe sur le clavier d'entrée le texte chiffré qui vient d'être obtenu sur les voyants apparaîtra lettre à lettre le texte clair. La machine, donc, peut chiffrer et déchiffrer, et son utilisation pour vous est désormais simple. L'expéditeur du message chiffre le message sur son Enigma—le destinataire lui, le déchiffre. Il a son Enigma. Il saît quelle configuration de machine adopter, il le déchiffre en remettant le texte chiffré et en récupérant le texte clair.

Vous venez de faire connaissance avec la caractéristique essentielle de cette machine, qui est la réversibilité, c'est à dire sa capacité de fonctionner en chiffrant et en déchiffrant: Vous constatez aussi que cette machine ne joue aucun rôle dans la transmission. Elle chiffre et déchiffre mais le texte chiffré doit ensuite être passé à un opérateur radio qui le transmettra normalement en morse tandis qu'à l'autre bout chez le destinataire un opérateur radio qui recevra le message, le transcrira et le passera ensuite à l'opérateur Enigma pour que celui-ci le déchiffre. Cette machine n'a pas que des qualités. . .

D'abord elle est gourmande en personnes: Elle exige au moins deux personnes: l'un qui tape le message et un autre qui lit les voyants qui apparaissent un à un—je répète que c'est une frappe lettre à lettre—qui lit les voyants et retransmêt ce qu'il lit sur les voyants sur une formule spéciale. Ce n'est pas rapide, cela signifie que pour une lettre il faut à peu près deux secondes: un message donc de 250 lettres prendra à peu près 10 minutes pour chiffrer, et pour déchiffrer. Car comme vous le voyez l'Enigma est donc lente du faît même de son mode de fonctionnement, et cette lenteur est encore accentuée par un autre facteur; vous voyez que le clavier ne comporte que des lettres; si donc j'ai des indications numériques à transmettre—et Dieu sait si dans un message militaire on a des numéros à transmettre ce qui allongera le message, allongera donc son cryptement et son décryptement. C'est un inconvénient grave de cette machine.

Dernier inconvénient—outre qu'elle est gourmande en personnel, qu'elle est lente, et qu'elle ne transmet pas de chiffres—la machine ne laisse aucune trace tangible des textes qu'elle enrégistre. Dans toutes les machines actuelles il sort une bande de papier qui est imprimée et marque ce que la machine a enregistré. Là, il n'y a rien. Il n'y a que ce que prend le deuxième opérateur. Les Allemands sont parfaitement conscients de ces inconvénients et travaillent à mettre au point un type dérivé de la machine. Ceci est une Enigma militaire Type I—ils travaillent à mettre au point un Type II, qui serait la même machine couplée à une imprimante. Vous auriez donc la possibilité d'une frappe réelle beaucoup plus rapide par un seul agent et avec une trace. Seul inconvénient—la manque de chiffres subsisterait.

Euh. . . ce Type II sera mis au point en 1932, essayé en campagne, c'est un fiasco total: la machine est complètement en panne—à peu près tout le temps-euh-dans ces conditions on en reste au Type I dont une centaine de milliers d'exemplaires seront construits entre 1930 et 1945.

Certes, les machines inventées et utilisées ensuite par les armées concurrentes—la Typex britannique qui est entrée en service en 1935 et la Sigmaba américaine qui sera mise au point en 39-40, sont des machines qui ne présentent pas les inconvénients de l'Enigma. Mais celle-ci n'en reste pas moins pour son temps une machine absolument remarquable et les Allemands débuteront la guerre avec, dans ce domaine, une supériorité marquée sur leurs adversaires, car, non seulement ils disposent d'une machine, mais ils ont pensé réellement leur système de transmission: ils ont établi tout un ensemble de règles, tout un réseau—ils n'ont pas attendu le général Gudérian pour dire que la guerre moderne exigerait des pénétrations blindées lontaines, donc des liaisons rapides, suivies et secrètes; ils ont donc réellement mis au point leur système, donc ils débuteront la guerre avec, dans ce domaine, une. . .euh. . .une supériorité marquée. Et la France dans tout cela? Eh bien la France s'est contentée en 36-37 de commander un millier d'exemplaires de machines à chiffrer C.36 au fabricant suédois Adler.

Ces machines ont été peu et mal utilisées au cours de la campagne 30-40. Comment s'efféctue le chiffrement à l'intérieur de cette machine? Le texte clair du message est transformé par la methode de substitution alphabétique, ce qui signifie simplement que chaque lettre du texte est remplacé par une autre lettre.

Il existe de mutiples méthodes de substitution alphabétique, la plus simple—vous la connaissez certainement, consiste à ecrire un alphabet normal A B C E F G . . . à mettre en dessous un alphabet de substitution désordonné, par exemple K en dessous de A, Z en dessous de B . . . et à remplacer dans le texte crypté chaque lettre claire du texte clair par son correspondant, c'est à dire A sera toujours chiffré par K, B par Z etc . . .

Il est clair qu'un tel système de substitution mono-alphabétique ne présente aucune garantie de sécurité: avec un message assez long, d'une centaine de lettres, ça prendra même pas dix minutes pour reconstituer l'alphabet de substitution et pour lire le message, pour autant que l'on puisse déterminer la langue dans laquelle il est écrit, mais rien n'interdit de faire des essais.

    Donc pour qu'une substitution alphabétique puisse avoir quelque chance d'assurer une sécurité il faut utiliser plusieurs alphabets de substitution. Du XVIe au XIXe siecle on a considéré que la méthode la plus élégante, la plus sûre, de faire une substitution polyalphabétique était d'utiliser ce qu'on appelle le carré de Vigenère qui mêt a la disposition de l'utilisateur vingt-six alphabets de substitution. Vous voyez pourquoi on l'appelle un carré—vingt-six alphabets dont chacun occupe une colonne de vingt six cases comme il y a vingt-six lettres cela fait vingt-six lignes:

```
A B C D E F G H I J K L M N O P Q R S T U V W X Y Z
B C D E F G H I J K L M N O P Q R S T U V W X Y Z A
C D E F G H I J K L M N O P Q R S T U V W X Y Z A B
D E F G H I J K L M N O P Q R S T U V W X Y Z A B C
E F G H I J K L M N O P Q R S T U V W X Y Z A B C D
F G H I J K L M N O P Q R S T U V W X Y Z A B C D E
G H I J K L M N O P Q R S T U V W X Y Z A B C D E F
H I J K L M N O P Q R S T U V W X Y Z A B C D E F G
I J K L M N O P Q R S T U V W X Y Z A B C D E F G H
J K L M N O P Q R S T U V W X Y Z A B C D E F G H I
K L M N O P Q R S T U V W X Y Z A B C D E F G H I J
L M N O P Q R S T U V W X Y Z A B C D E F G H I J K
M N O P Q R S T U V W X Y Z A B C D E F G H I J K L
N O P Q R S T U V W X Y Z A B C D E F G H I J K L M
O P Q R S T U V W X Y Z A B C D E F G H I J K L M N
P Q R S T U V W X Y Z A B C D E F G H I J K L M N O
Q R S T U V W X Y Z A B C D E F G H I J K L M N O P
R S T U V W X Y Z A B C D E F G H I J K L M N O P Q
S T U V W X Y Z A B C D E F G H I J K L M N O P Q R
T U V W X Y Z A B C D E F G H I J K L M N O P Q R S
U V W X Y Z A B C D E F G H I J K L M N O P Q R S T
V W X Y Z A B C D E F G H I J K L M N O P Q R S T U
W X Y Z A B C D E F G H I J K L M N O P Q R S T U V
X Y Z A B C D E F G H I J K L M N O P Q R S T U V W
Y Z A B C D E F G H I J K L M N O P Q R S T U V W X
Z A B C D E F G H I J K L M N O P Q R S T U V W X Y
```

    Ayant vingt-six alphabets de substitution à sa disposition l'utilisateur sélectionne les alphabets à utiliser, et l'ordre dans lequel ils vont être utilisés, en affectant chaque message d'un mot-clef, et c'est ce mot-clef qui détermine les alphabets à utiliser et leur rang. Alors tout cela semblait absolument parfait jusqu'en 1863 où un mathématicien allemand, avec un raisonnement très simple et des calculs pas compliqués du tout, démontra que ces substitutions poly-alphabétiques périodiques, pour autant que la période n'était pas très grande était parfaitement décryptables et on cessa donc à ce moment-là d'utiliser les substitutions poly-alphabétiques.

Vint la guerre de 14-18 qui fut marquée par pas mal de nouveautés, et parmi ces nouveautés figurait l'utilisation de la radio. Tout le monde, ami ou ennemi, peut capter le message radio—le problème du secret du message se posait donc de façon particulièrement aiguë et avec une ampleur inégalée et chacun des belligérants s'efforça de la résoudre par l'utilisation de divers systèmes de chiffrement—de chiffrement manuel—dont on dû bien vite reconnaître qu'ils présentaient de sérieux inconvénients, et tout en assurant une sécurité qui dans nombre de cas se révéla illusoire.

Il y eut donc un peu partout des gens qui se dirent qu'une machine ferait mieux le travail et qu'il serait possible de confier le travail de chiffrement à une machine. Euh, on commença par faire des projets, puis l'armistice de 1918 survint avant qu'aucune réalisation pratique n'aît été faite: mais du côté européen, en 1919 un ingénieur hollandais qui s'appelait Hugo KOCH prit un brevet pour une machine—à vrai dire il prit un brevet pour une idée d'une machine—Il ne la réalisa pas, mais alors un ingénieur allemand qui s'appelait Arthur Scherbius réalisa cette machine, la construisit réellement en 1923 et la baptisa Enigma et il entreprit sa fabrication industrielle en la destinant—car il semble bien qu'il aît été un peu naïf au secret des communications personelles; il n'a jamais prétendu que sa machine pourrait servir à des buts militaires. Bien entendu, la machine fut un complet fiasco commercial, et le Dr Scherbius mourut en 1926, c'est-à-dire à l'époque précise où les militaires commençaient à s'intéresser à son invention. Comment fonctionnait cette Enigma commerciale? Eh bien c'est ce que je vais essayer de vous montrer à l'aide de cette Enigma militaire, bien que cette Enigma militaire diffère en quelques points de l'Enigma commerciale.

Donc l'Enigma commercial comporte un clavier d'entrée, de 26 lettres rangées dans l'ordre normal d'un clavier de machine à écrire. C'est l'organe d'entrée; et elle comporte un tableau de voyants 26 voyants rangés dans le même ordre que le clavier d'entrée, qui est l'organe de sortie.

Qu'est ce qui se passe entre l'entrée et la sortie?

Eh bien, je vais vous le montrer . . . Ce clavier de 26 touches, vous allez mieux voir . . . Vous voyez ces rangées de lampes qui illuminent. Si j'enfonce une touche je ferme un circuit électrique qui relie la touche à un disque d'entrée qui se trouve ici. Ce disque d'entrée comprend des deux côtés 26 contacts électriques corréspondant aux touches du clavier d'entrée, les contacts se faisant dans l'ordre du clavier, c'est à dire Q W E R X, viennent ensuite 3 rotors mobiles calés sur le même axe. Ces rotors, les voilà! Ces 3 rotors sont numérotés I, II et III en chiffres romains. Voilà un rotor, il présente sur la droite 26 contacts électriques qui sont des plats à ressort et à la gauche 26 contacts électriques qui sont de petites plaques. Ces rotors sont creux et à l'intérieur les contacts situés de chaque côté sont reliés par des câblages internes. Chaque rotor a un système de câblage particulier: le rotor II a un câblage différent du rotor I, le rotor III a des câblages internes différents des rotors I et II, mais pour toutes les machines tous les rotors I ont le même câblage, tous les rotors II ont le même câblage, tous les rotors III ont le même câblage. Vous voyez que le montage des rotors assure la continuité électrique avec le disque d'entrée. A gauche de la machine il y a un tambour . . . le voilà . . . celui qui est marqué B qui s'appelle le tambour de renvoi. Ce tambour présente sur le côté gauche et seulement sur le côté gauche, 26 contacts électriques—des plats à ressort et ces contacts électriques sont reliés 2 à 2 à l'intérieur du tambour par des cablages internes: vous avez donc 13 liaisons, 26 divisés par 2.

Quel va être le rôle du tambour de renvoi? Remettons ces rotors en place . . . J'enfonce une touche le courant va donc passer à travers le disque d'entrée à travers les trois rotors de droite à gauche, passer à travers le tambour de renvoi, puis être renvoyé par ce tambour de gauche à droite à travers les 3 rotors selon un trajet complètment différent du trajet d'entrée—et ils vont aboutir au disque d'entrée qui devient un disque de sortie—c'est un disque d'entrée/sortie—et ils vont être renvoyés du disque de sortie vers le tableau de voyants, où l'enfoncement de la touche déterminera l'éclairement d'un voyant. Le circuit du courant est donc clair . . .

Maintenant qu'est ce qui se passe si j'enfonce la touche A? Un voyant du cadran va s'illuminer . . . ce sera peut-être . . . le voyant C.

Qu'est-ce qui se passe si je re-appuie ensuite sur la touche A? L'enfoncement de la touche détermine la rotation du tambour de droite . . . d'une position. Les circuits électriques vont donc se trouver complètement différents de ceux qui existaient lors de la première frappe, et bien que j'aie appuyé sur la même touche A ce ne sera plus le voyant C, ce sera peut-être le voyant K qui s'illuminera. La seule chose qui ne puisse pas arriver si vous appuyez sur la touche A c'est que ce soit le A qui apparaisse sur le clavier. Par construction de la machine il y a un principe d'exclusion qui fait qu'une lettre ne peut pas être cryptée par elle-meme. Si je continue à taper, toujours lettre à lettre, sur le clavier d'entrée, le tambour de droite va continuer à tourner et, à une certaine position, il y a un ergot qui va passer, et qui entrainera le déplacement d'une position du rotor central, et puis la même chose pour le rotor central: au bout d'un certain nombre de frappes il entrainera le décalage d'une position du rotor de gauche: c'est exactement comparable à un compteur d'eau, de gaz ou d'électricité, ce n'est pas plus compliqué que ça.

Regardons maintenant un peu les choses: je continue à taper, plus exactement j'ai commencé à taper à partir d'une certaine position des rotors: si je frappe quotidiennement sur ma machine, il va arriver un moment où les rotors vont revenir à leur position initiale; quand est-ce que ça arrivera? Chaque rotor a 26 positions; cela arrivera au bout de 26 frappes au cube, c'est-à-dire 17,576 positions. Et ces 17,576 frappes correspondent a 17,576 positions différentes du rotor; or, à chacune de ces positions différentes correspond l'utilisation d'un alphabet de substitution différent; 17,576 alphabets de substitution— vous voyez que nous sommes très loin des 26 alphabets de substitution que constituait le carré Vigière.

Mais ce n'est pas tout. Ces rotors sont interchangeables; je puis donc en changer l'ordre. Avec trois rotors j'ai 6 ordres possibles, j'ai donc à ma disposition . . . $17{,}576 \times 6$, soit plus de 105,000 alphabets de substitution. Et quand le 15 décembre 1936 les Allemands auront à ajouter à la panoplie de 3 tambours mobiles I, II et III deux tambours IV et V, l'arrangement possible de 3 tambours sur une panoplie de 5 remontera à 60; j'aurai à ce moment-là à ma disposition plus d'un million d'alphabets de substitution de quoi décourager le crypto-analyste le plus courageux. En outre, chaque message . . . avant cela une chose—la machine ne comporte aucun moteur: c'est l'enfoncement des touches qui détermine la fermeture du circuit électrique et le

mouvement des rotors—le courant est fourni par une pile accumulateur de 4 volts, 5 . . . que voilà . . . mais il n'y a aucun moteur. Chaque message en outre aura sa propre clef. Quelle sera cette clef? Ce sera la position de depart des rotors. En effet, refermons la machine . . . Les rotors sont d'autre part libres sur leur axe et ont à leur droite un petit secteur denté qui permet de les tourner à la main; ceci me permet donc de faire apparaître dans les fenêtres qui se trouvent ici un pour chacun de ces rotors—l'un des 26 secteurs chiffrés chacun de ces secteurs chiffrés correspondant en fait à une lettre, la correspondance est très simple:
1 = A 2 = B etc. Je vais donc choisir une position de départ, par exemple H S B, H S B cela correspond du point de vue lettres . . . elles sont ici, à . . . 08 19 02 . . . voici donc ma clef de message affiché je puis commencer la frappe de mon message. Alors il y a quandmême une petite difficulté: encore faut-il que le destinataire à l'autre bout sache que j'ai débuté avec, comme clef de message, H S B. Alors je vais donc convenir, dans les instructions du jour, que, ce jour-là les clefs de mes messages seront tapées sur ma machine à partir d'une autre position de départ qui sera la même pour tous les messages du jour. Je choisirai par exemple Z A H, je mettrai donc ma machine à Z A H qui fait 26 01 08. Je taperai H S B sur le clavier puis je ferai apparaître l'équivalent en chiffres d'H S B sur les fenêtres et je commencerai la frappe du message. J'ai donc de nouveau à ma disposition 26 au cube, 17,576 positions de départ possibles . . . mais là aussi, il y a une astuce: la machine . . . ressortons les rotors! Il y a une astuce: vous voyez la couronne qui se trouve sur le rotor; la couronne avec les 26 chiffres; eh bien, il y a un petit clip, ici . . . qui me permèt de rendre—ce qui est difficile à faire à l'envers—de rendre la couronne mobile. Et je peux la bloquer dans les 26 positions différentes; ça ne change pas le nombre instantané de mes positions de depart—17,576—mais cela fait que j'ai encore 17,576 moyens de faire correspondre à mes positions de depart des alphabets de substitution complêtement différents. Donc je me trouve encore à multiplier de façon incroyable les possibilités de réglage de la machine. En bref dans cette Enigma commercial j'ai, d'une part la configuration du jour, l'ordre des rotors et le réglage des couronnes et, d'autre part pour chaque message la clef spécifique du message. Je vais remonter . . . comme ça . . . là . . . vous comprendrez qu'avec de telles dispositions la machine intéresse les militaires qui cherchent le moyen

de transmettre des messages secrets—les militaires allemands notamment—la Marine allemande adopte le 9 février 1926 un dérivé de l'Enigma commerciale. Il n'est pas question d'adopter l'Enigma commerciale directement—ce sera le modèle C, tandis que l'Armée de Terre fait de même le 15 juillet 1929 en adoptant un autre modèle d'Enigma, le modèle G. Ceci fait, le colonel Fellgiebel qui est responsable des services de transmissions de l'Armée allemande, n'est quand même pas tranquille; alors il décide d'ouvrir le parapluie, et dans toutes les armées du monde, comme dans toutes les organisations civiles, ouvrir le parapluie consiste à nommer un comité d'experts—et le colonel Fellgiebel confie donc à un comité d'experts la vérification de la sécurité de la machine—ceci en l'année 1928. Et un jour, de 1929, les experts reviennent avec un verdict absolument surprenant: ils disent 'Cette machine n'est pas sûre! D'abord votre période—c'est une période de 17,576—ce n'est pas si gros que ça' et puis surtout les experts vont trouver qu'une méthode mathématique, assez complexe, il est vrai, permêt à l'aide du texte chiffré des messages—pas mal de textes chiffrés—de re-constituer la configuration de la machine utilisée pour leur déchiffrement. Consternation? non . . . car les experts disent: 'Mais il existe un moyen simple de rendre cette machine absolument sûre. On va lui ajouter un tableau de connections' Le voilà! Ce panneau de connections comporte 26 prises—doubles—correspondant aux 26 lettres et ces prises peuvent être réunies deux à deux par des fiches mobiles qu'on appelle des 'Steckers'. Vous en avez ici, vous avez deux exemplaires de fiches mobiles de réserve. En les réunissant deux à deux on crée un double surchiffrage, parce qu'on fait passer les courants à travers ces fiches—il passe alors deux fois, il passe à l'entrée et il passe à la sortie—on a donc un double surchiffrage, qui non seulement met en échec la méthode mathématique que les experts allemands avaient trouvée et que les experts allemands appellent la méthode des batons, mais en plus on multiplie les possibilités de combinaisons par un facteur infime: en effet si nous prenons simplement 11 connections, pas 13,—on peut avoir un maximum de 13 connections . . . (26 divisé par 2 ça fait 13)—si je prends 11 fiches et que j'entreprends de compter les manières différentes qu'il y a à réunir 11 connections . . . euh . . . de réunir 26 lettres par 11 connections ce qui fait exactement dans ce cas-là 22 seulement je trouve qu'il y en aura . . . le nombre de possibilités est de 2 suivi de 14 zéros, 200,000,000,000,000. Donc l'adoption de ce tableau de connections—des Steckers—disent les experts, rend la machine absolument certaine, absolument sûre. Voyons comment on peut évaluer la sécurité de cette machine. Cette sécurité est assurée à plusieurs échelons: le premier échelon de sécurité c'est la machine elle-même: même si vous disposez d'une description de la machine elle est impossible à reconstituer, pour une raison très simple: cette machine comporte cinq organes présentant des cablages internes: les 3 rotors, les tambours de renvoi, et également le cablage réunissant les touches du clavier avec le disque d'entrée et sortie. Eh bien les possibilités diverses d'effectuer ce cablage se montent à 10 euh! Pardon . . . à 5 suivi de 92 zeros: 500,000,000, 000,000,000,000,000,000,000,000,000,000,000,000,000,000,000,000, 000,000,000,000,000,000,000,000,000,000,000,000. Donc même si vous connaissez . . . même si vous avez une description générale de la machine il est hors de question d'essayer de reconstituer ce cablage.

Les Allemands ont parfaitement conscience d'un jour ou l'autre ce succes cessera c'est-à-dire qu'une machine, en paix ou en guerre, tombera entre les mains de l'ennemi ou que, pire, un traître communiquera les schémas de cablages. En attendant ils prennent des mesures de secret sur cette machine et ces mesures de secret seront efficaces.

Jamais les schémas de cablages ne quitteront les coffres secrets de la Reichswehr ou de la Wehrmacht, et il faudra attendre la campagne de Norvège pour que 3 Enigmas soient saisies par les forces armées britanniques: donc le secret de ce point de vue-là était efficace. Mais même si vous disposez de la machine, si vous la connaissez, si vous avez ses cablages, restent les configurations. Or les configurations possibles de la machine, compte tenu de l'adjonction des 'Steckers' se montent pour chaque jour—parceque les organes sont règlés chaque jour—à un chiffre de possibilités qui est exprimé par 27 suivi de 22 zeros: 270,000,000,000,000,000,000,000, impossible à nouveau de tenter d'explorer ces combinaisons pour retrouver celle qui a été effectivement employée: la machine n'est ni reconstructible, ni décryptible. *Et pourtant elle va être très rapidement reconstituée et décryptée.* Les experts allemands se sont séparés avec la certitude d'avoir avec l'Enigma militaire un engin garantissant l'absolue sécurité de leurs transmissions. Et compte tenu des moyens à l'époque ils ont parfaitement raison—il n'y a pas d'ironie du tout dans mes paroles et pourtant la machine va être reconstituée et décryptée.

Elle va l'être pour 4 raisons—la conjonction de 4 causes—
1. Une erreur cryptologique dans les procédures d'emploi,
2. La trahison—une trahison,
3. L'intervention d'un mathématicien de génie.
4. Des erreurs des opérateurs allemands.

1. Une erreur cryptologique

Les experts allemands n'ont pas poussé le détail des procédures d'emploi de la machine; ce sont d'autres experts, d'autres spécialistes qui vont le faire. Ces experts, ces spécialistes ont d'autres préoccupations que les experts précédents: on leur a dit que la machine était d'une sécurité parfaite, ils n'y reviendront pas.

Eux, ce qui les intéresse, c'est la pratique des transmissions; et ils sont hantés par une idée, ce sont les erreurs qui ne manquent pas de se produire dans les procédures de chiffrement. Ces erreurs, ils savent qu'elles vont se produire, ils y sont parfaitement résignés. Comment faire autrement d'ailleurs? Mais ce qu'ils veulent au moins c'est que les erreurs graves puissent etre décélées très rapidement. Et, parmi les erreurs graves figurent les erreurs qui peuvent se glisser dans le chiffrement de la clef spécifique du message. J'ai choisi comme clef H S B . . . il faut que, à l'autre bout le destinataire récupère bien L'H S B. Pour en être sûr, qu'est-ce que font les spécialistes? Ils disent: 'On ne va pas la transmettre une fois, on va la transmettre deux fois. Ceci sera chiffré par 6 lettres, euh, disons, par exemple que j'aurai X K Y W A C. J'aurai donc au début du message un groupe de 6 lettres dans lequel si je connais les procédures je suis sûr que la 1e lettre et la 4e, la 2e et la 5e, la 3e et la 6e résultent du chiffrement de la même lettre du texte clair. C'est une rédondance, ça parait parfaitement anodin, ça va ruiner la sécurité de l'ensemble du systeme.

2. La trahison

En octobre 1931 un fonctionnaire du service du Ministère Allemand de la Défense propose aux services de Renseignement Français de lui fournir des documents et, c'est ainsi que le 8 novembre, 1931 un officier du service de Renseignement, le capitaine Bertrand, rencontre à Verdier en Bélgique un traître qui a pour pseudonyme Asche. C'est Hans-Thilo Schmidt et à cette première rencontre ASCHE lui remèt deux documents. Ces documents—les voici! Il y a donc un **'Gebrauchsanweisung für die Chiffriermaschine ENIGMA'** c'est-à-dire une notice d'utilisation de la machine Enigma et il y le '**Schluesselanleitung fuer die Chiffriermaschine ENIGMA**' la description des procédures de chiffrement utilisé à ce moment-là. Bien entendu le Gebrauchsanweisung comporte une description générale de la machine, avec photos, s'il vous plaît, mais bien entendu ne comporte aucune indication sur les cablages internes. Bertrand emporte les documents, va trouver le Service Français du Chiffre qui, après examen, adopte exactement les mêmes conclusions que les experts allemands: la machine, disent-ils, ne peut être reconstituée, ne peut être décryptée, les documents sont inutiles. Bertrand est évidemment très déçu et il obient de ses chefs l'autorisation de transmettre les documents aux sources Alliés pour voir s'il n'y aurait pas éventuellement une exploitation commune. Alors, les premiers touches sont les Britanniques, nous sommes à la fin novembre 1931: les Britanniques déclarent qu'ils ne sont pas intéressés, l'Allemagne de 1931 ne leur apparaît pas dangereuse et aussi comme Asche coûte très cher ils ne tiennent pas du tout à partager les frais. Alors du 7 à 11 décembre, 1931 Bertrand va en Pologne. Et en Pologne il rencontre les représentants du Service du Chiffre Polonais qui sont le commandant Langer et le capitaine Ciezki. Le capitaine est le responsable du B S K, c'est-à-dire du Bureau du Chiffre chargé spécialement de l'Allemagne.

Bertrand est reçu avec enthousiasme. Les Polonais sont sur la question depuis 1928 et n'ont pratiquement pas réussi à démarrer; ils voient dans la livraison de ces documents l'occasion de reprendre leurs études. On fait une sorte de pacte. Bertrand va continuer à fournir les documents que lui remettra ASCHE et les Polonais—c'est joué c'est promis—tiendront Bertrand au courant de ce qu'ils feront. Alors les officiers polonais repartent à l'assaut de la machine Enigma. Ils savent—ils étaient arrivés donc en 1931—ils savaient que les Allemands utilisaient une machine, ils étaient certains que la machine était une Enigma commerciale modifiée, mais ils ne savaient pas du tout quelles étaient les modifications qu'on avait apportées à l'Enigma commerciale et puis ils avaient aussi remarqué que les six premières lettres de chaque message avaient des caractères particuliers et que ça devait être une clef de messages.

3. L'intervention d'un mathématicien de génie

Alors, nantis des documents de Bertrand les officiers polonais repartent à l'assaut—c'est à nouveau un échec complêt; impossible de reconstituer la machine. En déséspoir de cause Langer et Ciezki prennent une mesure heroïque . . . puisque les militaires n'aboutissent à rien, essayons des mathématiciens civils!

Le Bureau de chiffre dispose de trois mathématiciens civils, qu'il a été chercher en 1929 à l'université de Poznan; ces trois mathématiciens s'appellent Marian Rejewski, Jerzy Rozycki et Henryk Zygalski. Alors en séptembre 1932 on incorpore ces trois mathématiciens qui travaillent déjà l'allemand pour le Service du Chiffre, on les incorpore au Bureau du Chiffre à Varsovie. On les essaye et puis au début d'octobre on prend le plus brillant d'entre eux, Rejewski, et on lui confie comme mission ultra secrète la réconstitution et, si possible, le décryptement de l'Enigma. Marian Rejewski dispose d'une Enigma commerciale, des deux documents Asche donnés par Bertrand et du flot ininterrompu des interceptions de messages que captent chaque jour les Services d'Ecoute polonais. Rejewski réfléchit, se familiarise avec la machine et concentre ses efforts sur les six premières lettres des messages . . . Alors, je ne veux pas vous donner les arcanes mathématiques du raisonnement de Rejewski mais je peux vous faire reconstituer sa démarche intellectuelle et vous verrez qu'il est au fond simple.

Ces premières lettres de chaque message qui correspondent à la répétition chiffrée de la clef spécifique du message, Rejewki se dit que . . . qu'elles entrainent le mouvement de 6 positions du rotor de droite. Nous savons qu'il n'y a qu'une position du rotor de droite qui entraine le mouvement du rotor du milieu donc dans 20 cas sur 26, ces six lettres sont chiffrées avec le seul mouvement du rotor de droite, et dans ces cas-là on pourra considérer tout le reste de la machine comme un ensemble fixe. Compte tenu du fait que l'on sait qu'il s'agit d'une duplication de la clef qui a deux fois les mêmes lettres on peut exprimer le chiffrement de ces six lettres par six équations successives de permutation dont certaines propriétés sont connues, compte tenu de la duplication, et dans ce cas ce système de six équations est, au sens mathématique du terme, 'déterminé'; c'est-à-dire qu'il peut être résolu théoriquement. Théoriquement parceque pratiquement il n'existe à l'époque, compte tenu des moyens de calcul disponibles, absolument aucun moyen d'arriver à la résolution pratique.

Mais Rejewski poursuit son idée: la résolution de ces équations permettrait de reconstituer le cablage du tambour de droite; comme les trois tambours sont à des périodes différentes placés à droite on pourrait reconstituer les cablages des trois rotors; une fois qu'on aurait les cablages des trois rotors on pourrait reconstituer le cablage du tambour de renvoi, et donc reconstituer l'ensemble de la machine. Je répète que tout cela est parfaitement théorique. Mais Rejewski va expliquer ça à Rozycki et Zygalski qui sont éblouis par les capacités du jeune mathématicien—il a 27 ans en ce moment—et lui disent 'Oui, dans ce cas-là on va vous donner autre chose' et Cieski lui donne autres documents qui viennent d'être transmis par Bertrand: ces documents sont des fascicules mensuels donnant des configurations d'Enigma. Rejewski a les messages chiffrés pour les autres correspondants, il connait, grace à ces fascicules l'ordre des rotors, le réglage des couronnes, le réglage des 'Steckers', il peut simplifier ses équations, et ces simplifications lui permettent de les résoudre pratiquement. Dès lors, à la fin de 1932, les cablages intérieurs de la machine sont entièrement reconstitués, non sans peine car les premiers calculs de Rejewski ont échoué, et Rejewski s'est interrogé 'Pourquoi cet échec?' alors que son raisonnement est impeccable et il s'est dit que . . . il avait adopté pour le schéma des liaisons entre les touches et le disque d'entrée-sortie . . . il avait adopté le même schéma que dans l'Enigma commerciale, c'est-à-dire l'ordre des touches. 'Et si', se dit-il 'les Allemands avaient changé cet ordre? Les Allemands sont des gens sérieux, systématiques, ils n'ont certainement pas fait ça au hasard . . . s'ils ont fait ça . . . eh bien pourquoi ne l'auraient-ils pas reliés dans l'ordre de l'alphabet A B C D E . . .?' Il essaye, et c'est effectivement la modification qui a été faite! Au début de 1933 la machine est entièrement reconstituée—et on peut lancer la fabrication industrielle des répliques de l'Enigma Militaire allémande a Varsovie.

4. Des erreurs des operateurs allemands

Les opérateurs allemands ont été si négligents au cours de cette année '32 dans le choix des cléfs spécifiques du message, ils ont choisi . . . des cléfs . . . dans l'ordre du clavier, ils ont choisi des A B C, ils ont choisi les mèmes letres S S S ou des choses comme ça . . . que Rejewski et ses collègues ont pu élaborer des systèmes généraux qui permettent toujours à partir de cette faute que constitue la duplication de la cléf spécifique du message, qui permettent de reconstituer et la configuration de la machine et la cléf spécifique du message. Au debut de 1933 les Polonais ont non seulement reconstitué la machine, ils la décryptent couramment.

APPENDIX 2

The Manual for the Use of the Enigma Cipher Machine

The contents table shows the range of instructions:

			Page
I.	1–2	General.	3
II.	3–9	Preparation of the Machine for use.	3
III.	10–15	Setting up the key	4
IV.	16–18	Encipherment	
V.	19.	Decipherment	6
VI.	20–21	Typing mistakes and faults.	7
VII.	22–26	Current source and Glow-Lamps	7
VIII.	27–31	Interference	9
IX.	32–33	Maintenance of the Machine.	11

Notes: VI—deals with striking wrong keys, double strikes and indicates the message has to be re-done from the start.
VII deals with replacements of batteries and glow-lamps and testing of 'Steckers' to see that they are correctly connected.
VIII Indicates the action to be taken by operators when the corresponding lamps do not light up.

H. Dv. g. 13
L. Dv. g. 13

Geheim!

Prüf-Nr. 16044

Ungültig

Ln.-Betr.-Komp. (mot.)

Gebrauchsanleitung
für die
Chiffriermaschine Enigma

Vom 12. 1. 1937

Unveränderter Nachdruck

Berlin 1940
Gedruckt in der Reichsdruckerei

Inhaltsverzeichnis.

			Seite
I.	1.—2.	Allgemeines	3
II.	3.—9.	Vorbereiten der Maschine zum Betrieb	3
III.	10.—15.	Schlüsseleinstellung	4
IV.	16.—18.	Verschlüsseln	6
V.	19.	Entschlüsseln	6
VI.	20.—21.	Tastfehler und Versager	7
VII.	22.—26.	Stromquelle, Glühlampen	7
VIII.	27.—31.	Störungen	9
IX.	32.—33.	Wartung der Maschine	11

I. Allgemeines.

1. Die Chiffriermaschine Enigma ist ein geheimer Gegenstand im Sinne der Verschlußsachen-Vorschrift (H. Dv. 99). Sie ist nach den Bestimmungen dieser Vorschrift unter Verschluß zu halten.

2. Jeder Benutzer der Chiffriermaschine muß sich bewußt sein, daß die Art ihrer Konstruktion ein sorgfältiges Bedienen und Warten erfordert, damit die Maschine jederzeit betriebsfähig erhalten wird.

II. Vorbereiten der Maschine zum Betrieb.

3. Vor Inbetriebnahme ist die Chiffriermaschine auf richtiges Arbeiten zu prüfen. Hierzu sind der hölzerne Schutzkasten zu öffnen, die Haltevorrichtung (Bild I, 1) durch Anheben der Federknöpfe (I, 2) auszulösen, die Haltehebel (I, 3) herumzuschwenken, worauf die Abdeckplatte (I/II, 4) sich aufklappen läßt und die Einstellräder (II/IV, 5) freigibt.

4. Die Einstellräder (II/IV, 5) sind mehrmals gegeneinander zu verdrehen, damit die Kontakte der Chiffrierwalzen blank werden. Danach ist die Abdeckplatte (I/II, 4) wieder zu schließen und durch die Haltehebel (I, 3) zu sichern.

5. Zur Säuberung der Tastkontakte sind vor Einschalten des Stromes sämtliche Tasten (II, 6) mehrmals kräftig herunterzudrücken und rasch hochschnellen zu lassen. Dabei ist **eine Taste** in niedergedrücktem Zustande festzuhalten, um ein unnötiges Weiterschalten der Walzen zu vermeiden.

6. Der Schaltergriff (II, 7) für die Batterie ist bei frischer Batterie von Stellung »aus« auf »dunkel« zu stellen. Sobald die Spannung der Batterie nach längerem Gebrauch nachläßt, ist zum besseren Aufleuchten der Glühlampen die Schalterstellung »hell« zu verwenden. Zu frühes Benutzen der Stellung »hell« führt zu vorzeitigem Durchbrennen der Glühlampen.

7. Bei Sonnenschein und zur Schonung der Augen empfiehlt es sich, die grüne Zellonplatte (I/II, 8) durch Anheben und Drehen der Federknöpfe (I/II, 9) aus dem Holzdeckel zu lösen und mit der gleichen Vorrichtung über dem Buchstaben-Transparent (I, 10) zu befestigen. Die Zellonplatte dämpft das grelle Licht der Glühlampen und verdeckt alle Buchstaben, so daß nur der aufleuchtende Buchstabe sichtbar ist.

8. Zum Schutz gegen blendendes Sonnenlicht kann die Maschine dadurch abgeschattet werden, daß die Gelenke der Deckelscharniere (II, 1) nach vorn gezogen und der Holzdeckel halb heruntergeklappt wird.

9. Im Inneren des Holzdeckels ist ein Blatthalter (I, 42) angebracht, damit die Texte beim Schlüsseln bequem vor Augen stehen.

III. Schlüsseleinstellung.

10. Der zur Maschine ausgegebene Schlüssel legt folgende 4 verschiedene Einstellungen der Maschine fest:

 a) Reihenfolge der Chiffrierwalzen (III/IV, 12) (Walzenlage),
 b) Einstellung der Zahlen- oder Buchstabenringe (III/IV, 13) auf den 3 Chiffrierwalzen (Ringstellung),
 c) Einstellung der in den Fenstern (I/II, 16) sichtbaren Zahlen oder Buchstaben (Grundstellung),
 d) Herstellung der Steckerverbindungen mittels Doppelsteckerschnüren (II, 30) am Steckerbrett (II, 15) (Steckerverbindungen).

11. Die Schlüsseleinstellung geschieht folgendermaßen:

Der Metalldeckel (II/III, 17) der Maschine wird geöffnet, indem die beiden Halteschrauben (II, 18) durch Drehen gelöst werden, der Deckel an den Schrauben hochgezogen und aufgeklappt wird.

12. Die Walzen sind an der Seite der federnden Kontaktstifte (IV, 35) mit römischen Zahlen (IV, 34) und auf dem blanken Mittelteil mit einer diesen Zahlen entsprechenden Anzahl schwarzer Punkte (IV, 33) gekennzeichnet, so daß man die Reihenfolge der Walzen, zunächst ohne sie herausnehmen zu müssen, nachprüfen kann.

Zur Herstellung der richtigen Walzenlage (vgl. Ziff. 10a) wird der in der linken hinteren Ecke liegende Haltehebel (III, 19) nach vorn bis zum Anschlag geklappt und die Umkehrwalze (III, 20) scharf nach links herangeschoben; dann werden die Chiffrierwalzen (III/IV, 12) an den Einstellrädern (II/IV, 5) mit der rechten Hand nach links zusammengedrückt und zusammen mit der Achse (IV, 21) herausgehoben.

Die Walzen werden in der durch den Schlüssel angegebenen Reihenfolge auf die Achse geschoben und unter Zusammendrücken wieder in die Maschine eingesetzt. Beim Aufsetzen der Walzen auf die Achse ist darauf zu achten, daß die Seiten mit den glatten Kontaktflächen (IV, 36) stets auf die Seite des Achsenbundes (IV, 21a) der Welle weisen, und daß beim Einsetzen der drei auf die Achse geschobenen Walzen der Achsenbund (IV, 21) mit den glatten Kontaktflächen stets der Umkehrwalze zugekehrt ist. Nach dem Einsetzen der Walzen in die Maschine ist der Haltehebel (III, 9) wieder nach hinten bis zum Anschlag zu legen.

Das Herausnehmen und Wiedereinsetzen der Chiffrierwalzen hat so sorgfältig zu geschehen, daß mit dem linken Lagerzapfen der Achse nicht die vorstehenden Kontaktstifte der Umkehrwalze (III, 20) verbogen werden. Es ist ferner darauf zu achten, daß nach dem Zurücklegen des Haltehebels nach hinten die Walzen richtig gerastet sind, was daran zu erkennen ist, daß die Zahlen oder Buchstaben in der Mitte der Fenster stehen. (Nachprüfung durch Drehen der einzelnen Chiffrierwalzen.)

13. Zum Einstellen der richtigen Ringstellung (vgl. Ziff. 10 b) werden die Haltefedern (IV, 22) der Zahlen- oder Buchstabenringe (IV, 13) an dem an jeder Haltefeder sitzenden Knopf (IV, 23) mit der rechten Hand angehoben und die Ringe mit der linken Hand so weit gedreht, bis der — von Maschine Nr. 1253 an mit einer roten Kennmarke versehene — Federzapfen (IV, 24) in das Loch neben der durch den Schlüssel vorgeschriebenen Zahl einschnappt. Der Metalldeckel (II/III, 17) wird darauf geschlossen und durch die beiden Halteschrauben (II, 18) festgeschraubt.

14. Zum Einstellen der Grundstellung (vgl. Ziff. 10 c) wird die Abdeckplatte (I/II, 4) geöffnet, und die Chiffrierwalzen (III/IV, 12) werden mittels der Einstellräder (II/IV, 5) so lange gedreht, bis die durch den Schlüssel vorgeschriebenen Zahlen oder Buchstaben der Grundstellung in den Fenstern (I/II, 16) sichtbar sind. Die Abdeckplatte ist wieder zu schließen.

15. Zum Herstellen der Steckerverbindungen (vgl. Ziff. 10 d) sind die Haken (III, 26) an der Stirnwand (I/III, 25) zu lösen und die Stirnwand herunterzuklappen. Dadurch werden 26 Buchsenpaare (II, 31) frei, die mit den Buchstaben »A« bis »Z« und zugleich mit den entsprechenden Ziffern »1« bis »26« gekennzeichnet sind.

Die durch Kabel verbundenen Doppelsteckerpaare (II, 13) werden einzeln am Steckergriff herausgezogen (nicht an der Steckerschnur herausreißen!). Dann wird entsprechend den im Schlüssel vorgeschriebenen Steckerverbindungen eine Anzahl von Buchsenpaaren mittels der durch die Schnüre (II, 30) verbundenen Doppelstecker miteinander verbunden. Buchsen und Steckerpaare sind unverwechselbar ausgeführt. Es ist darauf zu achten, daß die Stecker bis zu ihrem Anschlag in die Buchsen fest hineingedrückt werden, damit ein gleichzeitiges Aufleuchten mehrerer Lampen verhütet wird. Die Stirnwand ist zu schließen und durch die Haken (III, 26) zu sichern.

IV. Verschlüsseln.

16. Nach dem Einstellen des Schlüssels (vgl. III) ist der Klartext Buchstabe für Buchstabe durch Niederdrücken der Tasten ähnlich wie bei einer Schreibmaschine zu schreiben. Die Tasten sind dabei ganz herunterzudrücken, bis in dem Transparent (I, 10) bzw. auf der darübergelegten Zellonplatte (II, 8) ein Buchstabe aufleuchtet. Die nächste Taste darf erst dann niedergedrückt werden, wenn die vorhergehende Taste losgelassen und in die Ruhestellung zurückgeschnellt ist. Über die Einzelheiten des Verschlüsselns vgl. die »Schlüsselanleitung zur Chiffriermaschine Enigma« (II. Dv. g. 14).

17. Nimmt eine Person das Verschlüsseln vor, so ist zweckmäßig mit der linken Hand der Klartext zu tasten und mit der rechten Hand der verschlüsselte Spruch niederzuschreiben. Stehen zum Verschlüsseln zwei Personen zur Verfügung, so bedient die eine die Maschine, die andere liest die aufleuchtenden Buchstaben ab und schreibt sie nieder.

18. Für die Schreibweise von Satzzeichen, Zahlen usw. gelten die Vorschriften in der »Schlüsselanleitung zur Chiffriermaschine Enigma« (II. Dv. g. 14).

V. Entschlüsseln.

19. Die Maschine ist nach dem vorgeschriebenen Schlüssel einzustellen (vgl. III) und das Entschlüsseln wie das Verschlüsseln nach IV. vorzunehmen, doch sind an Stelle der Klartextbuchstaben die Buchstaben des verschlüsselten Spruches zu tasten.

VI. Tastfehler und Versager.

20. Sind beim Schlüsseln (Ver- oder Entschlüsseln) durch Drücken falscher Tasten, Auslassen oder Doppelschreiben von Buchstaben oder durch Versager in der Maschine (Nichtaufleuchten von Lampen) Fehler entstanden, so muß das Schlüsseln vom **Spruchanfang** an wiederholt werden. Hierzu ist der Schlüssel in den Fenstern (II, 16) wie zu Anfang einzustellen. Um aber bei einem erst gegen Ende des Schlüsselns eingetretenen Fehler die Wiederholung der ganzen Schlüsselarbeit zu vermeiden, genügt es, nach neuer Einstellung des Schlüssels eine beliebige Taste so oft zu drücken, wie vor dem Fehler Buchstaben richtig geschlüsselt sind.

Beispiel: Ist beim Schlüsseln der 32. Buchstabe falsch getastet, so wird nach Wiedereinstellung des Schlüssels in dem Fenster ein beliebiger Buchstabe 30mal getastet, darauf der 31. Buchstabe des Spruches zur Kontrolle mit der entsprechenden Taste getastet und mit dem beim ersten Schlüsseln herausgekommenen Buchstaben verglichen. Ergibt der Vergleich denselben Buchstaben wie beim ersten Schlüsseln, so wird mit dem 32. und den folgenden Buchstaben in normaler Weise weitergeschlüsselt.

21. Bei längeren Sprüchen wird die Verbesserung vorgekommener Versehen beim Schlüsseln wesentlich erleichtert, wenn etwa bei jedem 50. Buchstaben die gleichzeitig in den Fenstern erscheinenden Zahlen niedergeschrieben werden. Es genügt dann zum Beseitigen von Fehlern, bis zu dem letzten so niedergeschriebenen Buchstaben zurückzugehen, die zugehörigen Zahlen in den Fenstern einzustellen und nur von da ab die Schlüsselarbeit zu wiederholen.

VII. Stromquelle, Glühlampen.

22. Eine allgemeine Betriebsanweisung (II, 32) ist im Deckel der Maschine angebracht, damit ohne die vorliegende Gebrauchsanleitung kleine Störungen an der Maschine beseitigt werden können.

23. Als Batterie wird die Batterie 4,5 KZT 5 verwendet. Sie wird bei dem Zeugamt (Nachr.) vorrätig gehalten und kann von dort bezogen werden. Ist keine brauchbare Batterie vorhanden, so ermöglichen die beiden Kordelschrauben (II, 28) den Anschluß einer beliebigen Stromquelle (Taschenlampenbatterie, Sammler u. dgl.), wobei jedoch darauf zu achten ist, daß diese Stromquelle eine Höchstspannung von 4 Volt besitzt. Zum Betrieb mit einer an die beiden Kordelschrauben (II, 28) angelegten Stromquelle wird der Schaltergriff (II, 7) auf Stellung »Sammler« gelegt.

24. Zum Auswechseln der Batterie in der Chiffriermaschine ist der Deckel des Batteriekastens (III, 27), der nach Öffnen des Metalldeckels (III, 17) zugänglich ist, zu öffnen, die erschöpfte Batterie herauszuziehen und durch eine neue zu ersetzen. Dabei ist zu beachten, daß die Kontaktfedern der einzusetzenden Batterie nach rechts zeigen (vgl. die Lage der Gegenkontaktfedern im Batteriekasten [III, 27]).

25. Die in der Chiffriermaschine verwendeten Glühlampen entsprechen folgenden Bedingungen: Halbkugelform, 12 mm, 3,5 Volt, 0,2 Ampère, säurefrei gelötet, vernickelter Lampensockel. In der Maschine befinden sich 10 Reservelampen auf einem Blechstreifen (I, 37) am oberen Rande des Holzdeckels. Handelsübliche Taschenlampenbirnen mit 12 mm Durchmesser können im äußersten Notfall verwendet werden, sie sind jedoch **baldmöglichst** auszutauschen, da sie leicht zu Störungen Anlaß geben.

Von Maschine Nr. 4388 ab ist auf der rechten Seite des Glühlampenfeldes (III, 38) eine Öffnung mit der Bezeichnung »Lampenprüfung« (III, 39) angebracht. Durch Einstecken der Glühlampen in diese Öffnung bei Stellung des Schaltergriffes auf »dunkel« bzw. »hell« können die einzelnen Glühlampen auf ihre Brauchbarkeit geprüft werden. (Achtung: Die Glühlampen müssen sofort nach der Prüfung aus dieser Öffnung wieder herausgezogen werden.)

26. Zu jeder Maschine gehören 8 Doppelsteckerschnüre, von denen 2 (I, 34) im Innern des Deckels der Maschine untergebracht werden können. Von der Maschine Nr. 4388 ab sind 2 Buchsen (die äußerste linke und äußerste rechte — durch rote Punkte gekennzeichnete — Buchse der mittleren Reihe am Steckerbrett — III, 41) und die Lampe mit der Bezeichnung »Kabelprüfung« (III, 40) auf der linken Seite des Glühlampenfeldes (III, 38) angebracht, damit die richtige Verbindung der Doppelsteckerschnüre und ihre Brauchbarkeit nachgeprüft werden können. Die beiden Buchsen sind unverwechselbar und so geschaltet, daß beim Einführen des entsprechenden Steckerstiftes eines jeden Doppelsteckers in diese Buchsen die Prüflampe aufleuchten muß, dabei ist die Doppelsteckerschnur (II, 30) durch Bewegen auf Brüche zu prüfen.

VIII. Störungen.

27. Störungen, die durch den Schlüßler behoben werden können, sind im allgemeinen Kontaktstörungen, zu deren Feststellung und Auffindung wie folgt vorzugehen ist.

28. Zur Feststellung, ob Glühlampen (V, 43), Walzenkontakte (V, 44) und Kurzschlußbleche des Steckerbrettes (V, 45) in Ordnung sind, wird bei beliebiger Schlüsseleinstellung die Q-Taste gedrückt, wodurch irgendein Buchstabe, z. B. der Buchstabe »W«, aufleuchtet. Unter Festhalten der niedergedrückten Q-Taste wird nun die Taste der korrespondierenden Lampe, in diesem Falle die W-Taste, gedrückt, wodurch nach Loslassen der Q-Taste der Buchstabe »Q« aufleuchten muß. Die W-Taste wird weiter festgehalten und nun z. B. die E-Taste niedergedrückt, wodurch wieder ein Buchstabe aufleuchtet, z. B. »R«. Jetzt wird die W-Taste losgelassen, die R-Taste gedrückt, die E-Taste losgelassen und dadurch der Buchstabe »E« zum Aufleuchten gebracht. Dann wird z. B. die T-Taste niedergedrückt usw. Auf diese Weise wird — ohne Veränderung der Schlüsseleinstellung im Fenster — das ganze Alphabet durchgeprüft.

29. Brennen bei dieser Durchprüfung eine oder zwei der korrespondierenden Lampen nicht, so sind folgende Untersuchungen anzustellen bzw. Fehler zu beseitigen:

a) Die Kontaktstifte der Chiffrierwalzen (IV, 35; V, 44) und die Umkehrwalze sind durch Drehen der Walzen in der Maschine oder nach Herausnahme der Walzen aus der Maschine durch Blankreiben der Kontaktkuppen mit Polierpapier zu reinigen. Gleichzeitig ist zu prüfen, ob sich einzelne dieser Kontaktstifte klemmen. In diesem Falle sind sie mit gereinigtem Benzin zu säubern und sodann mit harz- und säurefreiem Öl hauchdünn einzufetten. Ebenso sind die festen Kontakte der Walzen (IV, 36) bei dauerndem Gebrauch der Maschine alle 6 bis 8 Wochen, sonst in entsprechend längeren Zwischenräumen mit Polierpapier zu überschleifen und mit einem wenig getränkten Öllappen abzureiben. Alle übrigen Kontakte, Tastenkontakte (V, 46, 47), Lampenkontakte (V, 48) und Kurzschlußbleche (V, 45) sind sorgfältig vor Öl zu schützen.

b) Die Lampenkontakte sind durch Niederdrücken des Lampengegenkontaktes (V, 49) bei herausgeschraubten Glühlampen und durch Wiederfestschrauben der nicht brennenden Lampen auf richtige Kontakte zu prüfen, nachdem zuvor die beiden Glühlampen nach Ziff. 25 auf ihre Brauchbarkeit geprüft sind. (Sofern die Maschine noch keine Einrichtung zur Lampenprüfung besitzt, sind die Lampen zur Prüfung in unmittelbaren Kontakt mit den beiden Polen der Batterie zu bringen.)

c) Die entsprechenden Doppelsteckerschnüre sind nach Ziff. 26 zu prüfen. (Sofern die Maschine noch nicht die Einrichtung zur Kabelprüfung besitzt, muß das Kabel unter Benutzung einer Glühbirne in unmittelbaren Kontakt mit den beiden Polen der Batterie gebracht werden.) Gegebenenfalls sind schadhafte Schnüre auszuwechseln.

d) Durch mehrmaliges Einführen und rasches Herausziehen der Doppelstecker (II, 14) in die entsprechenden Buchsenpaare (II, 31) sind die federnden Kontaktblättchen (Kurzschlußbleche) (V, 45) von den Buchsen (V, 50) abzudrücken und gegen die Buchsen zurückschnellen zu lassen. (Vgl. Bild V, die eingeführten Stecker bei W und E im Gegensatz zu Q und R ohne Stecker.)

e) Zur Reinigung der betreffenden zwei Tastkontakte (V, 46, 47) sind die zugehörigen Tasten entsprechend Ziff. 5 mehrmals kräftig herunterzudrücken und rasch hochschnellen zu lassen, wobei eine dritte Taste dauernd gedrückt bleibt, um ein Weiterschalten der Walzen zu vermeiden.

Unter allen Umständen ist zu vermeiden, daß die einzelnen Kontakte mit den Händen berührt werden.

30. Wenn **alle** Lampen nicht brennen, so ist die Batterie verbraucht oder die Polenden haben keinen Kontakt mit den Federn des Batteriekastens. Behebung des Fehlers erfolgt durch Einsetzen einer Ersatzbatterie nach Ziff. 24 bzw. durch Ausbiegen der Federn, so daß sie Kontakt bekommen.

31. Sind die Störungen nach Prüfung in der oben geschilderten Weise nicht zu beheben, so sind weitere Instandsetzungsarbeiten nur in den Werkstätten der Nachr.-Abteilungen und der Heereszeugämter bzw. des Luft-Nachr.-Zeugamtes nach besonderen Richtlinien zulässig.

Instandsetzungsarbeiten an Chiffriermaschinen sind grundsätzlich verboten. Die Maschine ist in diesem Falle für den Bereich des O. K. H. an das Heeres-Zeugamt (Nachr.), für den Bereich des Ob. d. L. an das Luft-Nachr.-Zeugamt einzusenden.

IX. Wartung der Maschine.

32. Die Achse (IV, 21) der Chiffrierwalzen sowie die Lagerstellen der Antriebswelle sind bei dauerndem Gebrauch der Maschine im Abstand von 6 bis 8 Wochen, sonst etwa vierteljährlich zu reinigen und mit säure- und harzfreiem Öl leicht einzufetten. Dabei muß peinlichst vermieden werden, daß Öl an irgendeine Kontaktstelle (Tastkontakte, Lampenkontakte und Kurzschlußbleche) bringt.

33. Zum Schutz der Maschine gegen Eindringen von Staub u. dgl. ist der Metalldeckel (II/III, 17) und die Abdeckplatte (I/II, 4) immer geschlossen zu halten. Sobald die Maschine nicht mehr benutzt wird, ist der Schaltergriff (II, 7) für die Batterie auf »aus« zu stellen und der Deckel des Holzkastens zu schließen.

Berlin, den 12. Januar 1937.

**Der Reichskriegsminister
und Oberbefehlshaber der Wehrmacht.**

J. A.

Fellgiebel.

Bild 1

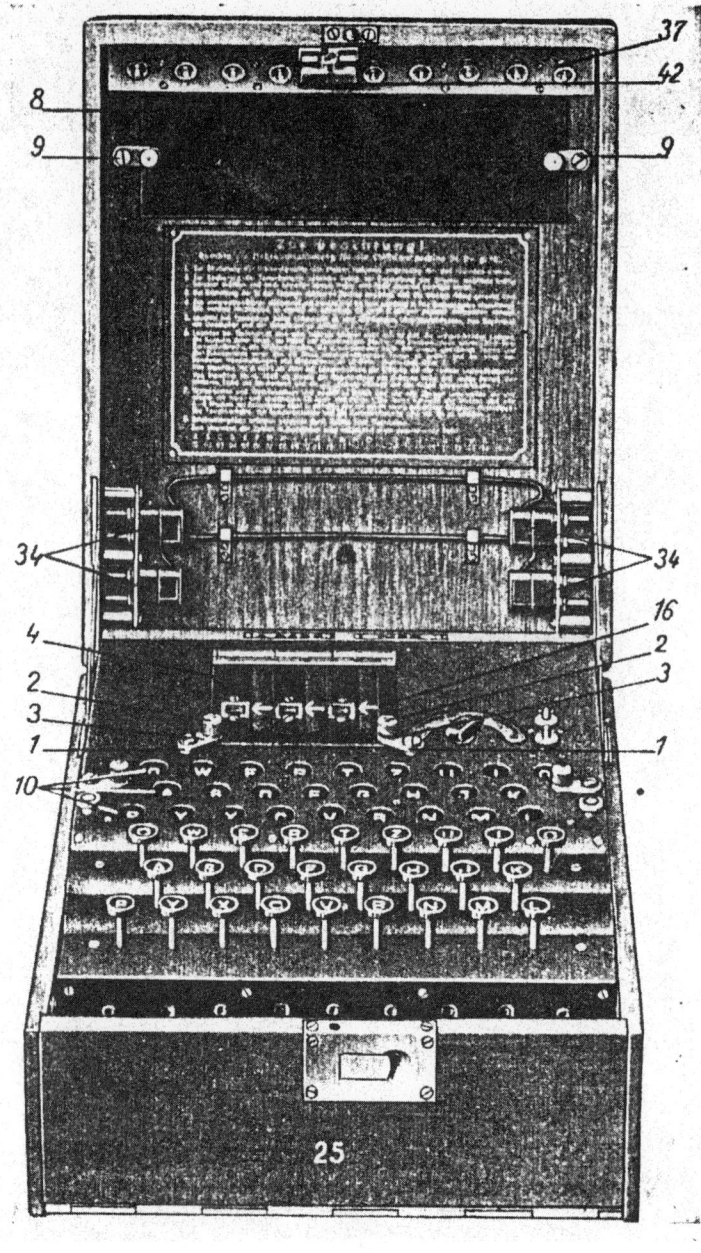

1 Haltevorrichtung	8 Zellenplatte	25 Stirnwand
2 Federknöpfe	9 Federknöpfe	34 Doppelsteckerschnüre
3 Haltehebel	10 Transparent	37 Reserveglühlampen
4 Abdeckplatte	16 Fenster	42 Blatthalter

Bild II

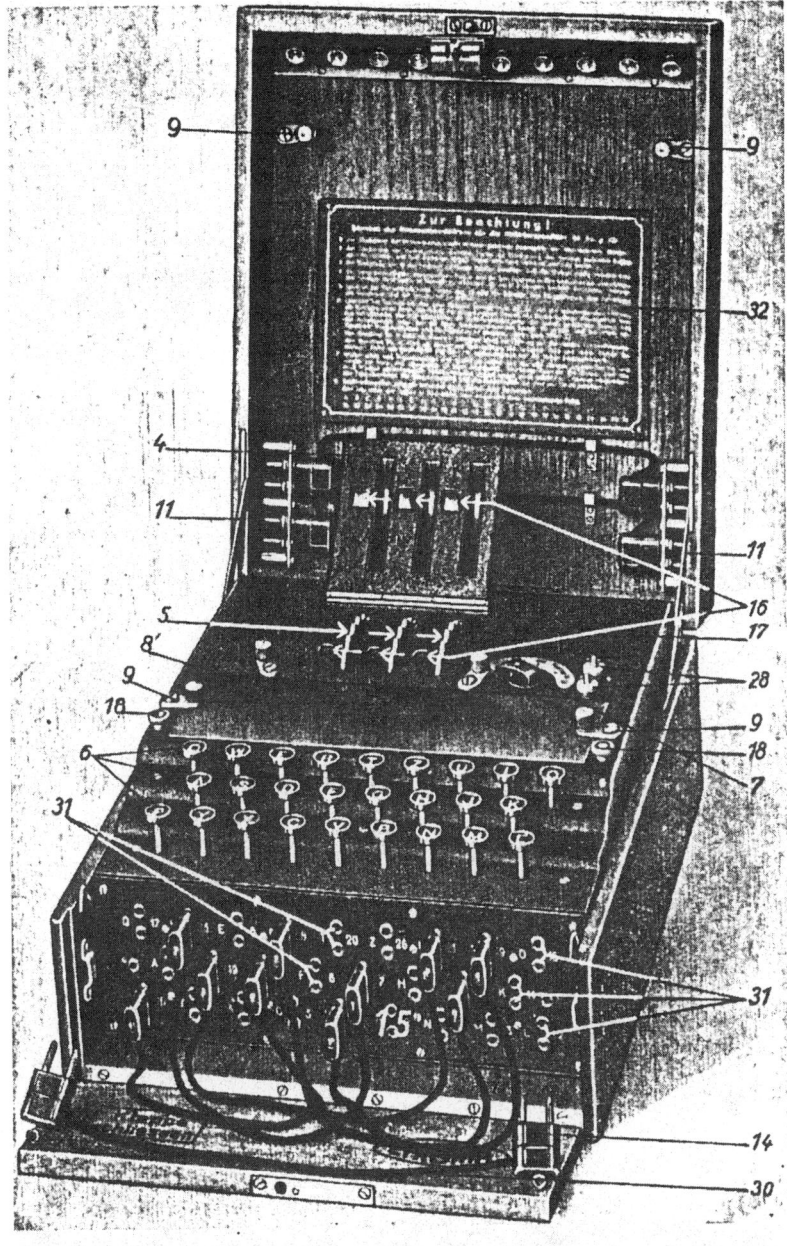

4 Abdeckplatte	8 Zellonplatte	15 Steckerbrett	28 Kordelschrauben
5 Einstellräder	9 Federknöpfe	16 Fenster	30 Doppelsteckerschnur
6 Tasten	11 Scharniere	17 Metalldeckel	31 Buchsenpaare
7 Schaltergriff	14 Doppelstecker	18 Halteschrauben	32 Betriebsanweisung

Bild III

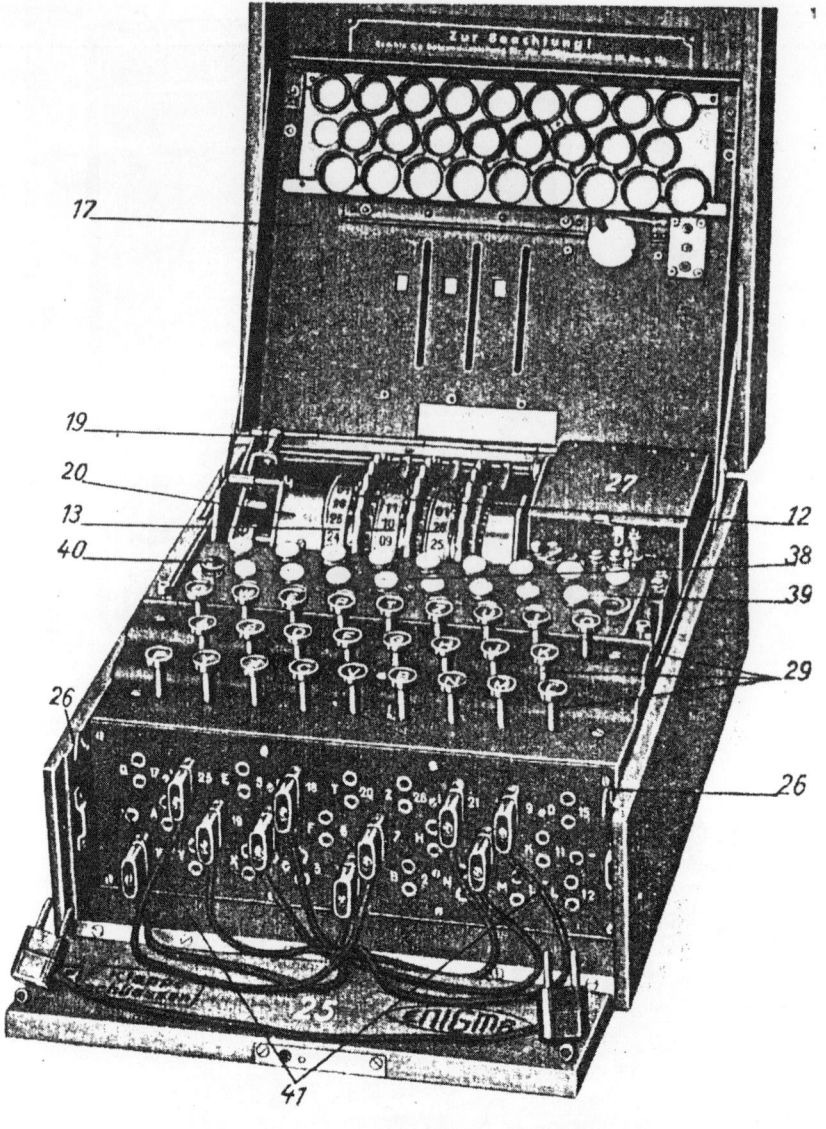

12 Chiffrierwalzen 20 Umkehrwalze 29 Tastenbolzen
13 Zahlenringe   25 Stirnwand   38 Glühlampenfeld
17 Metalldeckel   26 Haken   39 Lampenprüfung
19 Haltehebel   27 Batteriekasten 40 Kabelprüfung
41 Unverw. Buchsen zur Kabelprüfung

Bild IV

5 Einstellräder
12 Chiffrierwalzen
13 Zahlenring
21 Achse
21a Achsenbund
22 Halteseder
23 Knopf
24 Federzapfen
33 Kennzeichnung durch Punkte
34 Kennzeichnung durch röm. Zahl
35 Federnde Kontaktstifte
36 Glatte Kontaktflächen

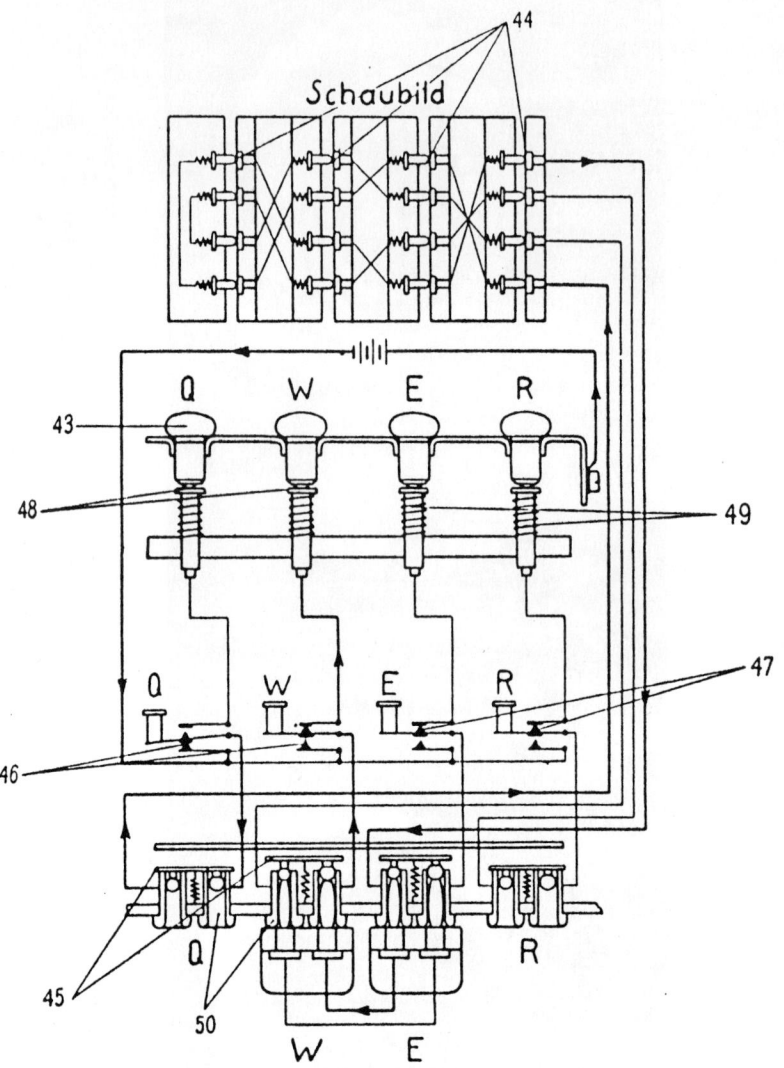

43 Glühlampen
44 Chiffr. Walzen-Kontakte
45 Kurzschlußbleche
46 Tastkontakte (Arbeitskontakte)
47 Tastkontakte (Ruhekontakte)
48 Lampenkontakte
49 Federnde Lampengegenkontakte
50 Buchsen im Steckerbrett

Key Instructions of the Enigma Cipher Machine

I.		Explanation of terms and descriptions.	3
II.	1–2	General	3
III.	3–5	Key Basics	3
IV.	6–9	Encipherment	5
V.	10–12	Characteristics of the Keys	6
VI.	13–15	Decipherment	7
VII.	16	Emergency Keys	7
VIII.	17–20	Examples	8

Notes: Under IV the operator is forbidden to choose as a key three identical letters (AAA) Words (IST) abbreviations (RGT), Q-code QRM, call-signs, letters in the order on the keyboard, ERT, in alphabetical order forwards or backwards (abc—cba).

For each message and each part of a multi-part message a new key must be used.

Under VIII the use of the emergency key is shown with an extract from the monthly key list showing order and settings of rotors and stecker connections (P.8)—excellent material for cryptographers.

Dv. g. 14
Dv. Nr. 168
Dv. g. 14

Prüf=Nr. 1812

Geheim!

Schlüsselanleitung
zur
Chiffriermaschine Enigma

Vom 8. 6. 37

—489—

Berlin 1937
Gedruckt in der Reichsdruckerei

Inhaltsverzeichnis.

			Seite
I.		Erklärung von Begriffen und Bezeichnungen	3
II.	1.—2.	Allgemeines	3
III.	3.—5.	Schlüsselunterlagen	3
IV.	6.—9.	Merkblätter	6
V.	10.—12.	Kennzeichnung des Schlüssels	6
VI.	13.—15.	Entschlüsseln	7
VII.	16.	Netzschlüssel	7
VIII.	17.—26.	Beispiel	8

I. Erklärung von Begriffen und Bezeichnungen.

Klartext ist ein in offener Sprache geschriebener Text.

Geheimtext oder **Schlüsseltext** ist ein nach einem bestimmten Schlüssel umgewandelter Klartext.

Verschlüsseln heißt Umwandeln eines Klartextes in Geheimtext.

Entschlüsseln heißt Umwandeln eines Geheimtextes in Klartext.

Schlüsseln kann sowohl Ver- als auch Entschlüsseln sein.

Schlüsselverfahren ist das Gesetz, nach dem geschlüsselt wird.

Schlüssel ist die wechselnde Ausführungsform für das Schlüsselverfahren (z. B. die Angaben zur Einstellung der Chiffriermaschine).

Schlüsselmittel ist der zum Schlüsseln erforderliche Gehilfe, z. B. Chiffriermaschine.

II. Allgemeines.

1. Die Verwendung der Chiffriermaschine Enigma wird vom Reichskriegsministerium gesondert befohlen.

2. Die allgemeinen Schlüsselregeln sind in der Vorschrift „Die Heeresschlüssel (H. Dv. g. 7)", Abschnitt IX, die Anweisung für die Bedienung der Chiffriermaschine Enigma ist in der „Gebrauchsanleitung für die Chiffriermaschine Enigma (H. Dv. g. 13)" enthalten.

III. Schlüsselunterlagen.

3. Der Schlüssel wechselt täglich (Tagesschlüssel). Die Schlüssel und ihre Kennzeichnungen (vgl. IV.) werden unter Zusammenfassung der einzelnen Tagesschlüssel und Kennzeichnungen in einer Schlüsseltafel mit aufgedruckter Kenngruppentafel und Kenngruppenweiser in der Regel für einen Monat ausgegeben.

4. Zur Einstellung der Chiffriermaschine enthält der Schlüssel folgende Angaben, die täglich wechseln:

a) Walzenlage (in römischen Zahlen),
b) Ringstellung,
c) ~~Grundstellung,~~
c d) Steckerverbindungen.

Mit Ausnahme von a werden die Schlüsselangaben durch Buchstaben oder durch Zahlen ausgedrückt, wobei die Zahlen an Stelle der Buchstaben gemäß ihrer Reihenfolge im Alphabet treten.

```
A   B   C   D   E   F   G   H   I   J   K   L   M
01  02  03  04  05  06  07  08  09  10  11  12  13
N   O   P   Q   R   S   T   U   V   W   X   Y   Z
14  15  16  17  18  19  20  21  22  23  24  25  26
```

(Beachte, daß neben I der Buchstabe J als besonderer Buchstabe bei der Chiffriermaschine vorhanden ist, so daß das Alphabet aus 26 Buchstaben besteht!) Die Schlüsselangaben sind in den folgenden Beispielen in Buchstaben eingesetzt und die entsprechenden Zahlen in Klammern darunter beigefügt.

5. Beispiele zu:

4a) Die Walzenlage bezeichnet die Reihenfolge, in der die einzelnen Chiffrierwalzen von links nach rechts in die Chiffriermaschine einzusetzen sind (vgl. H.Dv. g. 13, Ziff. 10a und 12)

z. B. II   I   III;

4b) Die Ringstellung zeigt die Einstellung der Buchstaben- oder Zahlenringe jeder einzelnen Walze an (vgl. H.Dv. g. 13, Ziff. 10b und 13)

z. B.   II   I   III
         M   H   K
        (13) (08) (11)

~~4c) Die Grundstellung schreibt die Zahlen oder Buchstaben vor, die in den 3 Fenstern der Chiffriermaschine von links nach rechts einzustellen sind (vgl. H.Dv. g. 13, Ziff. 10c und 14)~~

z. B.   W   E   P
       (23) (05) (16)

c.

44) Durch die Angabe der Steckerverbindungen werden die Buchsenpaare gekennzeichnet, welche durch die Doppelsteckerschnüre miteinander zu verbinden sind (vgl. H. Dv. g. 13, Ziff. 10d und 15). Jeder Buchstabe bzw. jede Zahl bezeichnet ein bestimmtes Buchsenpaar und zwei zusammenstehende Buchstaben oder zwei durch Schrägstrich verbundene Zahlen diejenigen Buchsenpaare, die miteinander verbunden werden sollen, also

AO EH KW RY QT MU
(1/15) (5/8) (11/23) (18/25) (17/20) (13/21).

IV. Verschlüsseln.

6. Die Chiffriermaschine wird auf Grund der Schlüsselangaben eingestellt. Diese Einstellung ist für alle mit demselben Schlüssel (z. B. Wehrmacht-Maschinenschlüssel) arbeitenden Stellen die gleiche. *)

7. Jeder Spruch ist sodann nach einem besonderen Spruchschlüssel zu verschlüsseln, den sich der Schlüssler selbst aus den Buchstaben bzw. Zahlen für die 3 Ringe A A A bis Z Z Z (01 01 01 bis 26 26 26) wählt. Bei der Wahl der einzelnen Spruchschlüssel ist es ausdrücklich verboten, gleiche Buchstaben (A A A), Wörter (ist), Abkürzungen (Rgt), Rufzeichen des eigenen Verkehrsbereiches, Verkehrszeichen (Q R M), Buchstaben in Tastaturreihenfolge der Chiffriermaschine (E R T) oder in alphabetischer Reihenfolge (vorwärts oder rückwärts: A B C — C B A) zu verwenden.

Für jeden Spruch und für jeden Teil eines mehrteiligen Spruches ist am gleichen Tage stets ein neuer Spruchschlüssel zu benutzen.

8. Der von dem Schlüssler gewählte Spruchschlüssel, z. B. X F R (24 06 18), wird nach Einstellung der Chiffriermaschine auf Grund des vorgeschriebenen Tagesschlüssels (vgl. Ziff. 6) zweimal nacheinander auf der Chiffriermaschine getastet. Die sich dabei ergebenden 6 Buchstaben werden dem mit dem Spruchschlüssel zu verschlüsselnden Spruch vorangesetzt.

9. Der Schlüssler stellt nunmehr in den Fenstern die als Spruchschlüssel gewählten Buchstaben, z. B. X F R (24 06 18), ein und tastet den Klartext. Die hierbei aufleuchtenden Buchstaben werden hinter die durch Tasten des Spruchschlüssels gewonnenen Buchstaben geschrieben und gemeinsam zu fünfstelligen Buchstabengruppen zusammengefaßt; der Platz für die Kenngruppe (vgl. Ziff. 10, die »Einsatzstelle«) ist dabei auszusparen.

V. Kennzeichnung des Schlüssels.

10. Die Kennzeichnung des in einem Spruch angewendeten Schlüssels erfolgt durch eine fünfstellige Buchstaben-Kenngruppe. Die beiden ersten Buchstaben (Füllbuchstaben) dieser Gruppe sind beliebig zu wählen und zur Tarnung der Kenngruppe für jeden Spruch zu wechseln. Die 3 letzten Buchstaben (Kenngruppenbuchstaben) werden der jedem Schlüssel aufgedruckten oder beigefügten »Kenngruppentafel« entnommen. Je Schlüsselbereich und Tag stehen mehrere Kenngruppen zu je 3 Buchstaben zur Verfügung. Diese einzelnen Buchstabengruppen sind abwechselnd zu verwenden; dabei ist die Reihenfolge der einzelnen Buchstaben innerhalb dieser Buchstabengruppen bei jedem Spruch zu ändern.

Bei mehrteiligen Sprüchen erfolgt die Kennzeichnung eines jeden Teiles für sich unter Verwendung verschiedener **Kenngruppenbuchstaben** und verschiedener **Füllbuchstaben**.

Die Kenngruppe (2 Füllbuchstaben und 3 Kenngruppenbuchstaben) wird in den in Gruppen zu 5 Buchstaben eingeteilten Text des verschlüsselten Spruches an einer vorher festgelegten und dafür ausgesparten Stelle (vgl. Ziff. 9) nachträglich eingefügt. Die 5 Buchstaben der Kenngruppe sind in die im Spruchkopf enthaltene Buchstabenzahl mit einzurechnen. Die täglich wechselnde »Einsatzstelle« der Kenngruppe ist aus dem mit dem Tagesschlüssel gemeinsam ausgegebenen »Kenngruppenweiser« zu entnehmen. Die Kenngruppen werden also **nicht mitverschlüsselt**, sondern in den **bereits verschlüsselten Spruch** eingefügt und vor dem **Entschlüsseln** nach Feststellung des Schlüsselbereiches **gestrichen** (vgl. Ziff. 13).

Ist als Kenngruppen-Einsatzstelle die 1. Gruppe vorgeschrieben, so wird die Kenngruppe an den Anfang des Spruches vor den verschlüsselten Spruchschlüssel gesetzt.

Die Kenngruppe ist dem verschlüsselten Spruch als letzte Gruppe dann anzufügen, wenn infolge der geringen Buchstabenzahl des Spruches die vorgeschriebene Einsatzstelle **nicht** eingehalten werden kann. Enthält hierbei die letzte Textgruppe des verschlüsselten Spruches weniger als 5 Buchstaben, so muß sie vor Anfügen der Kenngruppe durch Füllbuchstaben, die den Sinn des Spruches nicht stören dürfen und untereinander verschieden sein müssen, auf eine volle Gruppe ergänzt werden.

11. Die Mindestlänge eines mit der Chiffriermaschine geschlüsselten Spruches ist nicht begrenzt. Die Höchstlänge des zur Übermittlung fertigen Spruches darf 180 Buchstaben nicht überschreiten.

12. Der Spruchkopf enthält keine Kennzeichnung des Schlüsselverfahrens, sondern nur

a) Datum vierstellig z. B. 0405 (4. 5.)
b) Uhrzeit vierstellig z. B. 1755,
c) Buchstabenzahl einschl. der 6 Buchstaben des Spruchschlüssels und der 5 Buchstaben der Kenngruppe.

d) die gewählte Grundstellung (zweimal eingesetzt) z.B. ...

VI. Entschlüsseln.

13. Aus dem aufgenommenen Schlüsseltext ist auf Grund der den einzelnen Schlüsseltafeln beigedruckten Kenngruppentafeln und Kenngruppenweiser der verwendete Schlüssel festzustellen und die Kenngruppe zu streichen (vgl. Ziff. 10). *)

14. ~~Zum Entschlüsseln muß der Schlüßler zuerst den verwendeten Spruch-~~ schlüssel feststellen. Nach Einstellung der Chiffriermaschine ~~gemäß dem gültigen~~ Tagesschlüssel (siehe Datum im Spruchkopf) werden die ersten 6 Buchstaben ~~getastet; sie ergeben zweimal den dreistelligen Spruchschlüssel.~~ **)

15. Nunmehr stellt der Schlüßler die Walzen nach dem so gewonnenen Spruchschlüssel in den Fenstern der Maschine ein und tastet vom 7. Buchstaben ab den Schlüsseltext. Die hierbei aufleuchtenden Buchstaben werden aufgeschrieben und ergeben den Klartext.

VII. Notschlüssel.

16. Zu jedem Maschinenschlüssel wird ein Ersatzschlüssel ausgegeben, der nach dem Wehrmacht-Handschlüsselverfahren (H. Dv. g. 15a und 15b) zu benutzen ist. Bei Bloßstellung oder Verlust des Maschinenschlüssels tritt er bei allen Dienststellen, die mit der gleichen Schlüsseltafel arbeiten (vgl. H. Dv. g. 7, Ziff. 10), an die Stelle des Maschinenschlüssels.

Bei Störungen an der Chiffriermaschine dient er als Ersatzschlüssel.

VIII. Beispiel.

17. Gültiger Tagesschlüssel:
 (Ausschnitt aus der für die Verschlüsselung des Klartextes in Betracht kommenden Schlüsseltafel, z. B. ....
 Maschinenschlüssel für Monat Mai.)

Datum	Walzenlage	Ringstellung	Grundstellung
4.	I III II	16 11 13	01 12 22

Steckerverbindung	Kenngruppen-Einsatzstelle ...... Gruppe	Kenngruppen
CO DI FR HU JW LS TX	2	ndq nuz opw vxz

Nach diesem Tagesschlüssel ist die Chiffriermaschine einzustellen (vgl. Ziff. 4 und 5).

Der im nachfolgenden Beispiel eingesetzte Schlüsseltext ist aus Geheimhaltungsgründen nicht mit der Chiffriermaschine getastet, sondern willkürlich gewählt worden.

A. Verschlüsseln.

18. Zu verschlüsselnder Spruch:
 Tag 4. 5.,
 Abgangzeit 17,55 Uhr
 Korpskommando VI
 angreift 5. Mai 0045 Uhr mit 3. und 10. Div. Feind bei Maisach.
 Gef. Stand: Milbertshofen Nordausgang.

19. Für die Verschlüsselung ist der Klartext des Spruches gem. H.Dv.g. 7, Ziff. 40 wie folgt niederzuschreiben:
 Korpskommando roem x seqs angreift fuenften mai null drei vier fuenf uhr mit dritter und zehnter div x feind bei maisach x gef stand x milbertshofen nordausgang

20. Auf dem Spruchformular bezeichnet der Schlüssler die im Tagesschlüssel vorgeschriebene Einsatzstelle (im Beispiel 2. Gruppe) für die Kenngruppe und spart diese Gruppe beim Eintragen des Spruchschlüssels bzw. des Schlüsseltextes aus.

Der Schlüssler wählt für jeden Spruch bzw. bei mehreren Teilen eines Spruches für jeden Teil eine besondere Grundstellung, z.B. wer (23 05 16) und stellt diese Grundstellung in den Fenstern der Chiffrier-

21. Der Schlüßler wählt den Spruchschlüssel, z. B. XFR (24 06 18), und tastet diese 3 Buchstaben zweimal nacheinander, wobei sich die Buchstaben hfi kllz ergeben, die unter Berücksichtigung der nachträglich einzusetzenden Kenngruppe (vgl. Ziff. 20) als erste Buchstaben des zu befördernden Spruches niederzuschreiben sind.

22. Nunmehr stellt der Schlüßler bei sonst gleichbleibender Einstellung der Chiffriermaschine in den Fenstern die als Spruchschlüssel gewählten Buchstaben XFR (24 06 18) ein und tastet den Klartext. Die sich ergebenden Buchstaben werden im Anschluß an die 6 Buchstaben, die beim Tasten des Spruchschlüssels entstanden sind, niedergeschrieben. Dabei werden gleichzeitig Gruppen zu je 5 Buchstaben gebildet.

Es ergibt sich folgender Schlüsseltext:

hfikl	. . . . .	bsgex	nnfop	(hfikl . . . . . b
rsalm	cydrj	qqarz	ubhfe	verschlüsselter
mooxz	lgred	lfijy	acivd	Spruchschlüssel)
gnhye	xmjyr	aqztl	ssiwf	
uwfhe	lnarz	qeduw	jvsfa	
bskqu	dihxg	ncjpf	afohw	
egaim	fojrl	ekhhd	lpbme	
binge				

23. Zur Bezeichnung der für die Schlüsselung des Spruches verwendeten Schlüsseltafel ist aus dem Tagesschlüssel eine der 4 Kenngruppen, z. B. »nuz«, zu entnehmen, die z. B. in znu umgestellt wird und unter Voranstellen zweier Füllbuchstaben, z. B. »ul«, als Kenngruppe an der ausgesparten Stelle einzusetzen.

Unter gleichzeitiger Voransetzung des Spruchkopfes (vgl. Ziff. 12) lautet der zur Übermittlung fertige Spruch:

0405 — 1755 — 145 — ulp wep —

hfikl	ulznu	bsgex	nnfop
rsalm	cydrj	qqarz	ubhfe
mooxz	lgred	lfijy	acivd
gnhye	xmjyr	aqztl	ssiwf
uwfhe	lnarz	qeduw	jvsfa
bskqu	dihxg	ncjpf	afohw
egaim	fojrl	ekhhd	lpbme
binge			

B. Entschlüsseln.

24. Der zu entschlüsselnde Spruch laute wie vorstehend (Ziff. 23).

25. Aus den Schlüsseltafeln für den Monat Mai ergibt sich für den 4. des Monats als Einsatzstelle die 2. Gruppe, mithin nach Streichung der beiden Füllbuchstaben und nach alphabetischer Ordnung der restlichen 3 Buchstaben die Kenngruppe nuz.

Mit Hilfe dieser Kenngruppe wird der verwendete Schlüssel ermittelt und die Chiffriermaschine nach dem Tagesschlüssel eingestellt.

Nach Streichung der Kenngruppe sind die ersten 6 Buchstaben hfiklb zu tasten und gleichfalls im Spruch zu streichen. Der entschlüsselte Spruchschlüssel lautet: »xfr xfr«.

26. Nunmehr stellt der Schlüßler in den Fenstern der Chiffriermaschine die Buchstaben des Spruchschlüssels XFR (24 06 18) ein und tastet den Geheimtext. Dabei ergeben sich die Buchstaben:

korpskommando roem x s e q s angreift fuensten mai null drei vier fuenf uhr mit dritter und zehnter div x feind bei maisach x gef stand milbertshofen nordausgang

Der endgültige Klartext des Spruches lautet:

Korpskommando VI angreift 5. Mai 0345 Uhr mit 3. und 10. Div. Feind bei Maisach. Gef. Stand: Milbertshofen Nordausgang.

Berlin, den 8. Juni 1937.

Der Reichskriegsminister und Oberbefehlshaber der Wehrmacht.

J. A.

Fellgiebel.

Werkschrift R.V. 01/1

Nur für den Dienstgebrauch

Dezimeter-Gerät DMG 3 G

Beschreibung und Betriebsvorschrift

"Rudolf"

Heft 1

Hochfrequenz-Teil

Juni 1941

TELEFUNKEN
GESELLSCHAFT FÜR DRAHTLOSE TELEGRAPHIE M. B. H.
BERLIN-ZEHLENDORF

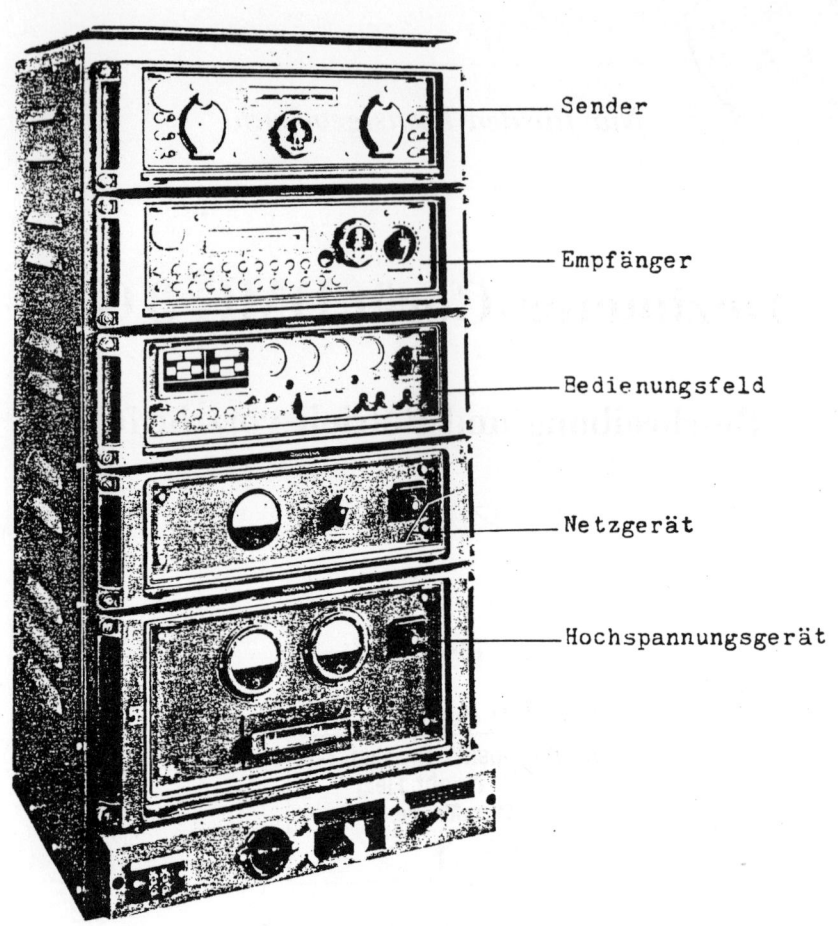

Front view of the complete apparatus

Dritter Teil: Betriebsvorschrift.

A. Inbetriebnahme des Dezimetergerätes.

Die erstmalige Abstimmung des Senders und des Empfängers, die Einstellung des Empfänger-Suchbereiches und der Nachstimm-Brückenschaltung sowie die Herstellung der Verbindungsleitungen vom Betriebsschrank zum Hellschreiber und zur Fernschreibmaschine werden vor bzw. bei der ersten Inbetriebnahme des Gerätes durch die Herstellerfirma vorgenommen. Die hierbei gefundenen Gradzahlen für die richtige Einstellung der Sender- und Empfängerskala sind auf einem Merkblatt zu notieren.

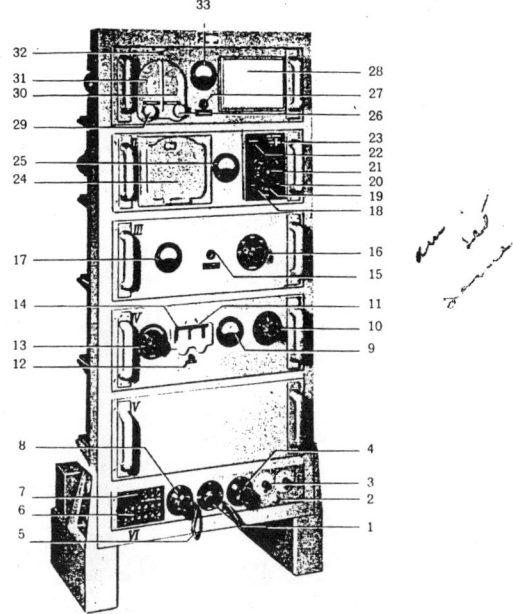

Bild 29. Bezeichnungen der Bedienungsgriffe und Überwachungsgeräte.

1 Netzschalter	12 Rufknopf	23 Umschalter für Suchen und Nachstimmen
2 Kontroll-Glimmlampe	13 Lautstärkeregler	
3 Sicherungsautomaten	14 Schauzeichen für abgegebenen Ruf	24 Klappdeckel für Empfängerskala
4 Umschalter für Kanal 1	15 Klinke „Pegelprüfung Empfänger"	25 Meßgerät für Feld II
5 Gabel für Mikrotelefon	16 Umschalter für Meßgerät	26 Frequenz-Einstellung
6 Klinkenfeld	17 Meßgerät für Feld III	27 Klinke „Pegelprüfung Sender"
7 Schauzeichen für ankommenden Ruf	18 Druckknopf „Diodenstrom"	28 Eichtafel
8 Umschalter für Kanal 2	19 Brückeneinstellung	29 Sender-Einstellung
9 Meßgerät für Feld IV	20 Druckknopf „Osz. Str."	30 Frequenzskala
10 Umschalter für Meßgerät	21 Halteschraube für Relaissatz	31 Senderskala
11 Schauzeichengruppe	22 Druckknopf für Brückenkontrolle	32 Druckknopf „Anodenstrom"
		33 Meßgerät für Feld I

Designation of the service controls and surveillance apparatus of DMG 4 ak 'Michael'

III. Betriebsvorschrift

A. Inbetriebnahme des DM-Gerätes

Die erstmalige Abstimmung des Senders und des Empfängers sowie die Herstellung der Verbindungsleitungen vom Betriebsschrank zum Hellschreiber, zu den WTZ-Gestellen und zur Fernschreibmaschine werden vor bzw. bei der ersten Inbetriebnahme des Gerätes vorgenommen.

Die Neueinschaltung des Gerätes wird folgendermaßen durchgeführt.

1. Prüfen, ob sämtliche Netzanschlüsse hergestellt sind.
2. Falls vor dem Gerät ein besonderer Netzhauptschalter vorhanden ist, diesen einschalten.
3. Sicherungsautomaten im Anschlußfeld eindrücken.
4. Schalter „Träger suchen" auf „Aus".
5. Schalter im Schubkasten III auf „Betrieb". Stellung „ÜTZ-Schleife" bzw. Entfernen des Steckers schaltet die Pegelhaltung aus und stört den gesamten Betrieb durch Hochregeln der Pegelung.
6. Steckumschalter im Schubkasten IV auf „Telefonie".
7. Einschalten des Hauptschalters. Glimmlampe des Anschlußfeldes leuchtet auf.
8. Nach $1/2$ Minute sämtliche Spannungen mit Spannungsmesser im Netzteil prüfen.

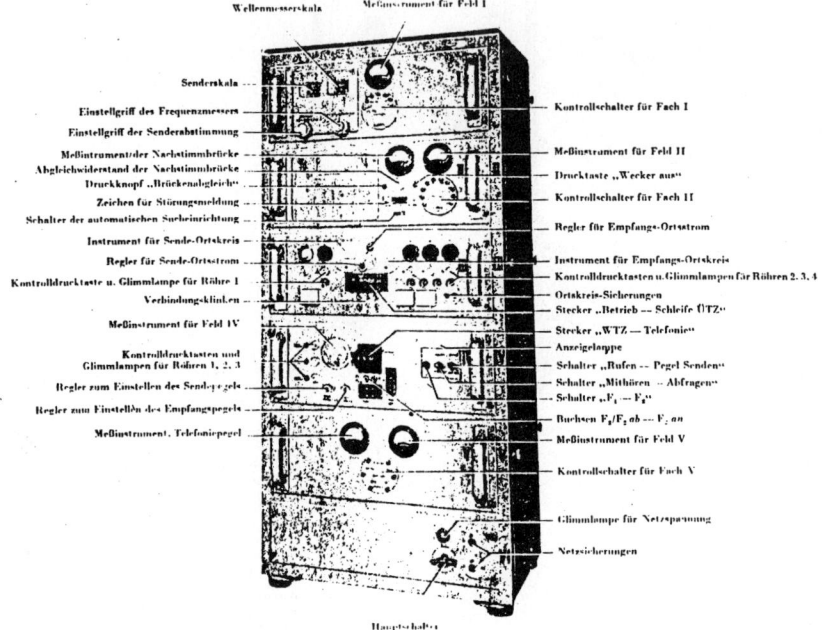

Designation of the controls of DMG 5 k

Index

Abwehr 26, 34, 114, 115, 119, 120, 123–134, 169
ACE Computer 99
Adler, Edward 4
Adler Tag (See Eagle Day) 4
Adstock 87
Afrika Korps 96
Agnes 85
Air Index 94
Albatross Key 105
Alexander, C.H.O'D. 98
Alsace (Battle of) 168
Anglo-Polish Pact 45
ANNA (Koenigsberg) 97, 145, 147, 153, 155
Asche (See Schmidt, Hans-Thilo)
Auschwitz 141
Autoclave (Autokey) 150, 151, 153
Avocet Key 106

Babbage, Dennis 79
Balme, Lieut D. 88
Barracuda key 88
Baudot code 96, 98
Bayly, Col B. 98
Beachey Head HDU 68
Beaumanor 72, 83, 92
Beck, Colonel 36
Beesley, Patrick 62
Bernard 109, 113, 123
Bertrand, Gustave 15, 19, 27, 35–48, 55, 56, 85, 86, 106, 129–132, 142, 161
Bertrand, Mary (See Mary)
Beurling, Arne 96
Biggin Hill 69
Bigot 80
Bill (Dunderdale) 134, 139
Birdbook 162
Bismarck 165
Bleak Key 103
Bloch, Gilbert 1, 26, 48, 92, 102

Block D 81
BLR 38, 39, 55
Blue Key 52, 86
Bolek 40, 51
Bomba 25, 57, 58, 65
Bombes 28, 79, 81, 83–88, 91, 99, 101
BP (Bletchley Park) 29, 59, 71–101, 105, 161
Bradley, Gen. Omar 165, 168
Brandl, Hermann (See Otto)
Bream key 103, 105
Britain, Battle of 62–70, 79, 168, 169
Browne, Tommy G.M. 91
Bruno (See Bertrand)
Bruno P.C. 48, 50, 54, 55, 58, 85
Buchenwald 140, 141
Bulldog HMS 50, 88

C.36 4.26
Cadix, P.C. 26, 163
Cairncross 105
Calvocoressi, Peter 62, 94
Canaris, Admiral 116
Central Party 52, 53
Chaffinch Key 57
Chatham 52, 59, 72, 83, 92, 161
Cheadle 67, 69, 70, 72, 92, 164
Chicksands 69, 72, 83, 92
Cieski, Major 16, 18, 49, 54, 133
Christopher von Hesse, Prince 34
Churchill, Winston 63, 65, 81, 99, 133
Clayton, Aileen 67, 92
Colman, John 84
Colossus 96, 98, 100, 101
Concentration Camps 141
Convoy Cipher 166, 167
Crawford, George 81
Creed, Typewriter Coy 72
Crete 65, 87, 96, 72
Crimea 152, 155
Crooner Key 106

Cupar 73
Cyclomètre 25, 57, 58

Dachau 142, 143
D-Day 83, 102, 104, 107, 166
Decoding Room 81, 82
Denmark Hill 98
Denning, Sir Norman 62–63
Denniston, Alastair 45, 46, 72, 76
Deutsch, Dr Harold 63
Dezimeter-geraet 97, 98
D/F 65, 164
Distant Waters Key 89
Dodds, Cdr George 89
Dollis Hill Research Est 100
Dolphin Key 89
Dowding, Sir Hugh AVM 63, 71, 163
Dunderdale, Cdr Wilfred 19, 37, 41
Duck 83

Eagle Day 62, 66, 80, 81
Eastcote 88
Elephant Book 163
Ellingworth, Cdr 52, 54, 73, 83
Enigma Machines 1–28, 30, 92–93
Equipe D 56, 89
Equipe Z 56, 58
Evans, Major P.W. 23

Fallot, Bernard (See Bernard)
Fasson, Lieut Tony RN, GC 92
Fellgiebel, Gen Erich 1, 64, 99, 159
Fish Traffic 97–104
Flowerdown Intercept 73
Flowers, T.H. 99
Forschungsamt 29–34, 141
Forschungsstellen 32–33
Fort Bridgewoods 73, 83, 84
France, Battle of 51, 162
Franco, General 58
Fredendall, General 166
Fresnoy, Raymond 143, 144
Freyberg, General 65
Fuehrer HQ 146

Gadfly Key 106
GAF (See Luftwaffe)
Gaulle, Gen C. de 10, 41
GC & CS 67, 72–101, 166
GCHQ (See GC & CS)
Geheimschreiber 23, 24, 97–103, 145, 162
German Army 11, 25, 27, 38, 82–3

German Navy 11, 29, 31, 38, 97, 103, 137, 168
Gestapo 26, 34, 41, 60, 101, 112, 114, 121, 124, 130, 133, 134, 136, 143
Gluender, Dip Ing Georg 145–161
Gneisenau 165
Good, Jack 100
Goering, Hermann 34, 63, 69, 80, 115
Gorilla Key 107
Gorleston HDU 68
Grazier, Colin GC 92
Green Key 52, 54
Grilse Key 104
Guderian, General 4–5
Gurnard Key 107
G-Zusatz 150, 153, 155, 157, 159, 161

Hagelin, Boris 23–26, 62
Harpenden 84
Hawkinge RAF 67–69
HDUs 67
Hebern, Edward 22
Henlein, Konrad 42
Henry, Capt 29
Herivel, John 76, 78, 80, 81
Hinsley, Sir H. 65, 71, 84, 92
Hitler A. 40–43, 46, 63, 65, 80, 98
Hitler Youth 42
Hodges, Andrew 100
Home Waters Key 89
Howard, Jean 81, 85
Hubatsch, Dr 64
Humbert, Lieut. 109, 110, 122, 143–4
Huts No 3 73, 74, 82–84
  No 4 74, 93
  No 6 74, 80, 82–85, 87
  No 8 73, 74, 83, 84.

Intercept Control Room 81

JABJAB 80
Jade-Amicol Gp(SOE) 141
Jeffreys, John 76, 81
Jellyfish Key 98

Kahn, David 62
Keen, Harold 'Doc' 87
Kesselring, Marshal 69
Kestrel key 88
Keun, Phillippe (See Philippe)
Kingfisher key 106
Kingsdown 68, 70, 71

Knockholt Intercept 97
Knox, Dillwyn 46, 76, 85
Koot, Capt 22
Koch, Hugo 7
Kurzsignale 88, 89

Langer, G. Col 16, 19, 35-48, 55, 56, 133, 163
Latvian E.M.G. 40
'Lauenberg' 26
Lemoine 43, 44, 114, 115, 125, 133
Lewin, Ronald 62
Liaison Section Hut 3 (3L) 80
Libya, Battle of 168
Light Blue Key 87
Lisicki, Tadeus Col 24, 57
Lofoten Islands 26, 92
Lorenz 96, 102, 44, 145, 149, 157
Luc (See Langer)
Luftwaffe 29, 50, 64, 68, 70, 79, 82, 86, 96, 102, 103, 105, 157, 162, 167, 168
    Luftflotte 2 69
    Luftflotte 3 69
    Luftflotte 5 69
    JagdGeschw 26 95
                   27 95
                   54 95
    Me 262 94, 95
Lympne 69

MacFarlane, Major 19, 41, 58, 163
Mache, Wolfgang 144
Machine Room 77, 80
Magnetophone 29-31, 34
Maidaneck 141
Mallard key 164
Manston RAF 69
Maquis 112
Marchant, Sir Herbert 62
Mary Bertrand 107, 109, 113, 118-9, 121-2, 127, 130-2, 133-6, 138
Masuy 108, 109, 113-5, 119-124, 126-7, 129, 131, 132, 135, 140, 142, 143
Mauthausen 141
Meacons 93
Menzies, Gen Stuart 45, 46, 132, 133, 139
MERS 165
Michael-geraet 97
Michie, Donald 99
Midway 65, 169
Mihailowich 81

Milner-Barry, Sir P.S. 84
'Muenchen' 20
Murray Code 96
Mustard Key 106

Nazi Party 169
Neptune Key 88
Newman, Max 98
Nijmegen 94
Nimitz, Admiral 65
Normandy, Battle of 101, 108

Oberg, General 116
Observer Corps 70
Octopus Key 105
Odic, Dr 140
Oeser, W/Cdr Oscar 81
OKH 97, 145, 147, 152-4, 157-159
OKW 64, 83, 98, 103, 127, 155
Olympia-geraet 97
Operation Flax 167
Operation Overlord 97
Operation Torch 165
Operations Room 67
Otto 60, 114, 119, 122, 142
Oyster Key 88

Paillole, Col Paul 32-34, 139
Pain, Mary 62
Pale, Erkki 62
Palluth, A. 25
Pantelleria Key 81
Passy, Colonel 139
Parkerismus 84
Patton, General 165
Paulus, General 164
Pearl Harbor 22, 65, 80
Peenemuende 81
Perch Key 105
Petard HMS 52, 91
Philip, Prince 34
Philippe 136-139, 140
Pike Key 88
Pilsudski, Marshal 36
Pink Key 87
Porpoise Key 105, 167
Puffin Key 103
Puma Key 103
Purple Machine 23, 25

Quail key 106

Radio-Abwehr   129, 142
Radio Luxemburg   30
Radley, Mr.   99
Raeder, Admiral   88
RAF   63, 79
   No. 11 Group   69
   No. 83 Group   93-95
RAF Y Service   92-95, 167
Raoul   38
Red Key   52, 77, 79, 86
Registration Room   80, 84
Reichswehr   13, 25
Rejewski, Marian   16-18, 6, 54, 55, 83
Remagen   95
Rex (See Lemoine)
Robin Key   164
Robinsons   98
Rohwer, Juergen   62, 64, 169
Rommel, F-M Erwin   85-87, 96, 167, 168
Rossberg, Erhard   102
Royal Navy   29
Rozycki, Jerzy   16, 54
Rudolf-geraet   97
Rundstedt, Gen von   98

SA   41
St. Albans Intercept   97
Saddam Hussein   86
Saegefisch (Sawfish)   96
Sandridge   72
Scharnhorst   90, 92
Scherbius, Arthur   7, 23, 25
Schmidt, Hans-Thilo   15, 25, 29, 36, 132, 169
Schmidt, Col-General Rudolf   36, 133, 169
Schofield, Vice-Admiral   62
Schussnig, Chancellor   41
Scott, Walter   43, 44
Sebastopol   87, 155-157
Sealion   63, 103
Shaftesbury Intercept   92
Shark Key   91-96, 165
Shrike Key   105
Siemens   96, 102, 144, 157, 159
Siemens & Halske   102, 145
Sigmaba   4
Sikorski   26
Sillies   75, 77, 79, 80, 86, 87
Simferopol   152, 153, 155
Sinclair, Admiral   71
Sixta Section   97

Slessor, Sir John   63
Special Wireless GP
   No. 1   59, 161
   No. 2   163-165
Special Wireless Sections
   No. 101   163, 164
      103   164
      105   164
      106   164
      109   164
Sparrow Key   105
Sperrle, General   69
Squid Key   105
SR (Service de Renseignement)   60
SS   26, 96, 116, 134, 159
Stalingrad   87, 164, 167, 169
Stanmore   87
Station in the Woods   46
Station X (See BP)
Straussberg Control   97
Strete HDU   68
Stumpf, General   69
Sturgeon Key   96
Sudetenlands   43
Sudeten Party SDP   43
Sunset Series   166
Super-Colossus   101
SYG   75
SZ 40 SZ 42   96, 102, 145, 156

T.52   102
Tape Recorder   32-35
Tangmere RAF   69
Tarpon Key   105
Taylor Telford, Col   81
Telefunken   97
Testery   98, 99
Thiele, General   98
Thomas, Col   141
Thrasher   103
Tito   81
Toadfish Key   103
Tonschreiber   29-31
Tracking Rooms   166
Traffic Analysis   65, 81-84
Traffic Register   84
Treblinka   141
Trenkle, Fritz   29-31
Triggerfish Key   103
Trout Key   105
Tunny Traffic   96, 103
Turing, Alan   75, 85, 98, 99

Typex 4, 72, 74

U-Boats 82, 91, 166, 167, 170
U.33 50, 88, 162
U.110 88, 91
U.155 162
U.505 91
U.559 28, 92
Ukraine 147
Ultra 63, 65, 83, 84, 133, 168, 170
US Army 83

V-1 Cipher 81
V-2 Cipher 81
Victor PC 58
Vigenère 6
Vulture Key 87

WAAF 67, 69, 72
Wavendon 87
Welchman, Gordon 51, 75, 77, 80, 83, 85, 98
West Kingsdown RAF 69
West Malling RAF 69
West, Nigel 71
Whiting Key 6
Wiazewski, Sisters 142

Wiegand, Capt 124–127, 134
Winterbotham, Gp/Capt 133
Wireless Intell. Unit 94, 165
Wireless Reconnaissance 62, 64
Wireless Units RAF 93, 168
  No. 270 Wing 93
  No. 329 Wing 93
  No. 61 WU 70
  No. 351 WU 93
  No. 371 WU 93, 94
  No. 380 WU 93, 94
  No. 382 WU 93–96
  No. 2 FU 94
  No. 3 FU 94
  No. 6 FU 94
  No. 9 FU 94
  No. 10 FU 94
  No. 25 FU 94

WRENS 88, 89, 102

YAK Key 107
Y Sections 59
Y Service 65, 163

Zossen 159, 160
Zygalski, Henryk 16, 54–56

SPIES
OF THE
AIRWAVES

Hugh Skillen

KNOWLEDGE STRENGTHENS THE ARM

Hugh Skillen